SELECTIONS FOR CONTRACTS

STATUTES, RESTATEMENT SECOND, FORMS

Compiled by

E. ALLAN FARNSWORTH
Alfred McCormack Professor of Law
Columbia University

WILLIAM F. YOUNG
James L. Dohr Professor of Law
Columbia University

Westbury, New York
THE FOUNDATION PRESS, INC.
1992

Selections for Contracts—FP

TEXT IS PRINTED ON 10% POST
CONSUMER RECYCLED PAPER

3rd Reprint—1995

TABLE OF CONTENTS

*

SELECTIONS FOR CONTRACTS

STATUTES, RESTATEMENT SECOND, FORMS

*

UNIFORM COMMERCIAL CODE

(Articles 1 and 2)

COMPILERS' NOTE

The law of contracts has been much affected by the Uniform Commercial Code. The relevant parts of the Code, Article 1 (General Provisions), Article 2 (Sale of Goods), an important section from Article 3 (Negotiable Instruments), and some sections from Article 9 (Secured Transactions, Sales of Accounts and Chattel Paper), are reproduced below. A little background is important to an understanding of this unique piece of uniform legislation.[a]

History. Until the seventeenth century contracts dealing with commercial matters were governed largely by the law merchant, a specialized body of customs made and administered by merchants themselves. Thus courts of merchants decided controversies that developed at the fairs which were the centers for much of early trade. Large bodies of mercantile practice were carried into the English common law of negotiable instruments and insurance. In substantial part this was the work of Lord Mansfield, who became Chief Justice of the King's Bench in 1756. In controversies between merchants, he made it a point to ascertain and apply the customs of the trade, sometimes using for this purpose a special merchants' jury to advise him on commercial practices. But as Professor Llewellyn pointed out, it is one of the ironies of the law that mercantile custom was not fully imported into the law of sales.[b] Llewellyn contended that this was an accident: the decisive sales cases did not come to Mansfield but to judges of a different bent who were content to decide mercantile disputes on the basis of concepts developed for a static land economy. At any rate, a complex body of common-law doctrine developed to govern sales of goods.

The British law of sales was reduced to statutory form in the Sale of Goods Act of 1893. The National Conference of Commissioners on Uniform State Laws entrusted to Professor Williston the task of producing a similar statute for the American states. His draft, to be known as the Uniform Sales Act, was approved by the Commissioners in 1906 and was eventually adopted by over thirty states. However, like its British cousin, it had relatively little to do with contractual problems arising out of the sale of goods and these remained largely governed by common-law rules. During the half-century after the Uniform Sales Act, a number of proposals were made for change, and some states

a. The following is adapted from E.A. Farnsworth and J. Honnold, Cases and Materials on Commercial Law 3–11 (4th ed. 1985) and J. Honnold, Cases and Materials on Sales and Sales Financing 2–6 (5th ed. 1984).

b. Llewellyn, Across Sales on Horseback, 52 Harv.L.Rev. 725 (1939).

passed amendments to certain sections. A federal sales act was proposed in Congress in 1940, but the Commissioners succeeded in having it postponed. Work began in that year on a Uniform Revised Sales Act and in 1945 this project was expanded to concentrate upon a comprehensive Uniform Commercial Code, to replace not only the Uniform Sales Act but other uniform acts dealing with commercial matters as well. The American Law Institute joined forces with the National Conference of Commissioners in this effort, with Professor Karl Llewellyn as Chief Reporter, and Soia Mentschikoff as Associate Chief Reporter. A final Official Draft with extensive comments was prepared at a cost of over $400,000, was approved by the two sponsoring organizations in 1952, and was promptly enacted by Pennsylvania in April 1953, effective July 1, 1954.

In many areas the Code took an entirely new approach to problems. The most important of these for our purposes was the reduction to statutory text and inclusion of many rules of contract law relating to sale of goods which had previously been left largely to the common law. The New York Law Revision Commission began to study the Code in 1953 and, in response to criticism, the sponsors of the Code published a number of amendments in 1955 in Supplement Number 1 to the 1952 Official Draft. The Commission held public hearings and retained consultants to study the draft, and in February 1956, after three years and the expenditure of some $300,000, it reported to the state legislature that the Code was not satisfactory and would require comprehensive reexamination and revision. Contemporaneous revision by the Editorial Board produced the 1956 Recommendations for the Uniform Commercial Code and these Recommendations became the 1957 Official Edition, which was published with Comments and minor revisions early in 1958.

By late 1961, thirteen states, including Pennsylvania, had adopted the 1958 Official Text of the Code, and the New York Law Revision Commission recommended its adoption in New York. It was enacted in 1962, effective on September 27, 1964. New York made, as had other states, a number of changes in the 1958 Official Text. In order to curb this tendency away from uniformity, a Permanent Editorial Board for the Uniform Commercial Code had been established in 1961. The Board passed upon the amendments made or proposed by each of the states and those of which it approved were incorporated in the 1962 Official Text. The Code has now been adopted in all states except Louisiana, and in the District of Columbia. The Code is divided into the following substantive articles: Article 1, General Provisions; Article 2, Sales; Article 2A, Leases; Commercial Paper; Article 4, Bank Deposits and Collections; Article 4A, Funds Transfers; Article 5, Letters of Credit; Article 6, Bulk Transfers [c]; Article 7, Warehouse Receipts, Bills of Lading and Other Documents of Title; Article 8, Invest-

c. The sponsors of the Code now recommend repeal of Article 6. The Code provisions reproduced here are those for use on repeal.

2

ment Securities; Article 9, Secured Transactions, Sales of Accounts and Chattel Paper.

Continuing Code Revision. As this list indicates, the original nine substantive articles have been significantly changed. In 1987 the sponsors of the Code promulgated a new Article 2A (Leases), and in 1990 amended it. A major purpose was to resolve "dissonances" between Article 2 (Sales) and Article 9 (Secured Transactions). The Article applies to a transaction in personal property that is "a lease rather than either a sale or a security interest as such." [d] Article 2A resembles Article 2 (Sales) in its structure and much of its text.

Use of the Code and Comments. The Code makes much less of an attempt than did the earlier codifications in Britain and the United States to follow existing formulations of the law. Very little of the language of the Uniform Sales Act is retained, and in some respects the Code takes a drastically new approach to the law. Professor Williston stated that some of the changes in the law of Sales under the Code "are not only iconoclastic but open to criticisms that I regard so fundamental as to preclude the desirability of enacting [the Sales Article] of the proposed Code." Professor Corbin was among those who took a different view. We shall have a chance to consider the soundness of some of the changes made by the Code.

One question in working with the Code is the extent to which recourse is to be had to prior drafts as an aid to interpretation. The 1952 edition of the Code attempted to close the door on such legislative history by providing in UCC 1–102(3)(g): "Prior drafts of text and comments may not be used to ascertain legislative intent." The drafting process had, of course, been in the hands of the sponsors of the Code and not the state legislatures which ultimately enacted it. The explanation given in the Comments for the provision was, however, somewhat different from this: "Frequently matters have been omitted as being implicit without statement and language has been changed or added solely for clarity. The only safe guide to intent lies in the final text and comments."

Subsection (3)(g) was deleted as the result of the revisions leading to the 1957 and 1958 editions of the Code. The Comments to the 1956 Recommendations of the Editorial Board for the Uniform Commercial Code state that "paragraph (3)(g) was deleted because the changes from the text enacted in Pennsylvania in 1953 are clearly legitimate legislative history." Is this intended to suggest that changes made prior to the 1952 edition adopted in Pennsylvania are *not* clearly legitimate legislative history? And to what extent *should* changes made by a drafting group, unconnected with the legislature, be considered as legitimate legislative history?

d. Foreword by the Chairman of the Permanent Editorial Board for the Uniform Commercial Code.

A comparable question is the extent to which, in interpreting the Code, recourse should be had to the draftsmen's Comments which follow each section. A hazard for the lazy mind, and a help for the responsible lawyer, the Comments raise troublesome problems about their place in the Code system which need to be faced at the outset. (Because of their bulk, only a few representative Comments have been reproduced here; the Comments run several times as long as the statutory text.)

The most obvious point about the Comments is the one which, curiously enough, is most often overlooked: The text to the Code was enacted by the legislature; the Comments were not. One is tempted to ignore this point because the Comments, written in an explanatory and non-statutory style, are easier to read. *Facilis est descensus Averno.* But the tempter will whisper: The draftsmen wrote these Comments, didn't they? If they say what the Code does, that's bound to be right, isn't it? Why bother then with this prickly statutory language? (You may find it easier to resist these temptations if you put yourself, in your mind's eye, in the role of a judge to whom this argument has been made and then imagine your comments to that hapless attorney.)

The problem of the force of the Comments is sufficiently important to justify some background. The 1952 edition of the Code included as UCC 1–102(3)(f) a significant provision about the Comments: "The Comments of the National Conference of Commissioners on Uniform State Laws and the American Law Institute may be consulted in the construction and application of this Act but, if text and comment conflict, text controls."

The 1956 Recommendations of the Editorial Board for the Uniform Commercial Code deleted UCC 1–102(3)(f), and did not substitute any new provision on the status of the Comments. The question immediately arises: Does this deletion imply the rejection of the idea behind the deleted provision so that reference to the Comments has become illegitimate? An answer appears in the Comments to the 1956 Recommendations. The reason for this and other changes was only briefly stated; the explanation for this change was as follows: "paragraph (3)(f) was deleted because the old comments were clearly out of date and it was not known when new ones could be prepared." [e]

Revised Comments accompanied the 1957 and 1958 versions of the Code, but without any statutory provision referring to them. But the role of the Comments is discussed in the Comments themselves. Thus, the Comment to the Title of the Code (1962 Official Text, page 1) in part reads:

> This Comment and those which follow are the Comments of the National Conference of Commissioners on Uniform State Laws and the American Law Institute. Uniformity through-

---

[e] 1956 Recommendations, p. 3. See also Braucher, The Legislative History of the Uniform Commercial Code, 58 Colum. L.Rev. 798, 808–10 (1958).

out American jurisdictions is one of the main objectives of this Code; and that objective cannot be obtained without substantial uniformity of construction. To aid in uniform construction these Comments set forth the purpose of various provisions of this Act to promote uniformity, to aid in viewing the Act as an integrated whole, and to safeguard against misconstruction.

This Comment continues with interesting material on the legislative history of the Code, but does not indicate to what extent the revision of the Comments was brought before the sponsoring organizations or reviewed by the draftsmen. Apparently this revision of the Comments was considered part of the final editorial work and entrusted to the faithful few who were carrying the Code project to its conclusion.

Embarrassing questions multiply if one subjects the Comments to the standards often imposed for recourse to legislative history. In some states the revised Comments had not yet been drafted at the time of the Code's adoption. In others it is highly doubtful that the Comments were laid before the legislators in the form of a committee report explaining the legislation which the legislators were asked to adopt.

It would be very wrong, however, to conclude that the Comments are without value to lawyers and to courts. Professor Williston's treatise on Sales has been given heavy weight by courts in construing the Uniform Sales Act on the ground that it reflected the intent of the draftsman, although it was written subsequent to the drafting of the Act; courts have repeatedly quoted the Comments in construing the Code.[f]

Surely the Comments may be given at least as much weight as an able article or treatise construing the Code. It is equally clear that the Comments do not approach the weight of legislation; if the statutory provisions adopted by the legislature contradict or fail to support the Comments, the Comments must be rejected. The point is significant, for there are instances, easily understood in the light of the Comments' bulk and the many successive revisions of the Code, where the Comments contradict the statute. More frequent are instances of enthusiastic discussion of significant problems on which the statute is silent. (See, e.g., the Comment to the Title quoted above.)

A thorough job of construing the Code calls for using the Comments to make sure one has found the pertinent language of the statute, as a double-check on a tentative construction, and as a secondary aid where the language of the statute is ambiguous. However, the editors warn their students that they sternly reject any reference to Comments until *after* the pertinent statutory language has been carefully examined in the light of the statutory definitions and the statuto-

f. See Braucher, note e supra at 809. The Code sponsors criticized this use of Professor Williston's treatise as a "delegation to private persons of essentially legislative power." Id. at note 73. Is this criticism applicable to the use of the Comments to the Code?

ry structure. Nuances concerning the precise weight which may be given the Comments must await further litigation testing the issue.

A word of caution is also in order concerning the "Definitional Cross References" which are contained in the Comments and which are set out in this Supplement. A careful lawyer will not rely on the completeness of these references in the Comments. For a thorough job, the lawyer will check Article 1, which contains important provisions applicable to the Code as a whole; UCC 1–201 contains the definitions (in alphabetical order) of forty-six terms used throughout the Code. In addition, the lawyer will check the definitions specially applicable to the article involved; in nearly every article the lawyer will find a helpful section, e.g., UCC 2–103, containing an "index of definitions."

UNIFORM COMMERCIAL CODE

1978 OFFICIAL TEXT [a]

Table of Contents

ARTICLE 1. GENERAL PROVISIONS

PART 1. SHORT TITLE, CONSTRUCTION, APPLICATION AND SUBJECT MATTER OF THE ACT

PART 2. GENERAL DEFINITIONS AND PRINCIPLES OF INTERPRETATION

ARTICLE 2. SALES

PART 1. SHORT TITLE, GENERAL CONSTRUCTION AND SUBJECT MATTER

ARTICLE 1. GENERAL PROVISIONS

PART 1

SHORT TITLE, CONSTRUCTION, APPLICATION AND SUBJECT MATTER OF THE ACT

§ 1—101. Short Title

This Act shall be known and may be cited as Uniform Commercial Code.

§ 1—102. Purposes; Rules of Construction; Variation by Agreement

(1) This Act shall be liberally construed and applied to promote its underlying purposes and policies.

(2) Underlying purposes and policies of this Act are

    (a) to simplify, clarify and modernize the law governing commercial transactions;

    (b) to permit the continued expansion of commercial practices through custom, usage and agreement of the parties;

    (c) to make uniform the law among the various jurisdictions.

(3) The effect of provisions of this Act may be varied by agreement, except as otherwise provided in this Act and except that the obligations

11

of good faith, diligence, reasonableness and care prescribed by this Act may not be disclaimed by agreement but the parties may by agreement determine the standards by which the performance of such obligations is to be measured if such standards are not manifestly unreasonable.

(4) The presence in certain provisions of this Act of the words "unless otherwise agreed" or words of similar import does not imply that the effect of other provisions may not be varied by agreement under subsection (3).

(5) In this Act unless the context otherwise requires

(a) words in the singular number include the plural, and in the plural include the singular;

(b) words of the masculine gender include the feminine and the neuter, and when the sense so indicates words of the neuter gender may refer to any gender.

§ 1—103. Supplementary General Principles of Law Applicable

Unless displaced by the particular provisions of this Act, the principles of law and equity, including the law merchant and the law relative to capacity to contract, principal and agent, estoppel, fraud, misrepresentation, duress, coercion, mistake, bankruptcy, or other validating or invalidating cause shall supplement its provisions.

§ 1—104. Construction Against Implicit Repeal

This Act being a general act intended as a unified coverage of its subject matter, no part of it shall be deemed to be impliedly repealed by subsequent legislation if such construction can reasonably be avoided.

§ 1—105. Territorial Application of the Act; Parties' Power to Choose Applicable Law

(1) Except as provided hereafter in this section, when a transaction bears a reasonable relation to this state and also to another state or nation the parties may agree that the law either of this state or of such other state or nation shall govern their rights and duties. Failing such agreement this Act applies to transactions bearing an appropriate relation to this state.

(2) Where one of the following provisions of this Act specifies the applicable law, that provision governs and a contrary agreement is effective only to the extent permitted by the law (including the conflict of laws rules) so specified:

Rights of creditors against sold goods. Section 2—402.

Applicability of the Article on Leases. Sections 2A—105 and 2A—106.

Applicability of the Article on Bank Deposits and Collections. Section 4—102.

Governing law in the Article on Funds Transfers. Section 4A—507.

Applicability of the Article on Investment Securities. Section 8—106.

Perfection provisions of the Article on Secured Transactions. Section 9—103.

§ 1—106. Remedies to Be Liberally Administered

(1) The remedies provided by this Act shall be liberally administered to the end that the aggrieved party may be put in as good a position as if the other party had fully performed but neither consequential or special nor penal damages may be had except as specifically provided in this Act or by other rule of law.

(2) Any right or obligation declared by this Act is enforceable by action unless the provision declaring it specifies a different and limited effect.

Definitional Cross References:

"Action". Section 1—201.
"Aggrieved party". Section 1—201.

"Party". Section 1—201.
"Remedy". Section 1—201.
"Rights". Section 1—201.

§ 1—107. Waiver or Renunciation of Claim or Right After Breach

Any claim or right arising out of an alleged breach can be discharged in whole or in part without consideration by a written waiver or renunciation signed and delivered by the aggrieved party.

Definitional Cross References:

"Aggrieved party". Section 1—201.
"Rights". Section 1—201.
"Signed". Section 1—201.
"Written". Section 1—201.

§ 1—108. Severability

If any provision or clause of this Act or application thereof to any person or circumstances is held invalid, such invalidity shall not affect other provisions or applications of the Act which can be given effect without the invalid provision or application, and to this end the provisions of this Act are declared to be severable.

Definitional Cross Reference:

"Person". Section 1—201.

§ 1—109. Section Captions

Section captions are parts of this Act.

PART 2

GENERAL DEFINITIONS AND PRINCIPLES OF INTERPRETATION

§ 1—201. General Definitions

Subject to additional definitions contained in the subsequent Articles of this Act which are applicable to specific Articles or Parts thereof, and unless the context otherwise requires, in this Act:

(1) "Action" in the sense of a judicial proceeding includes recoupment, counterclaim, set-off, suit in equity and any other proceedings in which rights are determined.

(2) "Aggrieved party" means a party entitled to resort to a remedy.

(3) "Agreement" means the bargain of the parties in fact as found in their language or by implication from other circumstances including course of dealing or usage of trade or course of performance as provided in this Act (Sections 1—205 and 2—208). Whether an agreement has legal consequences is determined by the provisions of this Act, if applicable; otherwise by the law of contracts (Section 1—103). (Compare "Contract".)

(4) "Bank" means any person engaged in the business of banking.

(5) "Bearer" means the person in possession of an instrument, document of title, or certificated security payable to bearer or indorsed in blank.

(6) "Bill of lading" means a document evidencing the receipt of goods for shipment issued by a person engaged in the business of transporting or forwarding goods, and includes an airbill. "Airbill" means a document serving for air transportation as a bill of lading does for marine or rail transportation, and includes an air consignment note or air waybill.

(7) "Branch" includes a separately incorporated foreign branch of a bank.

(8) "Burden of establishing" a fact means the burden of persuading the triers of fact that the existence of the fact is more probable than its non-existence.

(9) "Buyer in ordinary course of business" means a person who in good faith and without knowledge that the sale to him is in violation of the ownership rights or security interest of a third party in the goods buys in ordinary course from a person in the business of selling goods of that kind but does not include a pawnbroker. All persons who sell minerals or the like (including oil and gas) at wellhead or minehead shall be deemed to be persons in the business of selling goods of that kind. "Buying" may be for cash or by exchange of other property or on secured or unsecured credit and includes receiving goods or documents

of title under a preexisting contract for sale but does not include a transfer in bulk or as security for or in total or partial satisfaction of a money debt.

(10) "Conspicuous": A term or clause is conspicuous when it is so written that a reasonable person against whom it is to operate ought to have noticed it. A printed heading in capitals (as: NON–NEGOTIABLE BILL OF LADING) is conspicuous. Language in the body of a form is "conspicuous" if it is in larger or other contrasting type or color. But in a telegram any stated term is "conspicuous". Whether a term or clause is "conspicuous" or not is for decision by the court.

(11) "Contract" means the total legal obligation which results from the parties' agreement as affected by this Act and any other applicable rules of law. (Compare "Agreement".)

(12) "Creditor" includes a general creditor, a secured creditor, a lien creditor and any representative of creditors, including an assignee for the benefit of creditors, a trustee in bankruptcy, a receiver in equity and an executor or administrator of an insolvent debtor's or assignor's estate.

(13) "Defendant" includes a person in the position of defendant in a cross-action or counterclaim.

(14) "Delivery" with respect to instruments, documents of title, chattel paper, or certificated securities means voluntary transfer of possession.

(15) "Document of title" includes bill of lading, dock warrant, dock receipt, warehouse receipt or order for the delivery of goods, and also any other document which in the regular course of business or financing is treated as adequately evidencing that the person in possession of it is entitled to receive, hold and dispose of the document and the goods it covers. To be a document of title a document must purport to be issued by or addressed to a bailee and purport to cover goods in the bailee's possession which are either identified or are fungible portions of an identified mass.

(16) "Fault" means wrongful act, omission or breach.

(17) "Fungible" with respect to goods or securities means goods or securities of which any unit is, by nature or usage of trade, the equivalent of any other like unit. Goods which are not fungible shall be deemed fungible for the purposes of this Act to the extent that under a particular agreement or document unlike units are treated as equivalents.

(18) "Genuine" means free of forgery or counterfeiting.

(19) "Good faith" means honesty in fact in the conduct or transaction concerned.

(20) "Holder," with respect to a negotiable instrument, means the person in possession if the instrument is payable to bearer or, in the

case of an instrument payable to an identified person, if the identified person is in possession. "Holder" with respect to a document of title means the person in possession if the goods are deliverable to bearer or to the order of the person in possession.

(21) To "honor" is to pay or to accept and pay, or where a credit so engages to purchase or discount a draft complying with the terms of the credit.

(22) "Insolvency proceedings" includes any assignment for the benefit of creditors or other proceedings intended to liquidate or rehabilitate the estate of the person involved.

(23) A person is "insolvent" who either has ceased to pay his debts in the ordinary course of business or cannot pay his debts as they become due or is insolvent within the meaning of the federal bankruptcy law.

(24) "Money" means a medium of exchange authorized or adopted by a domestic or foreign government and includes a monetary unit of account established by an intergovernmental organization or by agreement between two or more nations.

(25) A person has "notice" of a fact when

    (a) he has actual knowledge of it; or

    (b) he has received a notice or notification of it; or

    (c) from all the facts and circumstances known to him at the time in question he has reason to know that it exists.

A person "knows" or has "knowledge" of a fact when he has actual knowledge of it. "Discover" or "learn" or a word or phrase of similar import refers to knowledge rather than to reason to know. The time and circumstances under which a notice or notification may cease to be effective are not determined by this Act.

(26) A person "notifies" or "gives" a notice or notification to another by taking such steps as may be reasonably required to inform the other in ordinary course whether or not such other actually comes to know of it. A person "receives" a notice or notification when

    (a) it comes to his attention; or

    (b) it is duly delivered at the place of business through which the contract was made or at any other place held out by him as the place for receipt of such communications.

(27) Notice, knowledge or a notice or notification received by an organization is effective for a particular transaction from the time when it is brought to the attention of the individual conducting that transaction, and in any event from the time when it would have been brought to his attention if the organization had exercised due diligence. An organization exercises due diligence if it maintains reasonable routines for communicating significant information to the person conducting the transaction and there is reasonable compliance with the

routines. Due diligence does not require an individual acting for the organization to communicate information unless such communication is part of his regular duties or unless he has reason to know of the transaction and that the transaction would be materially affected by the information.

(28) "Organization" includes a corporation, government or governmental subdivision or agency, business trust, estate, trust, partnership or association, two or more persons having a joint or common interest, or any other legal or commercial entity.

(29) "Party", as distinct from "third party", means a person who has engaged in a transaction or made an agreement within this Act.

(30) "Person" includes an individual or an organization (See Section 1—102).

(31) "Presumption" or "presumed" means that the trier of fact must find the existence of the fact presumed unless and until evidence is introduced which would support a finding of its non-existence.

(32) "Purchase" includes taking by sale, discount, negotiation, mortgage, pledge, lien, issue or re-issue, gift or any other voluntary transaction creating an interest in property.

(33) "Purchaser" means a person who takes by purchase.

(34) "Remedy" means any remedial right to which an aggrieved party is entitled with or without resort to a tribunal.

(35) "Representative" includes an agent, an officer of a corporation or association, and a trustee, executor or administrator of an estate, or any other person empowered to act for another.

(36) "Rights" includes remedies.

(37) "Security interest" means an interest in personal property or fixtures which secures payment or performance of an obligation. The retention or reservation of title by a seller of goods notwithstanding shipment or delivery to the buyer (Section 2–401) is limited in effect to a reservation of a "security interest". The term also includes any interest of a buyer of accounts or chattel paper which is subject to Article 9. The special property interest of a buyer of goods on identification of those goods to a contract for sale under Section 2–401 is not a "security interest", but a buyer may also acquire a "security interest" by complying with Article 9. Unless a consignment is intended as security, reservation of title thereunder is not a "security interest", but a consignment in any event is subject to the provisions on consignment sales (Section 2–326).

Whether a transaction creates a lease or security interest is determined by the facts of each case . . . .[a]

a. The definition continues with more than a dozen clauses bearing on the question whether, in specified circumstances, a transaction designated as a lease generates, instead, a "security interest." These provisions affect the subject matter of Article 9 of the Code (Secured Transactions).

(38) "Send" in connection with any writing or notice means to deposit in the mail or deliver for transmission by any other usual means of communication with postage or cost of transmission provided for and properly addressed and in the case of an instrument to an address specified thereon or otherwise agreed, or if there be none to any address reasonable under the circumstances. The receipt of any writing or notice within the time at which it would have arrived if properly sent has the effect of a proper sending.

(39) "Signed" includes any symbol executed or adopted by a party with present intention to authenticate a writing.

(40) "Surety" includes guarantor.

(41) "Telegram" includes a message transmitted by radio, teletype, cable, any mechanical method of transmission, or the like.

(42) "Term" means that portion of an agreement which relates to a particular matter.

(43) "Unauthorized" signature means one made without actual, implied, or apparent authority and includes a forgery.

(44) "Value". Except as otherwise provided with respect to negotiable instruments and bank collections (Sections 3—303, 4—208 and 4—209) a person gives "value" for rights if he acquires them

    (a) in return for a binding commitment to extend credit or for the extension of immediately available credit whether or not drawn upon and whether or not a charge-back is provided for in the event of difficulties in collection; or

    (b) as security for or in total or partial satisfaction of a pre-existing claim; or

    (c) by accepting delivery pursuant to a pre-existing contract for purchase; or

    (d) generally, in return for any consideration sufficient to support a simple contract.

(45) "Warehouse receipt" means a receipt issued by a person engaged in the business of storing goods for hire.

(46) "Written" or "writing" includes printing, typewriting or any other intentional reduction to tangible form.

§ 1—202. Prima Facie Evidence by Third Party Documents

A document in due form purporting to be a bill of lading, policy or certificate of insurance, official weigher's or inspector's certificate, consular invoice, or any other document authorized or required by the contract to be issued by a third party shall be prima facie evidence of its own authenticity and genuineness and of the facts stated in the document by the third party.

Definitional Cross References:

"Bill of lading". Section 1—201.
"Contract". Section 1—201.
"Genuine". Section 1—201.

§ 1—203. Obligation of Good Faith

Every contract or duty within this Act imposes an obligation of good faith in its performance or enforcement.

Definitional Cross References:

"Contract". Section 1—201.
"Good faith". Section 1—201; 2—103.

§ 1—204. Time; Reasonable Time; "Seasonably"

(1) Whenever this Act requires any action to be taken within a reasonable time, any time which is not manifestly unreasonable may be fixed by agreement.

(2) What is a reasonable time for taking any action depends on the nature, purpose and circumstances of such action.

(3) An action is taken "seasonably" when it is taken at or within the time agreed or if no time is agreed at or within a reasonable time.

Definitional Cross Reference:

"Agreement". Section 1—201.

§ 1—205. Course of Dealing and Usage of Trade

(1) A course of dealing is a sequence of previous conduct between the parties to a particular transaction which is fairly to be regarded as establishing a common basis of understanding for interpreting their expressions and other conduct.

(2) A usage of trade is any practice or method of dealing having such regularity of observance in a place, vocation or trade as to justify an expectation that it will be observed with respect to the transaction in question. The existence and scope of such a usage are to be proved as facts. If it is established that such a usage is embodied in a written trade code or similar writing the interpretation of the writing is for the court.

(3) A course of dealing between parties and any usage of trade in the vocation or trade in which they are engaged or of which they are or should be aware give particular meaning to and supplement or qualify terms of an agreement.

(4) The express terms of an agreement and an applicable course of dealing or usage of trade shall be construed wherever reasonable as consistent with each other; but when such construction is unreasonable express terms control both course of dealing and usage of trade and course of dealing controls usage of trade.

(5) An applicable usage of trade in the place where any part of performance is to occur shall be used in interpreting the agreement as to that part of the performance.

(6) Evidence of a relevant usage of trade offered by one party is not admissible unless and until he has given the other party such notice as the court finds sufficient to prevent unfair surprise to the latter.

Definitional Cross References:

"Agreement". Section 1—201.
"Contract". Section 1—201.
"Party". Section 1—201.
"Term". Section 1—201.

§ 1—206. Statute of Frauds for Kinds of Personal Property Not Otherwise Covered

(1) Except in the cases described in subsection (2) of this section a contract for the sale of personal property is not enforceable by way of action or defense beyond five thousand dollars in amount or value of remedy unless there is some writing which indicates that a contract for sale has been made between the parties at a defined or stated price, reasonably identifies the subject matter, and is signed by the party against whom enforcement is sought or by his authorized agent.

(2) Subsection (1) of this section does not apply to contracts for the sale of goods (Section 2—201) nor of securities (Section 8—319) nor to security agreements (Section 9—203).

Definitional Cross References:

"Action". Section 1—201.
"Agreement". Section 1—201.
"Contract". Section 1—201.
"Contract for sale". Section 2—106.
"Goods". Section 2—105.
"Party". Section 1—201.
"Sale". Section 2—106.
"Signed". Section 1—201.
"Writing". Section 1—201.

§ 1—207. Performance or Acceptance Under Reservation of Rights

(1) A party who with explicit reservation of rights performs or promises performance or assents to performance in a manner demanded or offered by the other party does not thereby prejudice the rights reserved. Such words as "without prejudice", "under protest" or the like are sufficient.

(2) Subsection (1) does not apply to an accord and satisfaction.

Definitional Cross References:

"Party". Section 1—201.
"Rights". Section 1—201.

§ 1—208. Option to Accelerate at Will

A term providing that one party or his successor in interest may accelerate payment or performance or require collateral or additional collateral "at will" or "when he deems himself insecure" or in words of similar import shall be construed to mean that he shall have power to do so only if he in good faith believes that the prospect of payment or performance is impaired. The burden of establishing lack of good faith is on the party against whom the power has been exercised.

Definitional Cross References:

"Burden of establishing". Section 1—201.

"Good faith". Section 1—201.

"Party". Section 1—201.

"Term". Section 1—201.

§ 1—209. Subordinated Obligations

[*Optional provision. Omitted.*—eds.]

ARTICLE 2. SALES

PART 1

SHORT TITLE, GENERAL CONSTRUCTION AND SUBJECT MATTER

§ 2—101. Short Title

This Article shall be known and may be cited as Uniform Commercial Code—Sales.

§ 2—102. Scope; Certain Security and Other Transactions Excluded From This Article

Unless the context otherwise requires, this Article applies to transactions in goods; it does not apply to any transaction which although in the form of an unconditional contract to sell or present sale is intended to operate only as a security transaction nor does this Article impair or repeal any statute regulating sales to consumers, farmers or other specified classes of buyers.

Definitional Cross References:

"Contract". Section 1—201.

"Contract for sale". Section 2—106.

"Present sale". Section 2—106.

"Sale". Section 2—106.

§ 2—103. Definitions and Index of Definitions

(1) In this Article unless the context otherwise requires

(a) "Buyer" means a person who buys or contracts to buy goods.

(b) "Good faith" in the case of a merchant means honesty in fact and the observance of reasonable commercial standards of fair dealing in the trade.

(c) "Receipt" of goods means taking physical possession of them.

21

    (d) "Seller" means a person who sells or contracts to sell goods.

    (2) Other definitions applying to this Article or to specified Parts thereof, and the sections in which they appear are:

"Acceptance". Section 2—606.

"Banker's credit". Section 2—325.

"Between merchants". Section 2—104.

"Cancellation". Section 2—106(4).

"Commercial unit". Section 2—105.

"Confirmed credit". Section 2—325.

"Conforming to contract". Section 2—106.

"Contract for sale". Section 2—106.

"Cover". Section 2—712.

"Entrusting". Section 2—403.

"Financing agency". Section 2—104.

"Future goods". Section 2—105.

"Goods". Section 2—105.

"Identification". Section 2—501.

"Installment contract". Section 2—612.

"Letter of Credit". Section 2—325.

"Lot". Section 2—105.

"Merchant". Section 2—104.

"Overseas". Section 2—323.

"Person in position of seller". Section 2—707.

"Present sale". Section 2—106.

"Sale". Section 2—106.

"Sale on approval". Section 2—326.

"Sale or return". Section 2—326.

"Termination". Section 2—106.

    (3) The following definitions in other Articles apply to this Article:

"Check". Section 3—104.

"Consignee". Section 7—102.

"Consignor". Section 7—102.

"Consumer goods". Section 9—109.

"Dishonor". Section 3—507.

"Draft". Section 3—104.

    (4) In addition Article 1 contains general definitions and principles of construction and interpretation applicable throughout this Article.

Definitional Cross Reference:

"Person". Section 1—201.

§ 2—104. Definitions: "Merchant"; "Between Merchants"; "Financing Agency"

(1) "Merchant" means a person who deals in goods of the kind or otherwise by his occupation holds himself out as having knowledge or skill peculiar to the practices or goods involved in the transaction or to whom such knowledge or skill may be attributed by his employment of an agent or broker or other intermediary who by his occupation holds himself out as having such knowledge or skill.

(2) "Financing agency" means a bank, finance company or other person who in the ordinary course of business makes advances against goods or documents of title or who by arrangement with either the seller or the buyer intervenes in ordinary course to make or collect payment due or claimed under the contract for sale, as by purchasing or paying the seller's draft or making advances against it or by merely taking it for collection whether or not documents of title accompany the draft. "Financing agency" includes also a bank or other person who similarly intervenes between persons who are in the position of seller and buyer in respect to the goods (Section 2—707).

(3) "Between merchants" means in any transaction with respect to which both parties are chargeable with the knowledge or skill of merchants.

Definitional Cross References:

"Bank". Section 1—201.
"Buyer". Section 2—103.

§ 2—105. Definitions: Transferability; "Goods"; "Future" Goods; "Lot"; "Commercial Unit"

(1) "Goods" means all things (including specially manufactured goods) which are movable at the time of identification to the contract for sale other than the money in which the price is to be paid, investment securities (Article 8) and things in action. "Goods" also includes the unborn young of animals and growing crops and other identified things attached to realty as described in the section on goods to be severed from realty (Section 2—107).

(2) Goods must be both existing and identified before any interest in them can pass. Goods which are not both existing and identified are "future" goods. A purported present sale of future goods or of any interest therein operates as a contract to sell.

(3) There may be a sale of a part interest in existing identified goods.

(4) An undivided share in an identified bulk of fungible goods is sufficiently identified to be sold although the quantity of the bulk is not

determined. Any agreed proportion of such a bulk or any quantity thereof agreed upon by number, weight or other measure may to the extent of the seller's interest in the bulk be sold to the buyer who then becomes an owner in common.

(5) "Lot" means a parcel or a single article which is the subject matter of a separate sale or delivery, whether or not it is sufficient to perform the contract.   ·

(6) "Commercial unit" means such a unit of goods as by commercial usage is a single whole for purposes of sale and division of which materially impairs its character or value on the market or in use. A commercial unit may be a single article (as a machine) or a set of articles (as a suite of furniture or an assortment of sizes) or a quantity (as a bale, gross, or carload) or any other unit treated in use or in the relevant market as a single whole.

Definitional Cross References:

"Buyer". Section 2—103.
"Contract". Section 1—201.
"Contract for sale". Section 2—106.

§ 2—106. Definitions: "Contract"; "Agreement"; "Contract for Sale"; "Sale"; "Present Sale"; "Conforming" to Contract; "Termination"; "Cancellation"

(1) In this Article unless the context otherwise requires "contract" and "agreement" are limited to those relating to the present or future sale of goods. "Contract for sale" includes both a present sale of goods and a contract to sell goods at a future time. A "sale" consists in the passing of title from the seller to the buyer for a price (Section 2—401). A "present sale" means a sale which is accomplished by the making of the contract.

(2) Goods or conduct including any part of a performance are "conforming" or conform to the contract when they are in accordance with the obligations under the contract.

(3) "Termination" occurs when either party pursuant to a power created by agreement or law puts an end to the contract otherwise than for its breach. On "termination" all obligations which are still executory on both sides are discharged but any right based on prior breach or performance survives.

(4) "Cancellation" occurs when either party puts an end to the contract for breach by the other and its effect is the same as that of "termination" except that the cancelling party also retains any remedy for breach of the whole contract or any unperformed balance.

Definitional Cross References:

"Agreement". Section 1—201.
"Buyer". Section 2—103.
"Contract". Section 1—201.

"Goods". Section 2—105.
"Party". Section 1—201.
"Remedy". Section 1—201.

"Rights". Section 1—201.
"Seller". Section 2—103.

§ 2—107. Goods to Be Severed From Realty: Recording

(1) A contract for the sale of minerals or the like (including oil and gas) or a structure or its materials to be removed from realty is a contract for the sale of goods within this Article if they are to be severed by the seller but until severance a purported present sale thereof which is not effective as a transfer of an interest in land is effective only as a contract to sell.

(2) A contract for the sale apart from the land of growing crops or other things attached to realty and capable of severance without material harm thereto but not described in subsection (1) or of timber to be cut is a contract for the sale of goods within this Article whether the subject matter is to be severed by the buyer or by the seller even though it forms part of the realty at the time of contracting, and the parties can by identification effect a present sale before severance.

(3) The provisions of this section are subject to any third party rights provided by the law relating to realty records, and the contract for sale may be executed and recorded as a document transferring an interest in land and shall then constitute notice to third parties of the buyer's rights under the contract for sale.

Definitional Cross References:

"Buyer". Section 2—103.
"Contract". Section 1—201.
"Contract for sale". Section 2—106.
"Goods". Section 2—105.

"Party". Section 1—201.
"Present sale". Section 2—106.
"Rights". Section 1—201.
"Seller". Section 2—103.

PART 2

FORM, FORMATION AND READJUSTMENT OF CONTRACT

§ 2—201. Formal Requirements; Statute of Frauds

(1) Except as otherwise provided in this section a contract for the sale of goods for the price of $500 or more is not enforceable by way of action or defense unless there is some writing sufficient to indicate that a contract for sale has been made between the parties and signed by the party against whom enforcement is sought or by his authorized agent or broker. A writing is not insufficient because it omits or incorrectly states a term agreed upon but the contract is not enforceable under this paragraph beyond the quantity of goods shown in such writing.

(2) Between merchants if within a reasonable time a writing in confirmation of the contract and sufficient against the sender is received and the party receiving it has reason to know its contents, it

satisfies the requirements of subsection (1) against such party unless written notice of objection to its contents is given within ten days after it is received.

(3) A contract which does not satisfy the requirements of subsection (1) but which is valid in other respects is enforceable

    (a) if the goods are to be specially manufactured for the buyer and are not suitable for sale to others in the ordinary course of the seller's business and the seller, before notice of repudiation is received and under circumstances which reasonably indicate that the goods are for the buyer, has made either a substantial beginning of their manufacture or commitments for their procurement; or

    (b) if the party against whom enforcement is sought admits in his pleading, testimony or otherwise in court that a contract for sale was made, but the contract is not enforceable under this provision beyond the quantity of goods admitted; or

    (c) with respect to goods for which payment has been made and accepted or which have been received and accepted (Sec. 2—606).

Official Comment

Prior Uniform Statutory Provision: Section 4, Uniform Sales Act (which was based on Section 17 of the Statute of 29 Charles II).

Changes: Completely rephrased; restricted to sale of goods. See also Sections 1—206, 8—319 and 9—203.

Purposes of Changes: The changed phraseology of this section is intended to make it clear that:

1. The required writing need not contain all the material terms of the contract and such material terms as are stated need not be precisely stated. All that is required is that the writing afford a basis for believing that the offered oral evidence rests on a real transaction. It may be written in lead pencil on a scratch pad. It need not indicate which party is the buyer and which the seller. The only term which must appear is the quantity term which need not be accurately stated but recovery is limited to the amount stated. The price, time and place of payment or delivery, the general quality of the goods, or any particular warranties may all be omitted.

Special emphasis must be placed on the permissibility of omitting the price term in view of the insistence of some courts on the express inclusion of this term even where the parties have contracted on the basis of a published price list. In many valid contracts for sale the parties do not mention the price in express terms, the buyer being bound to pay and the seller to accept a reasonable price which the trier of the fact may well be trusted to determine. Again, frequently the price is not mentioned since the parties have based their agreement on a price list or catalogue known to both of them and this list serves as an efficient safeguard against perjury. Finally, "market" prices and valuations that are current in the vicinity constitute a similar check. Thus if the price is not stated in the memorandum it can normally be supplied without danger of fraud. Of course if the "price" consists of goods rather than money the quantity of goods must be stated.

Only three definite and invariable requirements as to the memorandum are made by this subsection. First, it must evidence a contract for the sale of goods; second, it must be "signed", a word which includes any authentication which identifies the party to be charged; and third, it must specify a quantity.

2. "Partial performance" as a substitute for the required memorandum can validate the contract only for the goods which have been accepted or for which payment has been made and accepted.

Receipt and acceptance either of goods or of the price constitutes an unambiguous overt admission by both parties that a contract actually exists. If the court can make a just apportionment, therefore, the agreed price of any goods actually delivered can be recovered without a writing or, if the price has been paid, the seller can be forced to deliver an apportionable part of the goods. The overt actions of the parties make admissible evidence of the other terms of the contract necessary to a just apportionment. This is true even though the actions of the parties are not in themselves inconsistent with a different transaction such as a consignment for resale or a mere loan of money.

Part performance by the buyer requires the delivery of something by him that is accepted by the seller as such performance. Thus, part payment may be made by money or check, accepted by the seller. If the agreed price consists of goods or services, then they must also have been delivered and accepted.

3. Between merchants, failure to answer a written confirmation of a contract within ten days of receipt is tantamount to a writing under subsec-tion (2) and is sufficient against both parties under subsection (1). The only effect, however, is to take away from the party who fails to answer the defense of the Statute of Frauds; the burden of persuading the trier of fact that a contract was in fact made orally prior to the written confirmation is unaffected. Compare the effect of a failure to reply under Section 2—207.

4. Failure to satisfy the requirements of this section does not render the contract void for all purposes, but merely prevents it from being judicially enforced in favor of a party to the contract. For example, a buyer who takes possession of goods as provided in an oral contract which the seller has not meanwhile repudiated, is not a trespasser. Nor would the Statute of Frauds provisions of this section be a defense to a third person who wrongfully induces a party to refuse to perform an oral contract, even though the injured party cannot maintain an action for damages against the party so refusing to perform.

5. The requirement of "signing" is discussed in the comment to Section 1—201.

6. It is not necessary that the writing be delivered to anybody. It need not be signed or authenticated by both parties but it is, of course, not sufficient against one who has not signed it. Prior to a dispute no one can determine which party's signing of the memorandum may be necessary but from the time of contracting each party should be aware that to him it is signing by the other which is important.

7. If the making of a contract is admitted in court, either in a written pleading, by stipulation or by oral statement before the court, no additional writing is necessary for protection against fraud. Under this section it is no longer possible to admit the contract in court and still treat the Statute as a defense. However, the

contract is not thus conclusively established. The admission so made by a party is itself evidential against him of the truth of the facts so admitted and of nothing more; as against the other party, it is not evidential at all.

Cross References:

See Sections 1—201, 2—202, 2—207, 2—209 and 2—304.

Definitional Cross References:

"Action". Section 1—201.
"Between merchants". Section 2—104.
"Buyer". Section 2—103.
"Contract". Section 1—201.
"Contract for sale". Section 2—106.
"Goods". Section 2—105.
"Notice". Section 1—201.
"Party". Section 1—201.
"Reasonable time". Section 1—204.
"Sale". Section 2—106.
"Seller". Section 2—103.

§ 2—202. Final Written Expression: Parol or Extrinsic Evidence

Terms with respect to which the confirmatory memoranda of the parties agree or which are otherwise set forth in a writing intended by the parties as a final expression of their agreement with respect to such terms as are included therein may not be contradicted by evidence of any prior agreement or of a contemporaneous oral agreement but may be explained or supplemented

    (a) by course of dealing or usage of trade (Section 1—205) or by course of performance (Section 2—208); and

    (b) by evidence of consistent additional terms unless the court finds the writing to have been intended also as a complete and exclusive statement of the terms of the agreement.

Definitional Cross References:

"Agreed" and "agreement". Section 1—201.
"Course of dealing". Section 1—205.
"Parties". Section 1—201.
"Term". Section 1—201.
"Usage of trade". Section 1—205.
"Written" and "writing". Section 1—201.

§ 2—203. Seals Inoperative

The affixing of a seal to a writing evidencing a contract for sale or an offer to buy or sell goods does not constitute the writing a sealed instrument and the law with respect to sealed instruments does not apply to such a contract or offer.

Definitional Cross References:

"Contract for sale". Section 2—106.
"Goods". Section 2—105.
"Writing". Section 1—201.

§ 2—204. Formation in General

(1) A contract for sale of goods may be made in any manner sufficient to show agreement, including conduct by both parties which recognizes the existence of such a contract.

(2) An agreement sufficient to constitute a contract for sale may be found even though the moment of its making is undetermined.

(3) Even though one or more terms are left open a contract for sale does not fail for indefiniteness if the parties have intended to make a contract and there is a reasonably certain basis for giving an appropriate remedy.

Definitional Cross References:

"Agreement". Section 1—201.
"Contract". Section 1—201.
"Contract for sale". Section 2—106.

"Goods". Section 2—105.
"Party". Section 1—201.
"Remedy". Section 1—201.
"Term". Section 1—201.

§ 2—205. Firm Offers

An offer by a merchant to buy or sell goods in a signed writing which by its terms gives assurance that it will be held open is not revocable, for lack of consideration, during the time stated or if no time is stated for a reasonable time, but in no event may such period of irrevocability exceed three months; but any such term of assurance on a form supplied by the offeree must be separately signed by the offeror.

Definitional Cross References:

"Goods". Section 2—105.
"Merchant". Section 2—104.
"Signed". Section 1—201.
"Writing". Section 1—201.

§ 2—206. Offer and Acceptance in Formation of Contract

(1) Unless otherwise unambiguously indicated by the language or circumstances

    (a) an offer to make a contract shall be construed as inviting acceptance in any manner and by any medium reasonable in the circumstances;

    (b) an order or other offer to buy goods for prompt or current shipment shall be construed as inviting acceptance either by a prompt promise to ship or by the prompt or current shipment of conforming or non-conforming goods, but such a shipment of non-conforming goods does not constitute an acceptance if the seller seasonably notifies the buyer that the shipment is offered only as an accommodation to the buyer.

(2) Where the beginning of a requested performance is a reasonable mode of acceptance an offeror who is not notified of acceptance within a reasonable time may treat the offer as having lapsed before acceptance.

Definitional Cross References:

"Buyer". Section 2—103.
"Conforming". Section 2—106.

"Contract". Section 1—201.
"Goods". Section 2—105.

"Notifies". Section 1—201.
"Reasonable time". Section 1—204.

§ 2—207. Additional Terms in Acceptance or Confirmation

(1) A definite and seasonable expression of acceptance or a written confirmation which is sent within a reasonable time operates as an acceptance even though it states terms additional to or different from those offered or agreed upon, unless acceptance is expressly made conditional on assent to the additional or different terms.

(2) The additional terms are to be construed as proposals for addition to the contract. Between merchants such terms become part of the contract unless:

> (a) the offer expressly limits acceptance to the terms of the offer;
>
> (b) they materially alter it; or
>
> (c) notification of objection to them has already been given or is given within a reasonable time after notice of them is received.

(3) Conduct by both parties which recognizes the existence of a contract is sufficient to establish a contract for sale although the writings of the parties do not otherwise establish a contract. In such case the terms of the particular contract consist of those terms on which the writings of the parties agree, together with any supplementary terms incorporated under any other provisions of this Act.

Official Comment

Prior Uniform Statutory Provision: Sections 1 and 3, Uniform Sales Act.

Changes: Completely rewritten by this and other sections of this Article.

Purposes of Changes:

1. This section is intended to deal with two typical situations. The one is the written confirmation, where an agreement has been reached either orally or by informal correspondence between the parties and is followed by one or both of the parties sending formal memoranda embodying the terms so far as agreed upon and adding terms not discussed. The other situation is offer and acceptance, in which a wire or letter expressed and intended as an acceptance or the closing of an agreement adds further minor suggestions or proposals such as "ship by Tuesday," "rush," "ship draft against bill of lading inspection allowed," or the like. A frequent example of the second situation is the exchange of printed purchase order and acceptance (sometimes called "acknowledgment") forms. Because the forms are oriented to the thinking of the respective drafting parties, the terms contained in them often do not correspond. Often the seller's form contains terms different from or additional to those set forth in the buyer's form. Nevertheless, the parties proceed with the transaction. [Comment 1 was amended in 1966.]

2. Under this Article a proposed deal which in commercial understanding has in fact been closed is recognized as a contract. Therefore, any additional matter contained in the confirmation or in the acceptance falls

within subsection (2) and must be regarded as a proposal for an added term unless the acceptance is made conditional on the acceptance of the additional or different terms. [Comment 2 was amended in 1966.]

3. Whether or not additional or different terms will become part of the agreement depends upon the provisions of subsection (2). If they are such as materially to alter the original bargain, they will not be included unless expressly agreed to by the other party. If, however, they are terms which would not so change the bargain they will be incorporated unless notice of objection to them has already been given or is given within a reasonable time.

4. Examples of typical clauses which would normally "materially alter" the contract and so result in surprise or hardship if incorporated without express awareness by the other party are: a clause negating such standard warranties as that of merchantability or fitness for a particular purpose in circumstances in which either warranty normally attaches; a clause requiring a guaranty of 90% or 100% deliveries in a case such as a contract by cannery, where the usage of the trade allows greater quantity leeways; a clause reserving to the seller the power to cancel upon the buyer's failure to meet any invoice when due; a clause requiring that complaints be made in a time materially shorter than customary or reasonable.

5. Examples of clauses which involve no element of unreasonable surprise and which therefore are to be incorporated in the contract unless notice of objection is seasonably given are: a clause setting forth and perhaps enlarging slightly upon the seller's exemption due to supervening causes beyond his control, similar to those covered by the provision of this Article on merchant's excuse by failure of presupposed conditions or a clause fixing in advance any reasonable formula of proration under such circumstances; a clause fixing a reasonable time for complaints within customary limits, or in the case of a purchase for sub-sale, providing for inspection by the sub-purchaser; a clause providing for interest on overdue invoices or fixing the seller's standard credit terms where they are within the range of trade practice and do not limit any credit bargained for; a clause limiting the right of rejection for defects which fall within the customary trade tolerances for acceptance "with adjustment" or otherwise limiting remedy in a reasonable manner (see Sections 2—718 and 2—719).

6. If no answer is received within a reasonable time after additional terms are proposed, it is both fair and commercially sound to assume that their inclusion has been assented to. Where clauses on confirming forms sent by both parties conflict each party must be assumed to object to a clause of the other conflicting with one on the confirmation sent by himself. As a result the requirement that there be notice of objection which is found in subsection (2) is satisfied and the conflicting terms do not become a part of the contract. The contract then consists of the terms originally expressly agreed to, terms on which the confirmations agree, and terms supplied by his Act, including subsection (2). The written confirmation is also subject to Section 2—201. Under that section a failure to respond permits enforcement of a prior oral agreement; under this section a failure to respond permits additional terms to become part of the agreement. [Comment 6 was amended in 1966.]

7. In many cases, as where goods are shipped, accepted and paid for before any dispute arises, there is no question whether a contract has been

made. In such cases, where the writings of the parties do not establish a contract, it is not necessary to determine which act or document constituted the offer and which the acceptance. See Section 2—204. The only question is what terms are included in the contract, and subsection (3) furnishes the governing rule. [Comment 7 was added in 1966.]

Cross References:

See generally Section 2—302.

Point 5: Sections 2—513, 2—602, 2—607, 2—609, 2—612, 2—614, 2—615, 2—616, 2—718 and 2—719.

Point 6: Sections 1—102 and 2—104.

Definitional Cross References:

"Between merchants". Section 2—104.
"Contract". Section 1—201.
"Notification". Section 1—201.
"Reasonable time". Section 1—204.
"Seasonably". Section 1—204.
"Send". Section 1—201.
"Term". Section 1—201.
"Written". Section 1—201.

§ 2—208. Course of Performance or Practical Construction

(1) Where the contract for sale involves repeated occasions for performance by either party with knowledge of the nature of the performance and opportunity for objection to it by the other, any course of performance accepted or acquiesced in without objection shall be relevant to determine the meaning of the agreement.

(2) The express terms of the agreement and any such course of performance, as well as any course of dealing and usage of trade, shall be construed whenever reasonable as consistent with each other; but when such construction is unreasonable, express terms shall control course of performance and course of performance shall control both course of dealing and usage of trade (Section 1—205).

(3) Subject to the provisions of the next section on modification and waiver, such course of performance shall be relevant to show a waiver or modification of any term inconsistent with such course of performance.

Prior Uniform Statutory Provision: No such general provision but concept of this section recognized by terms such as "course of dealing", "the circumstances of the case," "the conduct of the parties," etc., in Uniform Sales Act.

§ 2—209. Modification, Rescission and Waiver

(1) An agreement modifying a contract within this Article needs no consideration to be binding.

(2) A signed agreement which excludes modification or rescission except by a signed writing cannot be otherwise modified or rescinded, but except as between merchants such a requirement on a form supplied by the merchant must be separately signed by the other party.

(3) The requirements of the statute of frauds section of this Article (Section 2—201) must be satisfied if the contract as modified is within its provisions.

(4) Although an attempt at modification or rescission does not satisfy the requirements of subsection (2) or (3) it can operate as a waiver.

(5) A party who has made a waiver affecting an executory portion of the contract may retract the waiver by reasonable notification received by the other party that strict performance will be required of any term waived, unless the retraction would be unjust in view of a material change of position in reliance on the waiver.

Definitional Cross References:

"Agreement". Section 1—201.

"Between merchants". Section 2—104.

"Contract". Section 1—201.

"Notification". Section 1—201.

"Signed." Section 1—201.

"Term". Section 1—201.

"Writing". Section 1—201.

§ 2—210. Delegation of Performance; Assignment of Rights

(1) A party may perform his duty through a delegate unless otherwise agreed or unless the other party has a substantial interest in having his original promisor perform or control the acts required by the contract. No delegation of performance relieves the party delegating of any duty to perform or any liability for breach.

(2) Unless otherwise agreed all rights of either seller or buyer can be assigned except where the assignment would materially change the duty of the other party, or increase materially the burden or risk imposed on him by his contract, or impair materially his chance of obtaining return performance. A right to damages for breach of the whole contract or a right arising out of the assignor's due performance of his entire obligation can be assigned despite agreement otherwise.

(3) Unless the circumstances indicate the contrary a prohibition of assignment of "the contract" is to be construed as barring only the delegation to the assignee of the assignor's performance.

(4) An assignment of "the contract" or of "all my rights under the contract" or an assignment in similar general terms is an assignment of rights and unless the language or the circumstances (as in an assignment for security) indicate the contrary, it is a delegation of performance of the duties of the assignor and its acceptance by the assignee constitutes a promise by him to perform those duties. This promise is enforceable by either the assignor or the other party to the original contract.

(5) The other party may treat any assignment which delegates performance as creating reasonable grounds for insecurity and may without prejudice to his rights against the assignor demand assurances from the assignee (Section 2—609).

Definitional Cross References:

"Agreement". Section 1—201.
"Buyer". Section 2—103.
"Contract". Section 1—201.

"Party". Section 1—201.
"Rights". Section 1—201.
"Seller". Section 2—103.
"Term". Section 1—201.

PART 3

GENERAL OBLIGATION AND CONSTRUCTION OF CONTRACT

§ 2—301. General Obligations of Parties

The obligation of the seller is to transfer and deliver and that of the buyer is to accept and pay in accordance with the contract.

Definitional Cross References:

"Buyer". Section 2—103.
"Contract". Section 1—201.

"Party". Section 1—201.
"Seller". Section 2—103.

§ 2—302. Unconscionable Contract or Clause

(1) If the court as a matter of law finds the contract or any clause of the contract to have been unconscionable at the time it was made the court may refuse to enforce the contract, or it may enforce the remainder of the contract without the unconscionable clause, or it may so limit the application of any unconscionable clause as to avoid any unconscionable result.

(2) When it is claimed or appears to the court that the contract or any clause thereof may be unconscionable the parties shall be afforded a reasonable opportunity to present evidence as to its commercial setting, purpose and effect to aid the court in making the determination.

Official Comment

Prior Uniform Statutory Provision: None.

Purposes:

1. This section is intended to make it possible for the courts to police explicitly against the contracts or clauses which they find to be unconscionable. In the past such policing has been accomplished by adverse construction of language, by manipulation of the rules of offer and acceptance or by determinations that the clause is contrary to public policy or to the dominant purpose of the contract. This section is intended to allow the court to pass directly on the unconscionability of the contract or particular clause therein and to make a conclusion of law as to its unconscionability. The basic test is whether, in the light of the general commercial background and the commercial needs of the particular trade or case, the clauses involved are so one-sided as to be unconscionable under the circumstances existing at the time of the making of the contract. Subsection (2) makes it clear that it is proper for the court to hear evidence upon these questions. The principle is one of the

prevention of oppression and unfair surprise (Cf. Campbell Soup Co. v. Wentz, 172 F.2d 80, 3d Cir.1948) and not of disturbance of allocation of risks because of superior bargaining power. The underlying basis of this section is illustrated by the results in cases such as the following:

Kansas City Wholesale Grocery Co. v. Weber Packing Corporation, 93 Utah 414, 73 P.2d 1272 (1937), where a clause limiting time for complaints was held inapplicable to latent defects in a shipment of catsup which could be discovered only by microscopic analysis; Hardy v. General Motors Acceptance Corporation, 38 Ga.App. 463, 144 S.E. 327 (1928), holding that a disclaimer of warranty clause applied only to express warranties, thus letting in a fair implied warranty; Andrews Bros. v. Singer & Co. (1934 CA) 1 K.B. 17, holding that where a car with substantial mileage was delivered instead of a "new" car, a disclaimer of warranties, including those "implied," left unaffected an "express obligation" on the description, even though the Sale of Goods Act called such an implied warranty; New Prague Flouring Mill Co. v. G.A. Spears, 194 Iowa 417, 189 N.W. 815 (1922), holding that a clause permitting the seller, upon the buyer's failure to supply shipping instructions, to cancel, ship, or allow delivery date to be indefinitely postponed 30 days at a time by the inaction, does not indefinitely postpone the date of measuring damages for the buyer's breach, to the seller's advantage; and Kansas Flour Mills Co. v. Dirks, 100 Kan. 376, 164 P. 273 (1917), where under a similar clause in a rising market the court permitted the buyer to measure his damages for non-delivery at the end of only one 30 day postponement; Green v. Arcos, Ltd. (1931 CA) 47 T.L.R. 336, where a blanket clause prohibiting rejection of shipments by the buyer was restricted to apply to shipments where discrepancies represented merely mercantile variations; Meyer v. Packard Cleveland Motor Co., 106 Ohio St. 328, 140 N.E. 118 (1922), in which the court held that a "waiver" of all agreements not specified did not preclude implied warranty of fitness of a rebuilt dump truck for ordinary use as a dump truck; Austin Co. v. J.H. Tillman Co., 104 Or. 541, 209 P. 131 (1922), where a clause limiting the buyer's remedy to return was held to be applicable only if the seller had delivered a machine needed for a construction job which reasonably met the contract description; Bekkevold v. Potts, 173 Minn. 87, 216 N.W. 790, 59 A.L.R. 1164 (1927), refusing to allow warranty of fitness for purpose imposed by law to be negated by clause excluding all warranties "made" by the seller; Robert A. Munroe & Co. v. Meyer (1930) 2 K.B. 312, holding that the warranty of description overrides a clause reading "with all faults and defects" where adulterated meat not up to the contract description was delivered.

2. Under this section the court, in its discretion, may refuse to enforce the contract as a whole if it is permeated by the unconscionability, or it may strike any single clause or group of clauses which are so tainted or which are contrary to the essential purpose of the agreement, or it may simply limit unconscionable clauses so as to avoid unconscionable results.

3. The present section is addressed to the court, and the decision is to be made by it. The commercial evidence referred to in subsection (2) is for the court's consideration, not the jury's. Only the agreement which results from the court's action on these matters is to be submitted to the general triers of the facts.

Definitional Cross Reference:

"Contract". Section 1—201.

§ 2—303. Allocation or Division of Risks

Where this Article allocates a risk or a burden as between the parties "unless otherwise agreed", the agreement may not only shift the allocation but may also divide the risk or burden.

Definitional Cross References:
"Agreement". Section 1—201.
"Party". Section 1—201.

§ 2—304. Price Payable in Money, Goods, Realty, or Otherwise

(1) The price can be made payable in money or otherwise. If it is payable in whole or in part in goods each party is a seller of the goods which he is to transfer.

(2) Even though all or part of the price is payable in an interest in realty the transfer of the goods and the seller's obligations with reference to them are subject to this Article, but not the transfer of the interest in realty or the transferor's obligations in connection therewith.

§ 2—305. Open Price Term

(1) The parties if they so intend can conclude a contract for sale even though the price is not settled. In such a case the price is a reasonable price at the time for delivery if

   (a) nothing is said as to price; or

   (b) the price is left to be agreed by the parties and they fail to agree; or

   (c) the price is to be fixed in terms of some agreed market or other standard as set or recorded by a third person or agency and it is not so set or recorded.

(2) A price to be fixed by the seller or by the buyer means a price for him to fix in good faith.

(3) When a price left to be fixed otherwise than by agreement of the parties fails to be fixed through fault of one party the other may at his option treat the contract as cancelled or himself fix a reasonable price.

(4) Where, however, the parties intend not to be bound unless the price be fixed or agreed and it is not fixed or agreed there is no contract. In such a case the buyer must return any goods already received or if unable so to do must pay their reasonable value at the time of delivery and the seller must return any portion of the price paid on account.

Definitional Cross References:

"Agreement". Section 1—201.
"Burden of establishing". Section 1—201.

"Buyer". Section 2—103.
"Cancellation". Section 2—106.
"Contract". Section 1—201.
"Contract for sale". Section 2—106.
"Fault". Section 1—201.

"Goods". Section 2—105.
"Party". Section 1—201.
"Receipt of goods". Section 2—103.

"Seller". Section 2—103.
"Term". Section 1—201.

§ 2—306. Output, Requirements and Exclusive Dealings

(1) A term which measures the quantity by the output of the seller or the requirements of the buyer means such actual output or requirements as may occur in good faith, except that no quantity unreasonably disproportionate to any stated estimate or in the absence of a stated estimate to any normal or otherwise comparable prior output or requirements may be tendered or demanded.

(2) A lawful agreement by either the seller or the buyer for exclusive dealing in the kind of goods concerned imposes unless otherwise agreed an obligation by the seller to use best efforts to supply the goods and by the buyer to use best efforts to promote their sale.

Definitional Cross References:

"Agreement". Section 1—201.
"Buyer". Section 2—103.
"Contract for sale". Section 2—106.
"Good faith". Section 1—201.

"Goods". Section 2—105.
"Party". Section 1—201.
"Term". Section 1—201.
"Seller". Section 2—103.

§ 2—307. Delivery in Single Lot or Several Lots

Unless otherwise agreed all goods called for by a contract for sale must be tendered in a single delivery and payment is due only on such tender but where the circumstances give either party the right to make or demand delivery in lots the price if it can be apportioned may be demanded for each lot.

Definitional Cross References:

"Contract for sale". Section 2—106.
"Goods". Section 2—105.

"Lot". Section 2—105.
"Party". Section 1—201.
"Rights". Section 1—201.

§ 2—308. Absence of Specified Place for Delivery

Unless otherwise agreed

(a) the place for delivery of goods is the seller's place of business or if he has none his residence; but

(b) in a contract for sale of identified goods which to the knowledge of the parties at the time of contracting are in some other place, that place is the place for their delivery; and

(c) documents of title may be delivered through customary banking channels.

Definitional Cross References:

"Contract for sale". Section 2—106.
"Delivery". Section 1—201.

"Document of title". Section 1—201.
"Goods". Section 2—105.
"Party". Section 1—201.
"Seller". Section 2—103.

37

§ 2—309. Absence of Specific Time Provisions; Notice of Termination

(1) The time for shipment or delivery or any other action under a contract if not provided in this Article or agreed upon shall be a reasonable time.

(2) Where the contract provides for successive performances but is indefinite in duration it is valid for a reasonable time but unless otherwise agreed may be terminated at any time by either party.

(3) Termination of a contract by one party except on the happening of an agreed event requires that reasonable notification be received by the other party and an agreement dispensing with notification is invalid if its operation would be unconscionable.

Definitional Cross References:

"Agreement". Section 1—201.
"Contract". Section 1—201.
"Notification". Section 1—201.

"Party". Section 1—201.
"Reasonable time". Section 1—204.
"Termination". Section 2—106.

§ 2—310. Open Time for Payment or Running of Credit; Authority to Ship Under Reservation

Unless otherwise agreed

(a) payment is due at the time and place at which the buyer is to receive the goods even though the place of shipment is the place of delivery; and

(b) if the seller is authorized to send the goods he may ship them under reservation, and may tender the documents of title, but the buyer may inspect the goods after their arrival before payment is due unless such inspection is inconsistent with the terms of the contract (Section 2—513); and

(c) if delivery is authorized and made by way of documents of title otherwise than by subsection (b) then payment is due at the time and place at which the buyer is to receive the documents regardless of where the goods are to be received; and

(d) where the seller is required or authorized to ship the goods on credit the credit period runs from the time of shipment but post-dating the invoice or delaying its dispatch will correspondingly delay the starting of the credit period.

Definitional Cross References:

"Buyer". Section 2—103.
"Delivery". Section 1—201.
"Document of title". Section 1—201.

"Goods". Section 2—105.
"Receipt of goods". Section 2—103.
"Seller". Section 2—103.
"Send". Section 1—201.
"Term". Section 1—201.

§ 2—311. Options and Cooperation Respecting Performance

(1) An agreement for sale which is otherwise sufficiently definite (subsection (3) of Section 2—204) to be a contract is not made invalid by the fact that it leaves particulars of performance to be specified by one of the parties. Any such specification must be made in good faith and within limits set by commercial reasonableness.

(2) Unless otherwise agreed specifications relating to assortment of the goods are at the buyer's option and except as otherwise provided in subsections (1)(c) and (3) of Section 2—319 specifications or arrangements relating to shipment are at the seller's option.

(3) Where such specification would materially affect the other party's performance but is not seasonably made or where one party's cooperation is necessary to the agreed performance of the other but is not seasonably forthcoming, the other party in addition to all other remedies

    (a) is excused for any resulting delay in his own performance; and

    (b) may also either proceed to perform in any reasonable manner or after the time for a material part of his own performance treat the failure to specify or to cooperate as a breach by failure to deliver or accept the goods.

Definitional Cross References:

"Agreement". Section 1—201.
"Buyer". Section 2—103.
"Contract for sale". Section 2—106.
"Goods". Section 2—105.

"Party". Section 1—201.
"Remedy". Section 1—201.
"Seasonably". Section 1—204.
"Seller". Section 2—103.

§ 2—312. Warranty of Title and Against Infringement; Buyer's Obligation Against Infringement

(1) Subject to subsection (2) there is in a contract for sale a warranty by the seller that

    (a) the title conveyed shall be good, and its transfer rightful; and

    (b) the goods shall be delivered free from any security interest or other lien or encumbrance of which the buyer at the time of contracting has no knowledge.

(2) A warranty under subsection (1) will be excluded or modified only by specific language or by circumstances which give the buyer reason to know that the person selling does not claim title in himself or that he is purporting to sell only such right or title as he or a third person may have.

(3) Unless otherwise agreed a seller who is a merchant regularly dealing in goods of the kind warrants that the goods shall be delivered free of the rightful claim of any third person by way of infringement or

the like but a buyer who furnishes specifications to the seller must hold the seller harmless against any such claim which arises out of compliance with the specifications.

Definitional Cross References:

"Buyer". Section 2—103.
"Contract for sale". Section 2—106.
"Goods". Section 2—105.

"Person". Section 1—201.
"Right". Section 1—201.
"Seller". Section 2—103.

§ 2—313. Express Warranties by Affirmation, Promise, Description, Sample

(1) Express warranties by the seller are created as follows:

    (a) Any affirmation of fact or promise made by the seller to the buyer which relates to the goods and becomes part of the basis of the bargain creates an express warranty that the goods shall conform to the affirmation or promise.

    (b) Any description of the goods which is made part of the basis of the bargain creates an express warranty that the goods shall conform to the description.

    (c) Any sample or model which is made part of the basis of the bargain creates an express warranty that the whole of the goods shall conform to the sample or model.

(2) It is not necessary to the creation of an express warranty that the seller use formal words such as "warrant" or "guarantee" or that he have a specific intention to make a warranty, but an affirmation merely of the value of the goods or a statement purporting to be merely the seller's opinion or commendation of the goods does not create a warranty.

Definitional Cross References:

"Buyer". Section 2—103.
"Conforming". Section 2—106.

"Goods". Section 2—105.
"Seller". Section 2—103.

§ 2—314. Implied Warranty: Merchantability; Usage of Trade

(1) Unless excluded or modified (Section 2—316), a warranty that the goods shall be merchantable is implied in a contract for their sale if the seller is a merchant with respect to goods of that kind. Under this section the serving for value of food or drink to be consumed either on the premises or elsewhere is a sale.

(2) Goods to be merchantable must be at least such as

    (a) pass without objection in the trade under the contract description; and

    (b) in the case of fungible goods, are of fair average quality within the description; and

    (c) are fit for the ordinary purposes for which such goods are used; and

(d) run, within the variations permitted by the agreement, of even kind, quality and quantity within each unit and among all units involved; and

(e) are adequately contained, packaged, and labeled as the agreement may require; and

(f) conform to the promises or affirmations of fact made on the container or label if any.

(3) Unless excluded or modified (Section 2—316) other implied warranties may arise from course of dealing or usage of trade.

Definitional Cross References:

"Agreement". Section 1—201.
"Contract". Section 1—201.
"Contract for sale". Section 2—106.

"Goods". Section 2—105.
"Merchant". Section 2—104.
"Seller". Section 2—103.

§ 2—315. Implied Warranty: Fitness for Particular Purpose

Where the seller at the time of contracting has reason to know any particular purpose for which the goods are required and that the buyer is relying on the seller's skill or judgment to select or furnish suitable goods, there is unless excluded or modified under the next section an implied warranty that the goods shall be fit for such purpose.

Definitional Cross References:

"Buyer". Section 2—103.
"Goods". Section 2—105.
"Seller". Section 2—103.

§ 2—316. Exclusion or Modification of Warranties

(1) Words or conduct relevant to the creation of an express warranty and words or conduct tending to negate or limit warranty shall be construed wherever reasonable as consistent with each other; but subject to the provisions of this Article on parol or extrinsic evidence (Section 2—202) negation or limitation is inoperative to the extent that such construction is unreasonable.

(2) Subject to subsection (3), to exclude or modify the implied warranty of merchantability or any part of it the language must mention merchantability and in case of a writing must be conspicuous, and to exclude or modify any implied warranty of fitness the exclusion must be by a writing and conspicuous. Language to exclude all implied warranties of fitness is sufficient if it states, for example, that "There are no warranties which extend beyond the description on the face hereof."

(3) Notwithstanding subsection (2)

(a) unless the circumstances indicate otherwise, all implied warranties are excluded by expressions like "as is", "with all faults" or other language which in common understanding calls the buyer's attention to the exclusion of

41

warranties and makes plain that there is no implied warranty; and

(b) when the buyer before entering into the contract has examined the goods or the sample or model as fully as he desired or has refused to examine the goods there is no implied warranty with regard to defects which an examination ought in the circumstances to have revealed to him; and

(c) an implied warranty can also be excluded or modified by course of dealing or course of performance or usage of trade.

(4) Remedies for breach of warranty can be limited in accordance with the provisions of this Article on liquidation or limitation of damages and on contractual modification of remedy (Sections 2—718 and 2—719).

Definitional Cross References:

"Agreement". Section 1—201.
"Buyer". Section 2—103.
"Contract". Section 1—201.
"Course of dealing". Section 1—205.

"Goods". Section 2—105.
"Remedy". Section 1—201.
"Seller". Section 2—103.
"Usage of trade". Section 1—205.

§ 2—317. Cumulation and Conflict of Warranties Express or Implied

Warranties whether express or implied shall be construed as consistent with each other and as cumulative, but if such construction is unreasonable the intention of the parties shall determine which warranty is dominant. In ascertaining that intention the following rules apply:

(a) Exact or technical specifications displace an inconsistent sample or model or general language of description.

(b) A sample from an existing bulk displaces inconsistent general language of description.

(c) Express warranties displace inconsistent implied warranties other than an implied warranty of fitness for a particular purpose.

Definitional Cross Reference:

"Party". Section 1—201.

§ 2—318. Third Party Beneficiaries of Warranties Express or Implied

Note: *If this Act is introduced in the Congress of the United States this section should be omitted. (States to select one alternative.)*

Alternative A

A seller's warranty whether express or implied extends to any natural person who is in the family or household of his buyer or who is a guest in his home if it is reasonable to expect that such person may use, consume or be affected by the goods and who is injured in person by breach of the warranty. A seller may not exclude or limit the operation of this section.

Alternative B

A seller's warranty whether express or implied extends to any natural person who may reasonably be expected to use, consume or be affected by the goods and who is injured in person by breach of the warranty. A seller may not exclude or limit the operation of this section.

Alternative C

A seller's warranty whether express or implied extends to any person who may reasonably be expected to use, consume or be affected by the goods and who is injured by breach of the warranty.

A seller may not exclude or limit the operation of this section with respect to injury to the person of an individual to whom the warranty extends.

§ 2—319. F.O.B. and F.A.S. Terms

(1) Unless otherwise agreed the term F.O.B. (which means "free on board") at a named place, even though used only in connection with the stated price, is a delivery term under which

  (a) when the term is F.O.B. the place of shipment, the seller must at that place ship the goods in the manner provided in this Article (Section 2—504) and bear the expense and risk of putting them into the possession of the carrier; or

  (b) when the term is F.O.B. the place of destination, the seller must at his own expense and risk transport the goods to that place and there tender delivery of them in the manner provided in this Article (Section 2—503);

  (c) when under either (a) or (b) the term is also F.O.B. vessel, car or other vehicle, the seller must in addition at his own expense and risk load the goods on board. If the term is F.O.B. vessel the buyer must name the vessel and in an appropriate case the seller must comply with the provisions of this Article on the form of bill of lading (Section 2—323).

(2) Unless otherwise agreed the term F.A.S. vessel (which means "free alongside") at a named port, even though used only in connection with the stated price, is a delivery term under which the seller must

    (a) at his own expense and risk deliver the goods alongside the vessel in the manner usual in that port or on a dock designated and provided by the buyer; and

    (b) obtain and tender a receipt for the goods in exchange for which the carrier is under a duty to issue a bill of lading.

(3) Unless otherwise agreed in any case falling within subsection (1)(a) or (c) or subsection (2) the buyer must seasonably give any needed instructions for making delivery, including when the term is F.A.S. or F.O.B. the loading berth of the vessel and in an appropriate case its name and sailing date. The seller may treat the failure of needed instructions as a failure of cooperation under this Article (Section 2—311). He may also at his option move the goods in any reasonable manner preparatory to delivery or shipment.

(4) Under the term F.O.B. vessel or F.A.S. unless otherwise agreed the buyer must make payment against tender of the required documents and the seller may not tender nor the buyer demand delivery of the goods in substitution for the documents.

Definitional Cross References:

"Agreed". Section 1—201.
"Bill of lading". Section 1—201.
"Buyer". Section 2—103.
"Goods". Section 2—105.
"Seasonably". Section 1—204.
"Seller". Section 2—103.
"Term". Section 1—201.

§ 2—320. C.I.F. and C. & F. Terms

(1) The term C.I.F. means that the price includes in a lump sum the cost of the goods and the insurance and freight to the named destination. The term C. & F. or C.F. means that the price so includes cost and freight to the named destination.

(2) Unless otherwise agreed and even though used only in connection with the stated price and destination, the term C.I.F. destination or its equivalent requires the seller at his own expense and risk to

    (a) put the goods into the possession of a carrier at the port for shipment and obtain a negotiable bill or bills of lading covering the entire transportation to the named destination; and

    (b) load the goods and obtain a receipt from the carrier (which may be contained in the bill of lading) showing that the freight has been paid or provided for; and

    (c) obtain a policy or certificate of insurance, including any war risk insurance, of a kind and on terms then current at the port of shipment in the usual amount, in the currency of the contract, shown to cover the same goods covered by the bill of lading and providing for payment of loss to the order of the buyer or for the account of whom it may concern; but the seller may add to the price the amount of the premium for any such war risk insurance; and

(d) prepare an invoice of the goods and procure any other documents required to effect shipment or to comply with the contract; and

(e) forward and tender with commercial promptness all the documents in due form and with any indorsement necessary to perfect the buyer's rights.

(3) Unless otherwise agreed the term C. & F. or its equivalent has the same effect and imposes upon the seller the same obligations and risks as a C.I.F. term except the obligation as to insurance.

(4) Under the term C.I.F. or C. & F. unless otherwise agreed the buyer must make payment against tender of the required documents and the seller may not tender nor the buyer demand delivery of the goods in substitution for the documents.

Definitional Cross References:

"Bill of lading". Section 1—201.
"Buyer". Section 2—103.
"Contract". Section 1—201.

"Goods". Section 2—105.
"Rights". Section 1—201.
"Seller". Section 2—103.
"Term". Section 1—201.

§ 2—321. C.I.F. or C. & F.: "Net Landed Weights"; "Payment on Arrival"; Warranty of Condition on Arrival

Under a contract containing a term C.I.F. or C. & F.

(1) Where the price is based on or is to be adjusted according to "net landed weights", "delivered weights", "out turn" quantity or quality or the like, unless otherwise agreed the seller must reasonably estimate the price. The payment due on tender of the documents called for by the contract is the amount so estimated, but after final adjustment of the price a settlement must be made with commercial promptness.

(2) An agreement described in subsection (1) or any warranty of quality or condition of the goods on arrival places upon the seller the risk of ordinary deterioration, shrinkage and the like in transportation but has no effect on the place or time of identification to the contract for sale or delivery or on the passing of the risk of loss.

(3) Unless otherwise agreed where the contract provides for payment on or after arrival of the goods the seller must before payment allow such preliminary inspection as is feasible; but if the goods are lost delivery of the documents and payment are due when the goods should have arrived.

Definitional Cross References:

"Agreement". Section 1—201.
"Contract". Section 1—201.
"Delivery". Section 1—201.

"Goods". Section 2—105.
"Seller". Section 2—103.
"Term". Section 1—201.

§ 2—322. Delivery "Ex–Ship"

(1) Unless otherwise agreed a term for delivery of goods "ex-ship" (which means from the carrying vessel) or in equivalent language is not restricted to a particular ship and requires delivery from a ship which has reached a place at the named port of destination where goods of the kind are usually discharged.

(2) Under such a term unless otherwise agreed

   (a) the seller must discharge all liens arising out of the carriage and furnish the buyer with a direction which puts the carrier under a duty to deliver the goods; and

   (b) the risk of loss does not pass to the buyer until the goods leave the ship's tackle or are otherwise properly unloaded.

Definitional Cross References:

"Buyer". Section 2—103.
"Goods". Section 2—105.
"Seller". Section 2—103.
"Term". Section 1—201.

§ 2—323. Form of Bill of Lading Required in Overseas Shipment; "Overseas"

(1) Where the contract contemplates overseas shipment and contains a term C.I.F. or C. & F. or F.O.B. vessel, the seller unless otherwise agreed must obtain a negotiable bill of lading stating that the goods have been loaded on board or, in the case of a term C.I.F. or C. & F., received for shipment.

(2) Where in a case within subsection (1) a bill of lading has been issued in a set of parts, unless otherwise agreed if the documents are not to be sent from abroad the buyer may demand tender of the full set; otherwise only one part of the bill of lading need be tendered. Even if the agreement expressly requires a full set

   (a) due tender of a single part is acceptable within the provisions of this Article on cure of improper delivery (subsection (1) of Section 2—508); and

   (b) even though the full set is demanded, if the documents are sent from abroad the person tendering an incomplete set may nevertheless require payment upon furnishing an indemnity which the buyer in good faith deems adequate.

(3) A shipment by water or by air or a contract contemplating such shipment is "overseas" insofar as by usage of trade or agreement it is subject to the commercial, financing or shipping practices characteristic of international deep water commerce.

Definitional Cross References:

"Bill of lading". Section 1—201.
"Buyer". Section 2—103.

"Contract". Section 1—201.
"Delivery". Section 1—201.
"Financing agency". Section 2—104.

"Person". Section 1—201.
"Seller". Section 2—103.

"Send". Section 1—201.
"Term". Section 1—201.

§ 2—324. "No Arrival, No Sale" Term

Under a term "no arrival, no sale" or terms of like meaning, unless otherwise agreed,

(a) the seller must properly ship conforming goods and if they arrive by any means he must tender them on arrival but he assumes no obligation that the goods will arrive unless he has caused the non-arrival; and

(b) where without fault of the seller the goods are in part lost or have so deteriorated as no longer to conform to the contract or arrive after the contract time, the buyer may proceed as if there had been casualty to identified goods (Section 2—613).

Definitional Cross References:

"Buyer". Section 2—103.
"Conforming". Section 2 106.
"Contract". Section 1—201.
"Fault". Section 1—201.

"Goods". Section 2—105.
"Sale". Section 2—106.
"Seller". Section 2—103.
"Term". Section 1—201.

§ 2—325. "Letter of Credit" Term; "Confirmed Credit"

(1) Failure of the buyer seasonably to furnish an agreed letter of credit is a breach of the contract for sale.

(2) The delivery to seller of a proper letter of credit suspends the buyer's obligation to pay. If the letter of credit is dishonored, the seller may on seasonable notification to the buyer require payment directly from him.

(3) Unless otherwise agreed the term "letter of credit" or "banker's credit" in a contract for sale means an irrevocable credit issued by a financing agency of good repute and, where the shipment is overseas, of good international repute. The term "confirmed credit" means that the credit must also carry the direct obligation of such an agency which does business in the seller's financial market.

Definitional Cross References:

"Buyer". Section 2—103.
"Contract for sale". Section 2—106.
"Draft". Section 3—104.
"Financing agency". Section 2—104.

"Notifies". Section 1—201.
"Overseas". Section 2—323.
"Purchaser". Section 1—201.
"Seasonably". Section 1—204.
"Seller". Section 2—103.
"Term". Section 1—201.

§ 2—326. Sale on Approval and Sale or Return; Consignment Sales and Rights of Creditors

(1) Unless otherwise agreed, if delivered goods may be returned by the buyer even though they conform to the contract, the transaction is

    (a) a "sale on approval" if the goods are delivered primarily for use, and

    (b) a "sale or return" if the goods are delivered primarily for resale.

(2) Except as provided in subsection (3), goods held on approval are not subject to the claims of the buyer's creditors until acceptance; goods held on sale or return are subject to such claims while in the buyer's possession.

(3) Where goods are delivered to a person for sale and such person maintains a place of business at which he deals in goods of the kind involved, under a name other than the name of the person making delivery, then with respect to claims of creditors of the person conducting the business the goods are deemed to be on sale or return. The provisions of this subsection are applicable even though an agreement purports to reserve title to the person making delivery until payment or resale or uses such words as "on consignment" or "on memorandum". However, this subsection is not applicable if the person making delivery

    (a) complies with an applicable law providing for a consignor's interest or the like to be evidenced by a sign, or

    (b) establishes that the person conducting the business is generally known by his creditors to be substantially engaged in selling the goods of others, or

    (c) complies with the filing provisions of the Article on Secured Transactions (Article 9).

(4) Any "or return" term of a contract for sale is to be treated as a separate contract for sale within the statute of frauds section of this Article (Section 2—201) and as contradicting the sale aspect of the contract within the provisions of this Article on parol or extrinsic evidence (Section 2—202).

Definitional Cross References:

"Between merchants". Section 2—104.

"Buyer". Section 2—103.

"Conform". Section 2—106.

"Contract for sale". Section 2—106.

"Creditor". Section 1—201.

"Goods". Section 2—105.

"Sale". Section 2—106.

"Seller". Section 2—103.

§ 2—327. Special Incidents of Sale on Approval and Sale or Return

(1) Under a sale on approval unless otherwise agreed

    (a) although the goods are identified to the contract the risk of loss and the title do not pass to the buyer until acceptance; and

    (b) use of the goods consistent with the purpose of trial is not acceptance but failure seasonably to notify the seller of election to return the goods is acceptance, and if the goods conform to the contract acceptance of any part is acceptance of the whole; and

(c) after due notification of election to return, the return is at the seller's risk and expense but a merchant buyer must follow any reasonable instructions.

(2) Under a sale or return unless otherwise agreed

(a) the option to return extends to the whole or any commercial unit of the goods while in substantially their original condition, but must be exercised seasonably; and

(b) the return is at the buyer's risk and expense.

Definitional Cross References:

"Agreed". Section 1—201.
"Buyer". Section 2—103.
"Commercial unit". Section 2—105.
"Conform". Section 2—106.
"Contract". Section 1—201.
"Goods". Section 2—105.

"Merchant". Section 2—104.
"Notifies". Section 1—201.
"Notification". Section 1—201.
"Sale on approval". Section 2—326.
"Sale or return". Section 2—326.
"Seasonably". Section 1—204.
"Seller". Section 2—103.

§ 2—328. Sale by Auction

(1) In a sale by auction if goods are put up in lots each lot is the subject of a separate sale.

(2) A sale by auction is complete when the auctioneer so announces by the fall of the hammer or in other customary manner. Where a bid is made while the hammer is falling in acceptance of a prior bid the auctioneer may in his discretion reopen the bidding or declare the goods sold under the bid on which the hammer was falling.

(3) Such a sale is with reserve unless the goods are in explicit terms put up without reserve. In an auction with reserve the auctioneer may withdraw the goods at any time until he announces completion of the sale. In an auction without reserve, after the auctioneer calls for bids on an article or lot, that article or lot cannot be withdrawn unless no bid is made within a reasonable time. In either case a bidder may retract his bid until the auctioneer's announcement of completion of the sale, but a bidder's retraction does not revive any previous bid.

(4) If the auctioneer knowingly receives a bid on the seller's behalf or the seller makes or procures such a bid, and notice has not been given that liberty for such bidding is reserved, the buyer may at his option avoid the sale or take the goods at the price of the last good faith bid prior to the completion of the sale. This subsection shall not apply to any bid at a forced sale.

Definitional Cross References:

"Buyer". Section 2—103.
"Good faith". Section 1—201.

"Goods". Section 2—105.
"Lot". Section 2—105.
"Notice". Section 1—201.

"Sale". Section 2—106.
"Seller". Section 2—103.

PART 4

TITLE, CREDITORS AND GOOD
FAITH PURCHASERS

§ 2—401. Passing of Title; Reservation for Security; Limited Application of This Section

Each provision of this Article with regard to the rights, obligations and remedies of the seller, the buyer, purchasers or other third parties applies irrespective of title to the goods except where the provision refers to such title. Insofar as situations are not covered by the other provisions of this Article and matters concerning title become material the following rules apply:

(1) Title to goods cannot pass under a contract for sale prior to their identification to the contract (Section 2—501), and unless otherwise explicitly agreed the buyer acquires by their identification a special property as limited by this Act. Any retention or reservation by the seller of the title (property) in goods shipped or delivered to the buyer is limited in effect to a reservation of a security interest. Subject to these provisions and to the provisions of the Article on Secured Transactions (Article 9), title to goods passes from the seller to the buyer in any manner and on any conditions explicitly agreed on by the parties.

(2) Unless otherwise explicitly agreed title passes to the buyer at the time and place at which the seller completes his performance with reference to the physical delivery of the goods, despite any reservation of a security interest and even though a document of title is to be delivered at a different time or place; and in particular and despite any reservation of a security interest by the bill of lading

    (a) if the contract requires or authorizes the seller to send the goods to the buyer but does not require him to deliver them at destination, title passes to the buyer at the time and place of shipment; but

    (b) if the contract requires delivery at destination, title passes on tender there.

(3) Unless otherwise explicitly agreed where delivery is to be made without moving the goods,

    (a) if the seller is to deliver a document of title, title passes at the time when and the place where he delivers such documents; or

(b) if the goods are at the time of contracting already identified and no documents are to be delivered, title passes at the time and place of contracting.

(4) A rejection or other refusal by the buyer to receive or retain the goods, whether or not justified, or a justified revocation of acceptance revests title to the goods in the seller. Such revesting occurs by operation of law and is not a "sale".

Definitional Cross References:

"Agreement". Section 1—201.
"Bill of lading". Section 1—201.
"Buyer". Section 2—103.
"Contract". Section 1—201.
"Contract for sale". Section 2—106.
"Delivery". Section 1—201.
"Document of title". Section 1—201.
"Good faith". Section 2—103.
"Goods". Section 2—105.

"Party". Section 1—201.
"Purchaser". Section 1—201.
"Receipt" of goods. Section 2—103.
"Remedy". Section 1—201.
"Rights". Section 1—201.
"Sale". Section 2—106.
"Security interest". Section 1—201.
"Seller". Section 2—103.
"Send". Section 1—201.

§ 2—402. Rights of Seller's Creditors Against Sold Goods.

(1) Except as provided in subsections (2) and (3), rights of unsecured creditors of the seller with respect to goods which have been identified to a contract for sale are subject to the buyer's rights to recover the goods under this Article (Sections 2—502 and 2—716).

(2) A creditor of the seller may treat a sale or an identification of goods to a contract for sale as void if as against him a retention of possession by the seller is fraudulent under any rule of law of the state where the goods are situated, except that retention of possession in good faith and current course of trade by a merchant-seller for a commercially reasonable time after a sale or identification is not fraudulent.

(3) Nothing in this Article shall be deemed to impair the rights of creditors of the seller

(a) under the provisions of the Article on Secured Transactions (Article 9); or

(b) where identification to the contract or delivery is made not in current course of trade but in satisfaction of or as security for a pre-existing claim for money, security or the like and is made under circumstances which under any rule of law of the state where the goods are situated would apart from this Article constitute the transaction a fraudulent transfer or voidable preference.

Definitional Cross References:

"Contract for sale". Section 2—106.
"Creditor". Section 1—201.
"Good faith". Section 2—103.

"Goods". Section 2—105.
"Merchant". Section 2—104.
"Money". Section 1—201.
"Reasonable time". Section 1—204.

"Rights". Section 1—201.
"Sale". Section 2—106.
"Seller". Section 2—103.

§ 2—403. Power to Transfer; Good Faith Purchase of Goods; "Entrusting"

(1) A purchaser of goods acquires all title which his transferor had or had power to transfer except that a purchaser of a limited interest acquires rights only to the extent of the interest purchased. A person with voidable title has power to transfer a good title to a good faith purchaser for value. When goods have been delivered under a transaction of purchase the purchaser has such power even though

(a) the transferor was deceived as to the identity of the purchaser, or

(b) the delivery was in exchange for a check which is later dishonored, or

(c) it was agreed that the transaction was to be a "cash sale", or

(d) the delivery was procured through fraud punishable as larcenous under the criminal law.

(2) Any entrusting of possession of goods to a merchant who deals in goods of that kind gives him power to transfer all rights of the entruster to a buyer in ordinary course of business.

(3) "Entrusting" includes any delivery and any acquiescence in retention of possession regardless of any condition expressed between the parties to the delivery or acquiescence and regardless of whether the procurement of the entrusting or the possessor's disposition of the goods have been such as to be larcenous under the criminal law.

(4) The rights of other purchasers of goods and of lien creditors are governed by the Articles on Secured Transactions (Article 9), Bulk Transfers (Article 6) and Documents of Title (Article 7).

Definitional Cross References:

"Buyer in ordinary course of business". Section 1—201.

"Good faith". Sections 1—201 and 2—103.

"Goods". Section 2—105.

"Person". Section 1—201.

"Purchaser". Section 1—201.

"Signed". Section 1—201.

"Term". Section 1—201.

"Value". Section 1—201.

PART 5

PERFORMANCE

§ 2—501. Insurable Interest in Goods; Manner of Identification of Goods

(1) The buyer obtains a special property and an insurable interest in goods by identification of existing goods as goods to which the contract refers even though the goods so identified are non-conforming and he has an option to return or reject them. Such identification can be made at any time and in any manner explicitly agreed to by the parties. In the absence of explicit agreement identification occurs

(a) when the contract is made if it is for the sale of goods already existing and identified;

(b) if the contract is for the sale of future goods other than those described in paragraph (c), when goods are shipped, marked or otherwise designated by the seller as goods to which the contract refers;

(c) when the crops are planted or otherwise become growing crops or the young are conceived if the contract is for the sale of unborn young to be born within twelve months after contracting or for the sale of crops to be harvested within twelve months or the next normal harvest season after contracting whichever is longer.

(2) The seller retains an insurable interest in goods so long as title to or any security interest in the goods remains in him and where the identification is by the seller alone he may until default or insolvency or notification to the buyer that the identification is final substitute other goods for those identified.

(3) Nothing in this section impairs any insurable interest recognized under any other statute or rule of law.

Definitional Cross References:

"Agreement". Section 1—201.
"Contract". Section 1—201.
"Contract for sale". Section 2—106.
"Future goods". Section 2—105.
"Goods". Section 2—105.

"Notification". Section 1—201.
"Party". Section 1—201.
"Sale". Section 2—106.
"Security interest". Section 1—201.
"Seller". Section 2—103.

§ 2—502. Buyer's Right to Goods on Seller's Insolvency

(1) Subject to subsection (2) and even though the goods have not been shipped a buyer who has paid a part or all of the price of goods in which he has a special property under the provisions of the immediately preceding section may on making and keeping good a tender of any unpaid portion of their price recover them from the seller if the seller

becomes insolvent within ten days after receipt of the first installment on their price.

(2) If the identification creating his special property has been made by the buyer he acquires the right to recover the goods only if they conform to the contract for sale.

Definitional Cross References:

"Buyer". Section 2—103.
"Conform". Section 2—106.
"Contract for sale". Section 2—106.

"Goods". Section 2—105.
"Insolvent". Section 1—201.
"Right". Section 1—201.
"Seller". Section 2—103.

§ 2—503. Manner of Seller's Tender of Delivery

(1) Tender of delivery requires that the seller put and hold conforming goods at the buyer's disposition and give the buyer any notification reasonably necessary to enable him to take delivery. The manner, time and place for tender are determined by the agreement and this Article, and in particular

(a) tender must be at a reasonable hour, and if it is of goods they must be kept available for the period reasonably necessary to enable the buyer to take possession; but

(b) unless otherwise agreed the buyer must furnish facilities reasonably suited to the receipt of the goods.

(2) Where the case is within the next section respecting shipment tender requires that the seller comply with its provisions.

(3) Where the seller is required to deliver at a particular destination tender requires that he comply with subsection (1) and also in any appropriate case tender documents as described in subsections (4) and (5) of this section.

(4) Where goods are in the possession of a bailee and are to be delivered without being moved

(a) tender requires that the seller either tender a negotiable document of title covering such goods or procure acknowledgment by the bailee of the buyer's right to possession of the goods; but

(b) tender to the buyer of a non-negotiable document of title or of a written direction to the bailee to deliver is sufficient tender unless the buyer seasonably objects, and receipt by the bailee of notification of the buyer's rights fixes those rights as against the bailee and all third persons; but risk of loss of the goods and of any failure by the bailee to honor the non-negotiable document of title or to obey the direction remains on the seller until the buyer has had a reasonable time to present the document or direction, and a refusal by the bailee to honor the document or to obey the direction defeats the tender.

(5) Where the contract requires the seller to deliver documents

    (a) he must tender all such documents in correct form, except as provided in this Article with respect to bills of lading in a set (subsection (2) of Section 2—323); and

    (b) tender through customary banking channels is sufficient and dishonor of a draft accompanying the documents constitutes non-acceptance or rejection.

Definitional Cross References:

"Agreement". Section 1—201.
"Bill of lading". Section 1—201.
"Buyer". Section 2—103.
"Conforming". Section 2—106.
"Contract". Section 1—201.
"Delivery". Section 1—201.
"Dishonor". Section 3—508.
"Document of title". Section 1—201.

"Draft". Section 3—104.
"Goods". Section 2—105.
"Notification". Section 1—201.
"Reasonable time". Section 1—204.
"Receipt" of goods. Section 2—103.
"Rights". Section 1—201.
"Seasonably". Section 1—204.
"Seller". Section 2—103.
"Written". Section 1—201.

§ 2—504. Shipment by Seller

Where the seller is required or authorized to send the goods to the buyer and the contract does not require him to deliver them at a particular destination, then unless otherwise agreed he must

    (a) put the goods in the possession of such a carrier and make such a contract for their transportation as may be reasonable having regard to the nature of the goods and other circumstances of the case; and

    (b) obtain and promptly deliver or tender in due form any document necessary to enable the buyer to obtain possession of the goods or otherwise required by the agreement or by usage of trade; and

    (c) promptly notify the buyer of the shipment.

Failure to notify the buyer under paragraph (c) or to make a proper contract under paragraph (a) is a ground for rejection only if material delay or loss ensues.

Definitional Cross References:

"Agreement". Section 1—201.
"Buyer". Section 2—103.
"Contract". Section 1—201.
"Delivery". Section 1—201.

"Goods". Section 2—105.
"Notifies". Section 1—201.
"Seller". Section 2—103.
"Send". Section 1—201.
"Usage of trade". Section 1—205.

§ 2—505. Seller's Shipment Under Reservation

(1) Where the seller has identified goods to the contract by or before shipment:

    (a) his procurement of a negotiable bill of lading to his own order or otherwise reserves in him a security interest in the goods. His procurement of the bill to the order of a financing agency or of the buyer indicates in addition only the seller's expectation of transferring that interest to the person named.

(b) a non-negotiable bill of lading to himself or his nominee reserves possession of the goods as security but except in a case of conditional delivery (subsection (2) of Section 2—507) a non-negotiable bill of lading naming the buyer as consignee reserves no security interest even though the seller retains possession of the bill of lading.

(2) When shipment by the seller with reservation of a security interest is in violation of the contract for sale it constitutes an improper contract for transportation within the preceding section but impairs neither the rights given to the buyer by shipment and identification of the goods to the contract nor the seller's powers as a holder of a negotiable document.

Definitional Cross References:

"Bill of lading". Section 1—201.
"Buyer". Section 2—103.
"Consignee". Section 7—102.
"Contract". Section 1—201.
"Contract for sale". Section 2—106.
"Delivery". Section 1—201.
"Financing agency". Section 2—104.

"Goods". Section 2—105.
"Holder". Section 1—201.
"Person". Section 1—201.
"Security interest". Section 1—201.
"Seller". Section 2—103.

§ 2—506. Rights of Financing Agency

(1) A financing agency by paying or purchasing for value a draft which relates to a shipment of goods acquires to the extent of the payment or purchase and in addition to its own rights under the draft and any document of title securing it any rights of the shipper in the goods including the right to stop delivery and the shipper's right to have the draft honored by the buyer.

(2) The right to reimbursement of a financing agency which has in good faith honored or purchased the draft under commitment to or authority from the buyer is not impaired by subsequent discovery of defects with reference to any relevant document which was apparently regular on its face.

Definitional Cross References:

"Buyer". Section 2—103.
"Document of title". Section 1—201.
"Draft". Section 3—104.
"Financing agency". Section 2—104.

"Good faith". Section 2—103.
"Goods". Section 2—105.
"Honor". Section 1—201.
"Purchase". Section 1—201.
"Rights". Section 1—201.
"Value". Section 1—201.

§ 2—507. Effect of Seller's Tender; Delivery on Condition

(1) Tender of delivery is a condition to the buyer's duty to accept the goods and, unless otherwise agreed, to his duty to pay for them. Tender entitles the seller to acceptance of the goods and to payment according to the contract.

(2) Where payment is due and demanded on the delivery to the buyer of goods or documents of title, his right as against the seller to retain or dispose of them is conditional upon his making the payment due.

Definitional Cross References:

"Buyer". Section 2—103.
"Contract". Section 1—201.
"Delivery". Section 1—201.
"Document of title". Section 1—201.

"Goods". Section 2—105.
"Rights". Section 1—201.
"Seller". Section 2—103.

§ 2—508. Cure by Seller of Improper Tender or Delivery; Replacement

(1) Where any tender or delivery by the seller is rejected because non-conforming and the time for performance has not yet expired, the seller may seasonably notify the buyer of his intention to cure and may then within the contract time make a conforming delivery.

(2) Where the buyer rejects a non-conforming tender which the seller had reasonable grounds to believe would be acceptable with or without money allowance the seller may if he seasonably notifies the buyer have a further reasonable time to substitute a conforming tender.

Definitional Cross References:

"Buyer". Section 2—103.
"Conforming". Section 2—106.
"Contract". Section 1—201.
"Money". Section 1—201.

"Notifies". Section 1—201.
"Reasonable time". Section 1—204.
"Seasonably". Section 1—204.
"Seller". Section 2—103.

§ 2—509. Risk of Loss in the Absence of Breach

(1) Where the contract requires or authorizes the seller to ship the goods by carrier

> (a) if it does not require him to deliver them at a particular destination, the risk of loss passes to the buyer when the goods are duly delivered to the carrier even though the shipment is under reservation (Section 2—505); but

> (b) if it does require him to deliver them at a particular destination and the goods are there duly tendered while in the possession of the carrier, the risk of loss passes to the buyer when the goods are there duly so tendered as to enable the buyer to take delivery.

(2) Where the goods are held by a bailee to be delivered without being moved, the risk of loss passes to the buyer

      (a) on his receipt of a negotiable document of title covering the goods; or

      (b) on acknowledgment by the bailee of the buyer's right to possession of the goods; or

      (c) after his receipt of a non-negotiable document of title or other written direction to deliver, as provided in subsection (4)(b) of Section 2—503.

(3) In any case not within subsection (1) or (2), the risk of loss passes to the buyer on his receipt of the goods if the seller is a merchant; otherwise the risk passes to the buyer on tender of delivery.

(4) The provisions of this section are subject to contrary agreement of the parties and to the provisions of this Article on sale on approval (Section 2—327) and on effect of breach on risk of loss (Section 2—510).

Definitional Cross References:

"Agreement". Section 1—201.
"Buyer". Section 2—103.
"Contract". Section 1—201.
"Delivery". Section 1—201.
"Document of title". Section 1—201.

"Goods". Section 2—105.
"Merchant". Section 2—104.
"Party". Section 1—201.
"Receipt" of goods. Section 2—103.
"Sale on approval". Section 2—326.
"Seller". Section 2—103.

§ 2—510. Effect of Breach on Risk of Loss

(1) Where a tender or delivery of goods so fails to conform to the contract as to give a right of rejection the risk of their loss remains on the seller until cure or acceptance.

(2) Where the buyer rightfully revokes acceptance he may to the extent of any deficiency in his effective insurance coverage treat the risk of loss as having rested on the seller from the beginning.

(3) Where the buyer as to conforming goods already identified to the contract for sale repudiates or is otherwise in breach before risk of their loss has passed to him, the seller may to the extent of any deficiency in his effective insurance coverage treat the risk of loss as resting on the buyer for a commercially reasonable time.

Definitional Cross References:

"Buyer". Section 2—103.
"Conform". Section 2—106.

"Contract for sale". Section 2—106.
"Goods". Section 2—105.
"Seller". Section 2—103.

§ 2—511. Tender of Payment by Buyer; Payment by Check

(1) Unless otherwise agreed tender of payment is a condition to the seller's duty to tender and complete any delivery.

(2) Tender of payment is sufficient when made by any means or in any manner current in the ordinary course of business unless the seller

demands payment in legal tender and gives any extension of time reasonably necessary to procure it.

(3) Subject to the provisions of this Act on the effect of an instrument on an obligation (Section 3—802), payment by check is conditional and is defeated as between the parties by dishonor of the check on due presentment.

Definitional Cross References:

"Buyer". Section 2—103.
"Check". Section 3—104.
"Dishonor". Section 3—508.

"Party". Section 1—201.
"Reasonable time". Section 1—204.
"Seller". Section 2—103.

§ 2—512. Payment by Buyer Before Inspection

(1) Where the contract requires payment before inspection non-conformity of the goods does not excuse the buyer from so making payment unless

    (a) the non-conformity appears without inspection; or

    (b) despite tender of the required documents the circumstances would justify injunction against honor under the provisions of this Act (Section 5—114).

(2) Payment pursuant to subsection (1) does not constitute an acceptance of goods or impair the buyer's right to inspect or any of his remedies.

Definitional Cross References:

"Buyer". Section 2—103.
"Conform". Section 2—106.
"Contract". Section 1—201.
"Financing agency". Section 2—104.

"Goods". Section 2—105.
"Remedy". Section 1—201.
"Rights". Section 1—201.

§ 2—513. Buyer's Right to Inspection of Goods

(1) Unless otherwise agreed and subject to subsection (3), where goods are tendered or delivered or identified to the contract for sale, the buyer has a right before payment or acceptance to inspect them at any reasonable place and time and in any reasonable manner. When the seller is required or authorized to send the goods to the buyer, the inspection may be after their arrival.

(2) Expenses of inspection must be borne by the buyer but may be recovered from the seller if the goods do not conform and are rejected.

(3) Unless otherwise agreed and subject to the provisions of this Article on C.I.F. contracts (subsection (3) of Section 2—321), the buyer is not entitled to inspect the goods before payment of the price when the contract provides

    (a) for delivery "C.O.D." or on other like terms; or

(b) for payment against documents of title, except where such payment is due only after the goods are to become available for inspection.

(4) A place or method of inspection fixed by the parties is presumed to be exclusive but unless otherwise expressly agreed it does not postpone identification or shift the place for delivery or for passing the risk of loss. If compliance becomes impossible, inspection shall be as provided in this section unless the place or method fixed was clearly intended as an indispensable condition failure of which avoids the contract.

Definitional Cross References:

"Buyer". Section 2—103.
"Conform". Section 2—106.
"Contract". Section 1—201.
"Contract for sale". Section 2—106.
"Document of title". Section 1—201.
"Goods". Section 2—105.

"Party". Section 1—201.
"Presumed". Section 1—201.
"Reasonable time". Section 1—204.
"Rights". Section 1—201.
"Seller". Section 2—103.
"Send". Section 1—201.
"Term". Section 1—201.

§ 2—514. When Documents Deliverable on Acceptance; When on Payment

Unless otherwise agreed documents against which a draft is drawn are to be delivered to the drawee on acceptance of the draft if it is payable more than three days after presentment; otherwise, only on payment.

Definitional Cross References:

"Delivery". Section 1—201.
"Draft". Section 3—104.

§ 2—515. Preserving Evidence of Goods in Dispute

In furtherance of the adjustment of any claim or dispute

(a) either party on reasonable notification to the other and for the purpose of ascertaining the facts and preserving evidence has the right to inspect, test and sample the goods including such of them as may be in the possession or control of the other; and

(b) the parties may agree to a third party inspection or survey to determine the conformity or condition of the goods and may agree that the findings shall be binding upon them in any subsequent litigation or adjustment.

Definitional Cross References:

"Conform". Section 2—106.
"Goods". Section 2—105.

"Notification". Section 1—201.
"Party". Section 1—201.

PART 6

BREACH, REPUDIATION AND EXCUSE

§ 2—601. Buyer's Rights on Improper Delivery

Subject to the provisions of this Article on breach in installment contracts (Section 2—612) and unless otherwise agreed under the sections on contractual limitations of remedy (Sections 2—718 and 2—719), if the goods or the tender of delivery fail in any respect to conform to the contract, the buyer may

(a) reject the whole; or

(b) accept the whole; or

(c) accept any commercial unit or units and reject the rest.

Definitional Cross References:

"Buyer". Section 2—103.
"Commercial unit". Section 2—105.
"Conform". Section 2—106.
"Contract". Section 1—201.
"Goods". Section 2—105.
"Installment contract". Section 2—612.
"Rights". Section 1—201.

§ 2—602. Manner and Effect of Rightful Rejection

(1) Rejection of goods must be within a reasonable time after their delivery or tender. It is ineffective unless the buyer seasonably notifies the seller.

(2) Subject to the provisions of the two following sections on rejected goods (Sections 2—603 and 2—604),

(a) after rejection any exercise of ownership by the buyer with respect to any commercial unit is wrongful as against the seller; and

(b) if the buyer has before rejection taken physical possession of goods in which he does not have a security interest under the provisions of this Article (subsection (3) of Section 2—711), he is under a duty after rejection to hold them with reasonable care at the seller's disposition for a time sufficient to permit the seller to remove them; but

(c) the buyer has no further obligations with regard to goods rightfully rejected.

(3) The seller's rights with respect to goods wrongfully rejected are governed by the provisions of this Article on Seller's remedies in general (Section 2—703).

Definitional Cross References:

"Buyer". Section 2—103.
"Commercial unit". Section 2—105.
"Goods". Section 2—105.
"Merchant". Section 2—104.
"Notifies". Section 1—201.
"Reasonable time". Section 1—204.
"Remedy". Section 1—201.

61

"Rights". Section 1—201.

"Seasonably". Section 1—204.

"Security interest". Section 1—201.

"Seller". Section 2—103.

§ 2—603. Merchant Buyer's Duties as to Rightfully Rejected Goods

(1) Subject to any security interest in the buyer (subsection (3) of Section 2—711), when the seller has no agent or place of business at the market of rejection a merchant buyer is under a duty after rejection of goods in his possession or control to follow any reasonable instructions received from the seller with respect to the goods and in the absence of such instructions to make reasonable efforts to sell them for the seller's account if they are perishable or threaten to decline in value speedily. Instructions are not reasonable if on demand indemnity for expenses is not forthcoming.

(2) When the buyer sells goods under subsection (1), he is entitled to reimbursement from the seller or out of the proceeds for reasonable expenses of caring for and selling them, and if the expenses include no selling commission then to such commission as is usual in the trade or if there is none to a reasonable sum not exceeding ten per cent on the gross proceeds.

(3) In complying with this section the buyer is held only to good faith and good faith conduct hereunder is neither acceptance nor conversion nor the basis of an action for damages.

Definitional Cross References:

"Buyer". Section 2—103.

"Good faith". Section 1—201.

"Goods". Section 2—105.

"Merchant". Section 2—104.

"Security interest". Section 1—201.

"Seller". Section 2—103.

§ 2—604. Buyer's Options as to Salvage of Rightfully Rejected Goods

Subject to the provisions of the immediately preceding section on perishables if the seller gives no instructions within a reasonable time after notification of rejection the buyer may store the rejected goods for the seller's account or reship them to him or resell them for the seller's account with reimbursement as provided in the preceding section. Such action is not acceptance or conversion.

Definitional Cross References:

"Buyer". Section 2—103.

"Notification". Section 1—201.

"Reasonable time". Section 1—204.

"Seller". Section 2—103.

§ 2—605. Waiver of Buyer's Objections by Failure to Particularize

(1) The buyer's failure to state in connection with rejection a particular defect which is ascertainable by reasonable inspection pre-

cludes him from relying on the unstated defect to justify rejection or to establish breach

> (a) where the seller could have cured it if stated seasonably; or
>
> (b) between merchants when the seller has after rejection made a request in writing for a full and final written statement of all defects on which the buyer proposes to rely.

(2) Payment against documents made without reservation of rights precludes recovery of the payment for defects apparent on the face of the documents.

Definitional Cross References:

"Between merchants". Section 2—104.

"Buyer". Section 2—103.

"Seasonably". Section 1—204.

"Seller". Section 2—103.

"Writing" and "written". Section 1—201.

§ 2—606. What Constitutes Acceptance of Goods

(1) Acceptance of goods occurs when the buyer

> (a) after a reasonable opportunity to inspect the goods signifies to the seller that the goods are conforming or that he will take or retain them in spite of their nonconformity; or
>
> (b) fails to make an effective rejection (subsection (1) of Section 2—602), but such acceptance does not occur until the buyer has had a reasonable opportunity to inspect them; or
>
> (c) does any act inconsistent with the seller's ownership; but if such act is wrongful as against the seller it is an acceptance only if ratified by him.

(2) Acceptance of a part of any commercial unit is acceptance of that entire unit.

Definitional Cross References:

"Buyer". Section 2—103.

"Commercial unit". Section 2—105.

"Goods". Section 2—105.

"Seller". Section 2—103.

§ 2—607. Effect of Acceptance; Notice of Breach; Burden of Establishing Breach After Acceptance; Notice of Claim or Litigation to Person Answerable Over

(1) The buyer must pay at the contract rate for any goods accepted.

(2) Acceptance of goods by the buyer precludes rejection of the goods accepted and if made with knowledge of a non-conformity cannot be revoked because of it unless the acceptance was on the reasonable assumption that the non-conformity would be seasonably cured but

acceptance does not of itself impair any other remedy provided by this Article for non-conformity.

    (3) Where a tender has been accepted

        (a) the buyer must within a reasonable time after he discovers or should have discovered any breach notify the seller of breach or be barred from any remedy; and

        (b) if the claim is one for infringement or the like (subsection (3) of Section 2—312) and the buyer is sued as a result of such a breach he must so notify the seller within a reasonable time after he receives notice of the litigation or be barred from any remedy over for liability established by the litigation.

    (4) The burden is on the buyer to establish any breach with respect to the goods accepted.

    (5) Where the buyer is sued for breach of a warranty or other obligation for which his seller is answerable over

        (a) he may give his seller written notice of the litigation. If the notice states that the seller may come in and defend and that if the seller does not do so he will be bound in any action against him by his buyer by any determination of fact common to the two litigations, then unless the seller after seasonable receipt of the notice does come in and defend he is so bound.

        (b) if the claim is one for infringement or the like (subsection (3) of Section 2—312) the original seller may demand in writing that his buyer turn over to him control of the litigation including settlement or else be barred from any remedy over and if he also agrees to bear all expense and to satisfy any adverse judgment, then unless the buyer after seasonable receipt of the demand does turn over control the buyer is so barred.

    (6) The provisions of subsection (3), (4) and (5) apply to any obligation of a buyer to hold the seller harmless against infringement or the like (subsection (3) of Section 2—312).

Definitional Cross References:

"Burden of establishing". Section 1—201.

"Buyer". Section 2—103.

"Conform". Section 2—106.

"Contract". Section 1—201.

"Goods". Section 2—105.

"Notifies". Section 1—201.

"Reasonable time". Section 1—204.

"Remedy". Section 1—201.

"Seasonably". Section 1—204.

§ 2—608. Revocation of Acceptance in Whole or in Part

    (1) The buyer may revoke his acceptance of a lot or commercial unit whose non-conformity substantially impairs its value to him if he has accepted it

(a) on the reasonable assumption that its non-conformity would be cured and it has not been seasonably cured; or

(b) without discovery of such non-conformity if his acceptance was reasonably induced either by the difficulty of discovery before acceptance or by the seller's assurances.

(2) Revocation of acceptance must occur within a reasonable time after the buyer discovers or should have discovered the ground for it and before any substantial change in condition of the goods which is not caused by their own defects. It is not effective until the buyer notifies the seller of it.

(3) A buyer who so revokes has the same rights and duties with regard to the goods involved as if he had rejected them.

Definitional Cross References:

"Buyer". Section 2—103.
"Commercial unit". Section 2—105.
"Conform". Section 2—106.
"Goods". Section 2—105.

"Lot". Section 2—105.
"Notifies". Section 1—201.
"Reasonable time". Section 1—204.
"Rights". Section 1—201.
"Seasonably". Section 1—204.
"Seller". Section 2—103.

§ 2—609. Right to Adequate Assurance of Performance

(1) A contract for sale imposes an obligation on each party that the other's expectation of receiving due performance will not be impaired. When reasonable grounds for insecurity arise with respect to the performance of either party the other may in writing demand adequate assurance of due performance and until he receives such assurance may if commercially reasonable suspend any performance for which he has not already received the agreed return.

(2) Between merchants the reasonableness of grounds for insecurity and the adequacy of any assurance offered shall be determined according to commercial standards.

(3) Acceptance of any improper delivery or payment does not prejudice the aggrieved party's right to demand adequate assurance of future performance.

(4) After receipt of a justified demand failure to provide within a reasonable time not exceeding thirty days such assurance of due performance as is adequate under the circumstances of the particular case is a repudiation of the contract.

Official Comment

Prior Uniform Statutory Provision: See Sections 53, 54(1)(b), 55 and 63(2), Uniform Sales Act.

Purposes:

1. The section rests on the recognition of the fact that the essential purpose of a contract between commercial men is actual performance and they do not bargain merely for a promise, or for a promise plus the right to win a lawsuit and that a continuing sense of reliance and security that the

promised performance will be forthcoming when due, is an important fea-
ture of the bargain. If either the willingness or the ability of a party to
perform declines materially between
the time of contracting and the time
for performance, the other party is
threatened with the loss of a substantial part of what he has bargained for.
A seller needs protection not merely
against having to deliver on credit to
a shaky buyer, but also against having
to procure and manufacture the
goods, perhaps turning down other
customers. Once he has been given
reason to believe that the buyer's performance has become uncertain, it is
an undue hardship to force him to
continue his own performance. Similarly, a buyer who believes that the
seller's deliveries have become uncertain cannot safely wait for the due
date of performance when he has been
buying to assure himself of materials
for his current manufacturing or to
replenish his stock of merchandise.

2. Three measures have been
adopted to meet the needs of commercial men in such situations. First, the
aggrieved party is permitted to suspend his own performance and any
preparation therefor, with excuse for
any resulting necessary delay, until
the situation has been clarified. "Suspend performance" under this section
means to hold up performance pending the outcome of the demand, and
includes also the holding up of any
preparatory action. This is the same
principle which governs the ancient
law of stoppage and seller's lien, and
also of excuse of a buyer from prepayment if the seller's actions manifest
that he cannot or will not perform.
(Original Act, Section 63(2).)

Secondly, the aggrieved party is giv-
en the right to require adequate assurance that the other party's performance will be duly forthcoming. This
principle is reflected in the familiar
clauses permitting the seller to curtail

deliveries if the buyer's credit becomes impaired, which when held
within the limits of reasonableness
and good faith actually express no
more than the fair business meaning
of any commercial contract.

Third, and finally, this section provides the means by which the aggrieved party may treat the contract
as broken if his reasonable grounds
for insecurity are not cleared up within a reasonable time. This is the
principle underlying the law of anticipatory breach, whether by way of defective part performance or by repudiation. The present section merges
these three principles of law and commercial practice into a single theory
of general application to all sales
agreements looking to future performance.

3. Subsection (2) of the present section requires that "reasonable"
grounds and "adequate" assurance as
used in subsection (1) be defined by
commercial rather than legal standards. The express reference to commercial standards carries no connota-
tion that the obligation of good faith is
not equally applicable here.

Under commercial standards and in
accord with commercial practice, a
ground for insecurity need not arise
from or be directly related to the contract in question. The law as to "de-
pendence" or "independence" of
promises within a single contract does
not control the application of the present section.

Thus a buyer who falls behind in
"his account" with the seller, even
though the items involved have to do
with separate and legally distinct contracts, impairs the seller's expectation
of due performance. Again, under the
same test, a buyer who requires preci-
sion parts which he intends to use
immediately upon delivery, may have
reasonable grounds for insecurity if he
discovers that his seller is making defective deliveries of such parts to oth-

er buyers with similar needs. Thus, too, in a situation such as arose in Jay Dreher Corporation v. Delco Appliance Corporation, 93 F.2d 275 (C.C.A. 2, 1937), where a manufacturer gave a dealer an exclusive franchise for the sale of his product but on two or three occasions breached the exclusive dealing clause, although there was no default in orders, deliveries or payments under the separate sales contract between the parties, the aggrieved dealer would be entitled to suspend his performance of the contract for sale under the present section and to demand assurance that the exclusive dealing contract would be lived up to. There is no need for an explicit clause tying the exclusive franchise into the contract for the sale of goods since the situation itself ties the agreements together.

The nature of the sales contract enters also into the question of reasonableness. For example, a report from an apparently trustworthy source that the seller had shipped defective goods or was planning to ship them would normally give the buyer reasonable grounds for insecurity. But when the buyer has assumed the risk of payment before inspection of the goods, as in a sales contract on C.I.F. or similar cash against documents terms, that risk is not to be evaded by a demand for assurance. Therefore no ground for insecurity would exist under this section unless the report went to a ground which would excuse payment by the buyer.

4. What constitutes "adequate" assurance of due performance is subject to the same test of factual conditions. For example, where the buyer can make use of a defective delivery, a mere promise by a seller of good repute that he is giving the matter his attention and that the defect will not be repeated, is normally sufficient. Under the same circumstances, however, a similar statement by a known

corner-cutter might well be considered insufficient without the posting of a guaranty or, if so demanded by the buyer, a speedy replacement of the delivery involved. By the same token where a delivery has defects, even though easily curable, which interfere with easy use by the buyer, no verbal assurance can be deemed adequate which is not accompanied by replacement, repair, money-allowance, or other commercially reasonable cure.

A fact situation such as arose in Corn Products Refining Co. v. Fasola, 94 N.J.L. 181, 109 A. 505 (1920) offers illustration both of reasonable grounds for insecurity and "adequate" assurance. In that case a contract for the sale of oils on 30 days' credit, 2% off for payment within 10 days, provided that credit was to be extended to the buyer only if his financial responsibility was satisfactory to the seller. The buyer had been in the habit of taking advantage of the discount but at the same time that he failed to make his customary 10 day payment, the seller heard rumors, in fact false, that the buyer's financial condition was shaky. Thereupon, the seller demanded cash before shipment or security satisfactory to him. The buyer sent a good credit report from his banker, expressed willingness to make payments when due on the 30 day terms and insisted on further deliveries under the contract. Under this Article the rumors, although false, were enough to make the buyer's financial condition "unsatisfactory" to the seller under the contract clause. Moreover, the buyer's practice of taking the cash discounts is enough, apart from the contract clause, to lay a commercial foundation for suspicion when the practice is suddenly stopped. These matters, however, go only to the justification of the seller's demand for security, or his "reasonable grounds for insecurity".

The adequacy of the assurance given is not measured as in the type of "satisfaction" situation affected with intangibles, such as in personal service cases, cases involving a third party's judgment as final, or cases in which the whole contract is dependent on one party's satisfaction, as in a sale on approval. Here, the seller must exercise good faith and observe commercial standards. This Article thus approves the statement of the court in James B. Berry's Sons Co. of Illinois v. Monark Gasoline & Oil Co., Inc., 32 F.2d 74 (C.C.A.8, 1929), that the seller's satisfaction under such a clause must be based upon reason and must not be arbitrary or capricious; and rejects the purely personal "good faith" test of the Corn Products Refining Co. case, which held that in the seller's sole judgment, if for any reason he was dissatisfied, he was entitled to revoke the credit. In the absence of the buyer's failure to take the 2% discount as was his custom, the banker's report given in that case would have been "adequate" assurance under this Act, regardless of the language of the "satisfaction" clause. However, the seller is reasonably entitled to feel insecure at a sudden expansion of the buyer's use of a credit term, and should be entitled either to security or to a satisfactory explanation.

The entire foregoing discussion as to adequacy of assurance by way of explanation is subject to qualification when repeated occasions for the application of this section arise. This Act recognizes that repeated delinquencies must be viewed as cumulative. On the other hand, commercial sense also requires that if repeated claims for assurance are made under this section, the basis for these claims must be increasingly obvious.

5. A failure to provide adequate assurance of performance and thereby to re-establish the security of expectation, results in a breach only "by repudiation" under subsection (4). Therefore, the possibility is continued of retraction of the repudiation under the section dealing with that problem, unless the aggrieved party has acted on the breach in some manner.

The thirty day limit on the time to provide assurance is laid down to free the question of reasonable time from uncertainty in later litigation.

6. Clauses seeking to give the protected party exceedingly wide powers to cancel or readjust the contract when ground for insecurity arises must be read against the fact that good faith is a part of the obligation of the contract and not subject to modification by agreement and includes, in the case of a merchant, the reasonable observance of commercial standards of fair dealing in the trade. Such clauses can thus be effective to enlarge the protection given by the present section to a certain extent, to fix the reasonable time within which requested assurance must be given, or to define adequacy of the assurance in any commercially reasonable fashion. But any clause seeking to set up arbitrary standards for action is ineffective under this Article. Acceleration clauses are treated similarly in the Articles on Commercial Paper and Secured Transactions.

Cross References:

Point 3: Section 1—203.
Point 5: Section 2—611.
Point 6: Sections 1—203 and 1—208 and Articles 3 and 9.

Definitional Cross References:

"Aggrieved party". Section 1—201.
"Between merchants". Section 2—104.
"Contract". Section 1—201.
"Contract for sale". Section 2—106.
"Party". Section 1—201.
"Reasonable time". Section 1—204.
"Rights". Section 1—201.
"Writing". Section 1—201.

§ 2—610. Anticipatory Repudiation

When either party repudiates the contract with respect to a performance not yet due the loss of which will substantially impair the value of the contract to the other, the aggrieved party may

(a) for a commercially reasonable time await performance by the repudiating party; or

(b) resort to any remedy for breach (Section 2—703 or Section 2—711), even though he has notified the repudiating party that he would await the latter's performance and has urged retraction; and

(c) in either case suspend his own performance or proceed in accordance with the provisions of this Article on the seller's right to identify goods to the contract notwithstanding breach or to salvage unfinished goods (Section 2—704).

Definitional Cross References:
"Aggrieved party". Section 1—201.
"Contract". Section 1—201.
"Party". Section 1—201.
"Remedy". Section 1—201.

§ 2—611. Retraction of Anticipatory Repudiation

(1) Until the repudiating party's next performance is due he can retract his repudiation unless the aggrieved party has since the repudiation cancelled or materially changed his position or otherwise indicated that he considers the repudiation final.

(2) Retraction may be by any method which clearly indicates to the aggrieved party that the repudiating party intends to perform, but must include any assurance justifiably demanded under the provisions of this Article (Section 2—609).

(3) Retraction reinstates the repudiating party's rights under the contract with due excuse and allowance to the aggrieved party for any delay occasioned by the repudiation.

Definitional Cross References:
"Aggrieved party". Section 1—201.
"Cancellation". Section 2—106.
"Contract". Section 1—201.
"Party". Section 1—201.
"Rights". Section 1—201.

§ 2—612. "Installment Contract"; Breach

(1) An "installment contract" is one which requires or authorizes the delivery of goods in separate lots to be separately accepted, even though the contract contains a clause "each delivery is a separate contract" or its equivalent.

(2) The buyer may reject any installment which is non-conforming if the non-conformity substantially impairs the value of that install-

ment and cannot be cured or if the non-conformity is a defect in the required documents; but if the non-conformity does not fall within subsection (3) and the seller gives adequate assurance of its cure the buyer must accept that installment.

(3) Whenever non-conformity or default with respect to one or more installments substantially impairs the value of the whole contract there is a breach of the whole. But the aggrieved party reinstates the contract if he accepts a non-conforming installment without seasonably notifying of cancellation or if he brings an action with respect only to past installments or demands performance as to future installments.

Definitional Cross References:

"Action". Section 1—201.
"Aggrieved party". Section 1—201.
"Buyer". Section 2—103.
"Cancellation". Section 2—106.
"Conform". Section 2—106.

"Contract". Section 1—201.
"Lot". Section 2—105.
"Notifies". Section 1—201.
"Seasonably". Section 1—204.
"Seller". Section 2—103.

§ 2—613. Casualty to Identified Goods

Where the contract requires for its performance goods identified when the contract is made, and the goods suffer casualty without fault of either party before the risk of loss passes to the buyer, or in a proper case under a "no arrival, no sale" term (Section 2—324) then

(a) if the loss is total the contract is avoided; and

(b) if the loss is partial or the goods have so deteriorated as no longer to conform to the contract the buyer may nevertheless demand inspection and at his option either treat the contract as avoided or accept the goods with due allowance from the contract price for the deterioration or the deficiency in quantity but without further right against the seller.

Definitional Cross References:

"Buyer". Section 2—103.
"Conform". Section 2—106.
"Contract". Section 1—201.
"Fault". Section 1—201.

"Goods". Section 2—105.
"Party". Section 1—201.
"Rights". Section 1—201.
"Seller". Section 2—103.

§ 2—614. Substituted Performance

(1) Where without fault of either party the agreed berthing, loading, or unloading facilities fail or an agreed type of carrier becomes unavailable or the agreed manner of delivery otherwise becomes commercially impracticable but a commercially reasonable substitute is available, such substitute performance must be tendered and accepted.

(2) If the agreed means or manner of payment fails because of domestic or foreign governmental regulation, the seller may withhold or stop delivery unless the buyer provides a means or manner of payment which is commercially a substantial equivalent. If delivery

has already been taken, payment by the means or in the manner provided by the regulation discharges the buyer's obligation unless the regulation is discriminatory, oppressive or predatory.

Definitional Cross References:

"Buyer". Section 2—103.
"Fault". Section 1—201.
"Party". Section 1—201.
"Seller". Section 2—103.

§ 2—615. Excuse by Failure of Presupposed Conditions

Except so far as a seller may have assumed a greater obligation and subject to the preceding section on substituted performance:

(a) Delay in delivery or non-delivery in whole or in part by a seller who complies with paragraphs (b) and (c) is not a breach of his duty under a contract for sale if performance as agreed has been made impracticable by the occurrence of a contingency the non-occurrence of which was a basic assumption on which the contract was made or by compliance in good faith with any applicable foreign or domestic governmental regulation or order whether or not it later proves to be invalid.

(b) Where the causes mentioned in paragraph (a) affect only a part of the seller's capacity to perform, he must allocate production and deliveries among his customers but may at his option include regular customers not then under contract as well as his own requirements for further manufacture. He may so allocate in any manner which is fair and reasonable.

(c) The seller must notify the buyer seasonably that there will be delay or non-delivery and, when allocation is required under paragraph (b), of the estimated quota thus made available for the buyer.

Official Comment

Prior Uniform Statutory Provision:
None.

Purposes:

1. This section excuses a seller from timely delivery of goods contracted for, where his performance has become commercially impracticable because of unforeseen supervening circumstances not within the contemplation of the parties at the time of contracting. The destruction of specific goods and the problem of the use of substituted performance on points other than delay or quantity, treated elsewhere in this Article, must be distinguished from the matter covered by this section.

2. The present section deliberately refrains from any effort at an exhaustive expression of contingencies and is to be interpreted in all cases sought to be brought within its scope in terms of its underlying reason and purpose.

3. The first test for excuse under this Article in terms of basic assumption is a familiar one. The additional test of commercial impracticability (as contrasted with "impossibility," "frustration of performance" or "frustra-

71

tion of the venture") has been adopted in order to call attention to the commercial character of the criterion chosen by this Article.

4. Increased cost alone does not excuse performance unless the rise in cost is due to some unforeseen contingency which alters the essential nature of the performance. Neither is a rise or a collapse in the market in itself a justification, for that is exactly the type of business risk which business contracts made at fixed prices are intended to cover. But a severe shortage of raw materials or of supplies due to a contingency such as war, embargo, local crop failure unforeseen shutdown of major sources of supply or the like, which either causes a marked increase in cost or altogether prevents the seller from securing supplies necessary to his performance, is within the contemplation of this section. (See Ford & Sons, Ltd., v. Henry Leetham & Sons, Ltd., 21 Com. Cas. 55 (1915, K.B.D.).)

5. Where a particular source of supply is exclusive under the agreement and fails through casualty, the present section applies rather than the provision on destruction or deterioration of specific goods. The same holds true where a particular source of supply is shown by the circumstances to have been contemplated or assumed by the parties at the time of contracting. (See Davis Co. v. Hoffmann–LaRoche Chemical Works, 178 App.Div. 855, 166 N.Y.S. 179 (1917) and International Paper Co. v. Rockefeller, 161 App.Div. 180, 146 N.Y.S. 371 (1914).) There is no excuse under this section, however, unless the seller has employed all due measures to assure himself that his source will not fail. (See Canadian Industrial Alcohol Co., Ltd., v. Dunbar Molasses Co., 258 N.Y. 194, 179 N.E. 383, 80 A.L.R. 1173 (1932) and Washington Mfg. Co. v. Midland Lumber Co., 113 Wash. 593, 194 P. 777 (1921).)

In the case of failure of production by an agreed source for causes beyond the seller's control, the seller should, if possible, be excused since production by an agreed source is without more a basic assumption of the contract. Such excuse should not result in relieving the defaulting supplier from liability nor in dropping into the seller's lap an unearned bonus of damages over. The flexible adjustment machinery of this Article provides the solution under the provision on the obligation of good faith. A condition to his making good the claim of excuse is the turning over to the buyer of his rights against the defaulting source of supply to the extent of the buyer's contract in relation to which excuse is being claimed.

6. In situations in which neither sense nor justice is served by either answer when the issue is posed in flat terms of "excuse" or "no excuse," adjustment under the various provisions of this Article is necessary, especially the sections on good faith, on insecurity and assurance and on the reading of all provisions in the light of their purposes, and the general policy of this Act to use equitable principles in furtherance of commercial standards and good faith.

7. The failure of conditions which go to convenience or collateral values rather than to the commercial practicability of the main performance does not amount to a complete excuse. However, good faith and the reason of the present section and of the preceding one may properly be held to justify and even to require any needed delay involved in a good faith inquiry seeking a readjustment of the contract terms to meet the new conditions.

8. The provisions of this section are made subject to assumption of greater liability by agreement and such agreement is to be found not only in the expressed terms of the contract but in the circumstances sur-

rounding the contracting, in trade usage and the like. Thus the exemptions of this section do not apply when the contingency in question is sufficiently foreshadowed at the time of contracting to be included among the business risks which are fairly to be regarded as part of the dickered terms, either consciously or as a matter of reasonable, commercial interpretation from the circumstances. (See Madeirense Do Brasil, S.A. v. Stulman–Emrick Lumber Co., 147 F.2d 399 (C.C.A., 2 Cir., 1945).) The exemption otherwise present through usage of trade under the present section may also be expressly negated by the language of the agreement. Generally, express agreements as to exemptions designed to enlarge upon or supplant the provisions of this section are to be read in the light of mercantile sense and reason, for this section itself sets up the commercial standard for normal and reasonable interpretation and provides a minimum beyond which agreement may not go.

Agreement can also be made in regard to the consequences of exemption as laid down in paragraphs (b) and (c) and the next section on procedure on notice claiming excuse.

9. The case of a farmer who has contracted to sell crops to be grown on designated land may be regarded as falling either within the section on casualty to identified goods or this section, and he may be excused, when there is a failure of the specific crop, either on the basis of the destruction of identified goods or because of the failure of a basic assumption of the contract.

Exemption of the buyer in the case of a "requirements" contract is covered by the "Output and Requirements" section both as to assumption and allocation of the relevant risks. But when a contract by a manufacturer to buy fuel or raw material makes no specific reference to a particular venture and no such reference may be drawn from the circumstances, commercial understanding views it as a general deal in the general market and not conditioned on any assumption of the continuing operation of the buyer's plant. Even when notice is given by the buyer that the supplies are needed to fill a specific contract of a normal commercial kind, commercial understanding does not see such a supply contract as conditioned on the continuance of the buyer's further contract for outlet. On the other hand, where the buyer's contract is in reasonable commercial understanding conditioned on a definite and specific venture or assumption as, for instance, a war procurement subcontract known to be based on a prime contract which is subject to termination, or a supply contract for a particular construction venture, the reason of the present section may well apply and entitle the buyer to the exemption.

10. Following its basic policy of using commercial practicability as a test for excuse, this section recognizes as of equal significance either a foreign or domestic regulation and disregards any technical distinctions between "law," "regulation," "order" and the like. Nor does it make the present action of the seller depend upon the eventual judicial determination of the legality of the particular governmental action. The seller's good faith belief in the validity of the regulation is the test under this Article and the best evidence of his good faith is the general commercial acceptance of the regulation. However, governmental interference cannot excuse unless it truly "supervenes" in such a manner as to be beyond the seller's assumption of risk. And any action by the party claiming excuse which causes or colludes in inducing the governmental action preventing his performance

would be in breach of good faith and would destroy his exemption.

11. An excused seller must fulfill his contract to the extent which the supervening contingency permits, and if the situation is such that his customers are generally affected he must take account of all in supplying one. Subsections (a) and (b), therefore, explicitly permit in any proration a fair and reasonable attention to the needs of regular customers who are probably relying on spot orders for supplies. Customers at different stages of the manufacturing process may be fairly treated by including the seller's manufacturing requirements. A fortiori, the seller may also take account of contracts later in date than the one in question. The fact that such spot orders may be closed at an advanced price causes no difficulty, since any allocation which exceeds normal past requirements will not be reasonable. However, good faith requires, when prices have advanced, that the seller exercise real care in making his allocations, and in case of doubt his contract customers should be favored and supplies prorated evenly among them regardless of price. Save for the extra care thus required by changes in the market, this section seeks to leave every reasonable business leeway to the seller.

Cross References:

Point 1: Sections 2—613 and 2—614.

Point 2: Section 1—102.

Point 5: Sections 1—203 and 2—613.

Point 6: Sections 1—102, 1—203 and 2—609.

Point 7: Section 2—614.

Point 8: Sections 1—201, 2—302 and 2—616.

Point 9: Sections 1—102, 2—306 and 2—613.

Definitional Cross References:

"Between merchants". Section 2—104.

"Buyer". Section 2—103.

"Contract". Section 1—201.

"Contract for sale". Section 2—106.

"Good faith". Section 1—201.

"Merchant". Section 2—104.

"Notifies". Section 1—201.

"Seasonably". Section 1—204.

"Seller". Section 2—103.

§ 2—616. Procedure on Notice Claiming Excuse

(1) Where the buyer receives notification of a material or indefinite delay or an allocation justified under the preceding section he may by written notification to the seller as to any delivery concerned, and where the prospective deficiency substantially impairs the value of the whole contract under the provisions of this Article relating to breach of installment contracts (Section 2—612), then also as to the whole,

> (a) terminate and thereby discharge any unexecuted portion of the contract; or

> (b) modify the contract by agreeing to take his available quota in substitution.

(2) If after receipt of such notification from the seller the buyer fails so to modify the contract within a reasonable time not exceeding thirty days the contract lapses with respect to any deliveries affected.

(3) The provisions of this section may not be negated by agreement except in so far as the seller has assumed a greater obligation under the preceding section.

Definitional Cross References:

"Buyer". Section 2—103.
"Contract". Section 1—201.
"Installment contract". Section 2—612.

"Notification". Section 1—201.
"Reasonable time". Section 1—204.
"Seller". Section 2—103.
"Termination". Section 2—106.
"Written". Section 1—201.

PART 7

REMEDIES

§ 2—701. Remedies for Breach of Collateral Contracts Not Impaired

Remedies for breach of any obligation or promise collateral or ancillary to a contract for sale are not impaired by the provisions of this Article.

Definitional Cross References:

"Contract for sale". Section 2—106.
"Remedy". Section 1—201.

§ 2—702. Seller's Remedies on Discovery of Buyer's Insolvency

(1) Where the seller discovers the buyer to be insolvent he may refuse delivery except for cash including payment for all goods theretofore delivered under the contract, and stop delivery under this Article (Section 2—705).

(2) Where the seller discovers that the buyer has received goods on credit while insolvent he may reclaim the goods upon demand made within ten days after the receipt, but if misrepresentation of solvency has been made to the particular seller in writing within three months before delivery the ten day limitation does not apply. Except as provided in this subsection the seller may not base a right to reclaim goods on the buyer's fraudulent or innocent misrepresentation of solvency or of intent to pay.

(3) The seller's right to reclaim under subsection (2) is subject to the rights of a buyer in ordinary course or other good faith purchaser under this Article (Section 2—403). Successful reclamation of goods excludes all other remedies with respect to them.

Definitional Cross References:

"Buyer". Section 2—103.
"Buyer in ordinary course of business". Section 1—201.
"Contract". Section 1—201.
"Good faith". Section 1—201.

"Goods". Section 2—105.
"Insolvent". Section 1—201.
"Person". Section 1—201.
"Purchaser". Section 1—201.
"Receipt" of goods. Section 2—103.
"Remedy". Section 1—201.
"Rights". Section 1—201.

"Seller". Section 2—103.
"Writing". Section 1—201.

§ 2—703. Seller's Remedies in General

Where the buyer wrongfully rejects or revokes acceptance of goods or fails to make a payment due on or before delivery or repudiates with respect to a part or the whole, then with respect to any goods directly affected and, if the breach is of the whole contract (Section 2—612), then also with respect to the whole undelivered balance, the aggrieved seller may

    (a) withhold delivery of such goods;

    (b) stop delivery by any bailee as hereafter provided (Section 2—705);

    (c) proceed under the next section respecting goods still un-identified to the contract;

    (d) resell and recover damages as hereafter provided (Section 2—706);

    (e) recover damages for non-acceptance (Section 2—708) or in a proper case the price (Section 2—709);

    (f) cancel.

Definitional Cross References:

"Aggrieved party". Section 1—201.
"Buyer". Section 2—103.
"Cancellation". Section 2—106.

"Contract". Section 1—201.
"Goods". Section 2—105.
"Remedy". Section 1—201.
"Seller". Section 2—103.

§ 2—704. Seller's Right to Identify Goods to the Contract Notwithstanding Breach or to Salvage Unfinished Goods

(1) An aggrieved seller under the preceding section may

    (a) identify to the contract conforming goods not already identified if at the time he learned of the breach they are in his possession or control;

    (b) treat as the subject of resale goods which have demonstrably been intended for the particular contract even though those goods are unfinished.

(2) Where the goods are unfinished an aggrieved seller may in the exercise of reasonable commercial judgment for the purposes of avoiding loss and of effective realization either complete the manufacture and wholly identify the goods to the contract or cease manufacture and resell for scrap or salvage value or proceed in any other reasonable manner.

Definitional Cross References:

"Aggrieved party". Section 1—201.
"Conforming". Section 2—106.
"Contract". Section 1—201.

"Goods". Section 2—105.
"Rights". Section 1—201.
"Seller". Section 2—103.

§ 2—705. Seller's Stoppage of Delivery in Transit or Otherwise

(1) The seller may stop delivery of goods in the possession of a carrier or other bailee when he discovers the buyer to be insolvent (Section 2—702) and may stop delivery of carload, truckload, planeload or larger shipments of express or freight when the buyer repudiates or fails to make a payment due before delivery or if for any other reason the seller has a right to withhold or reclaim the goods.

(2) As against such buyer the seller may stop delivery until

    (a) receipt of the goods by the buyer; or

    (b) acknowledgment to the buyer by any bailee of the goods except a carrier that the bailee holds the goods for the buyer; or

    (c) such acknowledgment to the buyer by a carrier by reshipment or as warehouseman; or

    (d) negotiation to the buyer of any negotiable document of title covering the goods.

(3) (a) To stop delivery the seller must so notify as to enable the bailee by reasonable diligence to prevent delivery of the goods.

    (b) After such notification the bailee must hold and deliver the goods according to the directions of the seller but the seller is liable to the bailee for any ensuing charges or damages.

    (c) If a negotiable document of title has been issued for goods the bailee is not obliged to obey a notification to stop until surrender of the document.

    (d) A carrier who has issued a non-negotiable bill of lading is not obliged to obey a notification to stop received from a person other than the consignor.

Definitional Cross References:

"Buyer". Section 2—103.
"Contract for sale". Section 2—106.
"Document of title". Section 1—201.
"Goods". Section 2—105.

"Insolvent". Section 1—201.
"Notification". Section 1—201.
"Receipt" of goods. Section 2—103.
"Rights". Section 1—201.
"Seller". Section 2—103.

§ 2—706. Seller's Resale Including Contract for Resale

(1) Under the conditions stated in Section 2—703 on seller's remedies, the seller may resell the goods concerned or the undelivered balance thereof. Where the resale is made in good faith and in a commercially reasonable manner the seller may recover the difference between the resale price and the contract price together with any incidental damages allowed under the provisions of this Article (Section 2—710), but less expenses saved in consequence of the buyer's breach.

(2) Except as otherwise provided in subsection (3) or unless otherwise agreed resale may be at public or private sale including sale by way of one or more contracts to sell or of identification to an existing contract of the seller. Sale may be as a unit or in parcels and at any time and place and on any terms but every aspect of the sale including the method, manner, time, place and terms must be commercially reasonable. The resale must be reasonably identified as referring to the broken contract, but it is not necessary that the goods be in existence or that any or all of them have been identified to the contract before the breach.

(3) Where the resale is at private sale the seller must give the buyer reasonable notification of his intention to resell.

(4) Where the resale is at public sale

(a) only identified goods can be sold except where there is a recognized market for a public sale of futures in goods of the kind; and

(b) it must be made at a usual place or market for public sale if one is reasonably available and except in the case of goods which are perishable or threaten to decline in value speedily the seller must give the buyer reasonable notice of the time and place of the resale; and

(c) if the goods are not to be within the view of those attending the sale the notification of sale must state the place where the goods are located and provide for their reasonable inspection by prospective bidders; and

(d) the seller may buy.

(5) A purchaser who buys in good faith at a resale takes the goods free of any rights of the original buyer even though the seller fails to comply with one or more of the requirements of this section.

(6) The seller is not accountable to the buyer for any profit made on any resale. A person in the position of a seller (Section 2—707) or a buyer who has rightfully rejected or justifiably revoked acceptance must account for any excess over the amount of his security interest, as hereinafter defined (subsection (3) of Section 2—711).

Definitional Cross References:

"Buyer". Section 2—103.
"Contract". Section 1—201.
"Contract for sale". Section 2—106.
"Good faith". Section 2—103.
"Goods". Section 2—105.
"Merchant". Section 2—104.
"Notification". Section 1—201.

"Person in position of seller". Section 2—707.
"Purchase". Section 1—201.
"Rights". Section 1—201.
"Sale". Section 2—106.
"Security interest". Section 1—201.
"Seller". Section 2—103.

§ 2—707. "Person in the Position of a Seller"

(1) A "person in the position of a seller" includes as against a principal an agent who has paid or become responsible for the price of goods on behalf of his principal or anyone who otherwise holds a security interest or other right in goods similar to that of a seller.

(2) A person in the position of a seller may as provided in this Article withhold or stop delivery (Section 2—705) and resell (Section 2—706) and recover incidental damages (Section 2—710).

Definitional Cross References:

"Consignee". Section 7—102.
"Consignor". Section 7—102.
"Goods". Section 2—105.

"Security interest". Section 1—201.
"Seller". Section 2—103.

§ 2—708. Seller's Damages for Non-acceptance or Repudiation

(1) Subject to subsection (2) and to the provisions of this Article with respect to proof of market price (Section 2—723), the measure of damages for non-acceptance or repudiation by the buyer is the difference between the market price at the time and place for tender and the unpaid contract price together with any incidental damages provided in this Article (Section 2—710), but less expenses saved in consequence of the buyer's breach.

(2) If the measure of damages provided in subsection (1) is inadequate to put the seller in as good a position as performance would have done then the measure of damages is the profit (including reasonable overhead) which the seller would have made from full performance by the buyer, together with any incidental damages provided in this Article (Section 2—710), due allowance for costs reasonably incurred and due credit for payments or proceeds of resale.

Definitional Cross References:

"Buyer". Section 2—103.
"Contract". Section 1—201
"Seller". Section 2—103.

§ 2—709. Action for the Price

(1) When the buyer fails to pay the price as it becomes due the seller may recover, together with any incidental damages under the next section, the price

    (a) of goods accepted or of conforming goods lost or damaged within a commercially reasonable time after risk of their loss has passed to the buyer; and

    (b) of goods identified to the contract if the seller is unable after reasonable effort to resell them at a reasonable price or the circumstances reasonably indicate that such effort will be unavailing.

(2) Where the seller sues for the price he must hold for the buyer any goods which have been identified to the contract and are still in his control except that if resale becomes possible he may resell them at any time prior to the collection of the judgment. The net proceeds of any such resale must be credited to the buyer and payment of the judgment entitles him to any goods not resold.

(3) After the buyer has wrongfully rejected or revoked acceptance of the goods or has failed to make a payment due or has repudiated (Section 2—610), a seller who is held not entitled to the price under this section shall nevertheless be awarded damages for non-acceptance under the preceding section.

Definitional Cross References:

"Action". Section 1—201.
"Buyer". Section 2—103.
"Conforming". Section 2—106.
"Contract". Section 1—201.
"Goods". Section 2—105.
"Seller". Section 2—103.

§ 2—710. Seller's Incidental Damages

Incidental damages to an aggrieved seller include any commercially reasonable charges, expenses or commissions incurred in stopping delivery, in the transportation, care and custody of goods after the buyer's breach, in connection with return or resale of the goods or otherwise resulting from the breach.

Definitional Cross References:

"Aggrieved party". Section 1—201.
"Buyer". Section 2—103.
"Goods". Section 2—105.
"Seller". Section 2—103.

§ 2—711. Buyer's Remedies in General; Buyer's Security Interest in Rejected Goods

(1) Where the seller fails to make delivery or repudiates or the buyer rightfully rejects or justifiably revokes acceptance then with respect to any goods involved, and with respect to the whole if the breach goes to the whole contract (Section 2—612), the buyer may cancel and whether or not he has done so may in addition to recovering so much of the price as has been paid

  (a) "cover" and have damages under the next section as to all the goods affected whether or not they have been identified to the contract; or

  (b) recover damages for non-delivery as provided in this Article (Section 2—713).

(2) Where the seller fails to deliver or repudiates the buyer may also

  (a) if the goods have been identified recover them as provided in this Article (Section 2—502); or

(b) in a proper case obtain specific performance or replevy the goods as provided in this Article (Section 2—716).

(3) On rightful rejection or justifiable revocation of acceptance a buyer has a security interest in goods in his possession or control for any payments made on their price and any expenses reasonably incurred in their inspection, receipt, transportation, care and custody and may hold such goods and resell them in like manner as an aggrieved seller (Section 2—706).

Definitional Cross References:

"Aggrieved party". Section 1—201.
"Buyer". Section 2—103.
"Cancellation". Section 2—106.
"Contract". Section 1—201.
"Cover". Section 2—712.
"Goods". Section 2—105.

"Notifies". Section 1—201.
"Receipt" of goods. Section 2—103.
"Remedy". Section 1—201.
"Security interest". Section 1—201.
"Seller". Section 2—103.

§ 2—712. "Cover"; Buyer's Procurement of Substitute Goods

(1) After a breach within the preceding section the buyer may "cover" by making in good faith and without unreasonable delay any reasonable purchase of or contract to purchase goods in substitution for those due from the seller.

(2) The buyer may recover from the seller as damages the difference between the cost of cover and the contract price together with any incidental or consequential damages as hereinafter defined (Section 2—715), but less expenses saved in consequence of the seller's breach.

(3) Failure of the buyer to effect cover within this section does not bar him from any other remedy.

Definitional Cross References:

"Buyer". Section 2—103.
"Contract". Section 1—201.
"Good faith". Section 2—103.

"Goods". Section 2—105.
"Purchase". Section 1—201.
"Remedy". Section 1—201.
"Seller". Section 2—103.

§ 2—713. Buyer's Damages for Non-delivery or Repudiation

(1) Subject to the provisions of this Article with respect to proof of market price (Section 2—723), the measure of damages for non-delivery or repudiation by the seller is the difference between the market price at the time when the buyer learned of the breach and the contract price together with any incidental and consequential damages provided in this Article (Section 2—715), but less expenses saved in consequence of the seller's breach.

(2) Market price is to be determined as of the place for tender or, in cases of rejection after arrival or revocation of acceptance, as of the place of arrival.

Definitional Cross References:

"Buyer". Section 2—103.
"Contract". Section 1—201.
"Seller". Section 2—103.

§ 2—714. Buyer's Damages for Breach in Regard to Accepted Goods

(1) Where the buyer has accepted goods and given notification (subsection (3) of Section 2—607) he may recover as damages for any non-conformity of tender the loss resulting in the ordinary course of events from the seller's breach as determined in any manner which is reasonable.

(2) The measure of damages for breach of warranty is the difference at the time and place of acceptance between the value of the goods accepted and the value they would have had if they had been as warranted, unless special circumstances show proximate damages of a different amount.

(3) In a proper case any incidental and consequential damages under the next section may also be recovered.

Definitional Cross References:

"Buyer". Section 2—103.
"Conform". Section 2—106.

"Goods". Section 1—201.
"Notification". Section 1—201.
"Seller". Section 2—103.

§ 2—715. Buyer's Incidental and Consequential Damages

(1) Incidental damages resulting from the seller's breach include expenses reasonably incurred in inspection, receipt, transportation and care and custody of goods rightfully rejected, any commercially reasonable charges, expenses or commissions in connection with effecting cover and any other reasonable expense incident to the delay or other breach.

(2) Consequential damages resulting from the seller's breach include

    (a) any loss resulting from general or particular requirements and needs of which the seller at the time of contracting had reason to know and which could not reasonably be prevented by cover or otherwise; and

    (b) injury to person or property proximately resulting from any breach of warranty.

Definitional Cross References:

"Cover". Section 2—712.
"Goods". Section 1—201.

"Person". Section 1—201.
"Receipt" of goods. Section 2—103.
"Seller". Section 2—103.

§ 2—716. Buyer's Right to Specific Performance or Replevin

(1) Specific performance may be decreed where the goods are unique or in other proper circumstances.

(2) The decree for specific performance may include such terms and conditions as to payment of the price, damages, or other relief as the court may deem just.

(3) The buyer has a right of replevin for goods identified to the contract if after reasonable effort he is unable to effect cover for such goods or the circumstances reasonably indicate that such effort will be unavailing or if the goods have been shipped under reservation and satisfaction of the security interest in them has been made or tendered.

Definitional Cross References:

"Buyer". Section 2—103.
"Goods". Section 1—201.
"Rights". Section 1—201.

§ 2—717. Deduction of Damages From the Price

The buyer on notifying the seller of his intention to do so may deduct all or any part of the damages resulting from any breach of the contract from any part of the price still due under the same contract.

Definitional Cross References:

"Buyer". Section 2—103.
"Notifies". Section 1—201.

§ 2—718. Liquidation or Limitation of Damages; Deposits

(1) Damages for breach by either party may be liquidated in the agreement but only at an amount which is reasonable in the light of the anticipated or actual harm caused by the breach, the difficulties of proof of loss, and the inconvenience or non-feasibility of otherwise obtaining an adequate remedy. A term fixing unreasonably large liquidated damages is void as a penalty.

(2) Where the seller justifiably withholds delivery of goods because of the buyer's breach, the buyer is entitled to restitution of any amount by which the sum of his payments exceeds

    (a) the amount to which the seller is entitled by virtue of terms liquidating the seller's damages in accordance with subsection (1), or

    (b) in the absence of such terms, twenty per cent of the value of the total performance for which the buyer is obligated under the contract or $500, whichever is smaller.

(3) The buyer's right to restitution under subsection (2) is subject to offset to the extent that the seller establishes

    (a) a right to recover damages under the provisions of this Article other than subsection (1), and

    (b) the amount or value of any benefits received by the buyer directly or indirectly by reason of the contract.

(4) Where a seller has received payment in goods their reasonable value or the proceeds of their resale shall be treated as payments for the purposes of subsection (2); but if the seller has notice of the buyer's breach before reselling goods received in part performance, his resale is subject to the conditions laid down in this Article on resale by an aggrieved seller (Section 2—706).

Definitional Cross References:

"Aggrieved party". Section 1—201.
"Agreement". Section 1—201.
"Buyer". Section 2—103.
"Goods". Section 2—105.

"Notice". Section 1—201.
"Party". Section 1—201.
"Remedy". Section 1—201.
"Seller". Section 2—103.
"Term". Section 1—201.

§ 2—719. Contractual Modification or Limitation of Remedy

(1) Subject to the provisions of subsections (2) and (3) of this section and of the preceding section on liquidation and limitation of damages,

    (a) the agreement may provide for remedies in addition to or in substitution for those provided in this Article and may limit or alter the measure of damages recoverable under this Article, as by limiting the buyer's remedies to return of the goods and repayment of the price or to repair and replacement of non-conforming goods or parts; and

    (b) resort to a remedy as provided is optional unless the remedy is expressly agreed to be exclusive, in which case it is the sole remedy.

(2) Where circumstances cause an exclusive or limited remedy to fail of its essential purpose, remedy may be had as provided in this Act.

(3) Consequential damages may be limited or excluded unless the limitation or exclusion is unconscionable. Limitation of consequential damages for injury to the person in the case of consumer goods is prima facie unconscionable but limitation of damages where the loss is commercial is not.

Definitional Cross References:

"Agreement". Section 1—201.
"Buyer". Section 2—103.
"Conforming". Section 2—106.

"Contract". Section 1—201.
"Goods". Section 2—105.
"Remedy". Section 1—201.
"Seller". Section 2—103.

§ 2—720. Effect of "Cancellation" or "Rescission" on Claims for Antecedent Breach

Unless the contrary intention clearly appears, expressions of "cancellation" or "rescission" of the contract or the like shall not be construed as a renunciation or discharge of any claim in damages for an antecedent breach.

Definitional Cross References:

"Cancellation". Section 2—106.
"Contract". Section 1—201.

§ 2—721. Remedies for Fraud

Remedies for material misrepresentation or fraud include all remedies available under this Article for non-fraudulent breach. Neither rescission or a claim for rescission of the contract for sale nor rejection or return of the goods shall bar or be deemed inconsistent with a claim for damages or other remedy.

Definitional Cross References:

"Contract for sale". Section 2—106.
"Goods". Section 1—201.
"Remedy". Section 1—201.

§ 2—722. Who Can Sue Third Parties for Injury to Goods

Where a third party so deals with goods which have been identified to a contract for sale as to cause actionable injury to a party to that contract

    (a) a right of action against the third party is in either party to the contract for sale who has title to or a security interest or a special property or an insurable interest in the goods; and if the goods have been destroyed or converted a right of action is also in the party who either bore the risk of loss under the contract for sale or has since the injury assumed that risk as against the other;

    (b) if at the time of the injury the party plaintiff did not bear the risk of loss as against the other party to the contract for sale and there is no arrangement between them for disposition of the recovery, his suit or settlement is, subject to his own interest, as a fiduciary for the other party to the contract;

    (c) either party may with the consent of the other sue for the benefit of whom it may concern.

Definitional Cross References:

"Action". Section 1—201.
"Buyer". Section 2—103.
"Contract for sale". Section 2—106.
"Goods". Section 2—105.
"Party". Section 1—201.
"Rights". Section 1—201.
"Security interest". Section 1—201.

§ 2—723. Proof of Market Price: Time and Place

(1) If an action based on anticipatory repudiation comes to trial before the time for performance with respect to some or all of the goods, any damages based on market price (Section 2—708 or Section 2—713) shall be determined according to the price of such goods prevailing at the time when the aggrieved party learned of the repudiation.

(2) If evidence of a price prevailing at the times or places described in this Article is not readily available the price prevailing within any reasonable time before or after the time described or at any other place

which in commercial judgment or under usage of trade would serve as a reasonable substitute for the one described may be used, making any proper allowance for the cost of transporting the goods to or from such other place.

(3) Evidence of a relevant price prevailing at a time or place other than the one described in this Article offered by one party is not admissible unless and until he has given the other party such notice as the court finds sufficient to prevent unfair surprise.

Definitional Cross References:

"Action". Section 1—201.
"Aggrieved party". Section 1—201.
"Goods". Section 2—105.

"Notifies". Section 1—201.
"Party". Section 1—201.
"Reasonable time". Section 1—204.
"Usage of trade". Section 1—205.

§ 2—724. Admissibility of Market Quotations

Whenever the prevailing price or value of any goods regularly bought and sold in any established commodity market is in issue, reports in official publications or trade journals or in newspapers or periodicals of general circulation published as the reports of such market shall be admissible in evidence. The circumstances of the preparation of such a report may be shown to affect its weight but not its admissibility.

Definitional Cross Reference:

"Goods". Section 2—105.

§ 2—725. Statute of Limitations in Contracts for Sale

(1) An action for breach of any contract for sale must be commenced within four years after the cause of action has accrued. By the original agreement the parties may reduce the period of limitation to not less than one year but may not extend it.

(2) A cause of action accrues when the breach occurs, regardless of the aggrieved party's lack of knowledge of the breach. A breach of warranty occurs when tender of delivery is made, except that where a warranty explicitly extends to future performance of the goods and discovery of the breach must await the time of such performance the cause of action accrues when the breach is or should have been discovered.

(3) Where an action commenced within the time limited by subsection (1) is so terminated as to leave available a remedy by another action for the same breach such other action may be commenced after the expiration of the time limited and within six months after the termination of the first action unless the termination resulted from voluntary discontinuance or from dismissal for failure or neglect to prosecute.

(4) This section does not alter the law on tolling of the statute of limitations nor does it apply to causes of action which have accrued before this Act becomes effective.

Definitional Cross References:

"Action". Section 1—201.
"Aggrieved party". Section 1—201.
"Agreement". Section 1—201.
"Contract for sale". Section 2—106.

"Goods". Section 2—105.
"Party". Section 1—201.
"Remedy". Section 1—201.
"Term". Section 1—201.
"Termination". Section 2—106.

[REVISED] ARTICLE 3. NEGOTIABLE INSTRUMENTS

. . .

§ 3—311. Accord and Satisfaction by Use of Instrument

(a) If a person against whom a claim is asserted proves that (i) that person in good faith tendered an instrument to the claimant as full satisfaction of the claim, (ii) the amount of the claim was unliquidated or subject to a bona fide dispute, and (iii) the claimant obtained payment of the instrument, the following subsections apply.

(b) Unless subsection (c) applies, the claim is discharged if the person against whom the claim is asserted proves that the instrument or an accompanying written communication contained a conspicuous statement to the effect that the instrument was tendered as full satisfaction of the claim.

(c) Subject to subsection (d), a claim is not discharged under subsection (b) if either of the following applies:

(1) The claimant, if an organization, proves that (i) within a reasonable time before the tender, the claimant sent a conspicuous statement to the person against whom the claim is asserted that communications concerning disputed debts, including an instrument tendered as full satisfaction of a debt, are to be sent to a designated person, office, or place, and (ii) the instrument or accompanying communication was not received by that designated person, office, or place.

(2) The claimant, whether or not an organization, proves that within 90 days after payment of the instrument, the claimant tendered repayment of the amount of the instrument to the person against whom the claim is asserted. This paragraph does not apply if the claimant is an organization that sent a statement complying with paragraph (1)(i).

(d) A claim is discharged if the person against whom the claim is asserted proves that within a reasonable time before collection of the instrument was initiated, the claimant, or an agent of the claimant having direct responsibility with respect to the disputed obligation, knew that the instrument was tendered in full satisfaction of the claim.

. . .

ARTICLE 9. SECURED TRANSACTIONS; SALES OF ACCOUNTS AND CHATTEL PAPER

PART 1

SHORT TITLE, APPLICABILITY AND DEFINITIONS

§ 9—101. Short Title

This Article shall be known and may be cited as Uniform Commercial Code—Secured Transactions.

§ 9—102. Policy and Subject Matter of Article

(1) Except as otherwise provided in Section 9—104 on excluded transactions, this Article applies

(a) to any transaction (regardless of its form) which is intended to create a security interest in personal property or fixtures including goods, documents, instruments, general intangibles, chattel paper or accounts; and also

(b) to any sale of accounts or chattel paper.

(2) This Article applies to security interests created by contract including pledge, assignment, chattel mortgage, chattel trust, trust deed, factor's lien, equipment trust, conditional sale, trust receipt, other lien or title retention contract and lease or consignment intended as security. This Article does not apply to statutory liens except as provided in Section 9—310.

Definitional Cross References:

"Account". Section 9—106.

"Chattel paper". Section 9—105.

"Contract". Section 1—201.

. . .

"General intangibles". Section 9—106.

. . .

"Security interest". Section 1—201.

. . .

§ 9—104. Transactions Excluded From Article

This Article does not apply

. . .

(d) to a transfer of a claim for wages, salary or other compensation of an employee; or

. . .

(f) to a sale of accounts or chattel paper as part of a sale of the business out of which they arose, or an assignment of accounts or chattel paper which is for the purpose of collection only, or a transfer of a right to payment under a contract to an assignee who is also to do the performance under the contract or a transfer of a single account to an assignee in whole or partial satisfaction of a preexisting indebtedness; or

. . .

(k) to a transfer in whole or in part of any claim arising out of tort; or

. . .

§ 9—105. Definitions and Index of Definitions

(1) In this Article unless the context otherwise requires:

(a) "Account debtor" means the person who is obligated on an account, chattel paper or general intangible;

(b) "Chattel paper" means a writing or writings which evidence both a monetary obligation and a security interest in or a lease of specific goods, but a charter or other contract involving the use or hire of a vessel is not chattel paper. When a transaction is evidenced both by such a security agreement or a lease and by an instrument or a series of instruments, the group of writings taken together constitutes chattel paper;

(c) "Collateral" means the property subject to a security interest, and includes accounts and chattel paper which have been sold;

. . .

(*l*) "Security agreement" means an agreement which creates or provides for a security interest;

. . .

(4) In addition Article 1 contains general definitions and principles of construction and interpretation applicable throughout this Article.

§ 9—106. Definitions: "Account"; "General Intangibles"

"Account" means any right to payment for goods sold or leased or for services rendered which is not evidenced by an instrument or chattel paper, whether or not it has been earned by performance. "General intangibles" means any personal property (including things in action) other than goods, accounts, chattel paper, documents, instruments, and money. All rights to payment earned or unearned under a charter or other contract involving the use or hire of a vessel and all rights incident to the charter or contract are accounts.

Definitional Cross References:

"Chattel paper". Section 9—105.
"Contract". Section 1—201.

"Document". Section 9—105.
"Goods". Section 9—105.
"Instrument". Section 9—105.

. . .

§ 9—109. Classification of Goods; "Consumer Goods"; "Equipment"; "Farm Products"; "Inventory"

Goods are

(1) "consumer goods" if they are used or bought for use primarily for personal, family or household purposes; . . .

. . .

PART 2

VALIDITY OF SECURITY AGREEMENT AND RIGHTS OF PARTIES THERETO

§ 9—201. General Validity of Security Agreement

Except as otherwise provided by this Act a security agreement is effective according to its terms between the parties, against purchasers of the collateral and against creditors. Nothing in this Article validates any charge or practice illegal under any statute or regulation thereunder governing usury, small loans, retail installment sales, or the like, or extends the application of any such statute or regulation to any transaction not otherwise subject thereto.

Definitional Cross References:

"Collateral". Section 9—105.
"Creditor". Section 1—201.
"Party". Section 1—201.

"Purchaser". Section 1—201.
"Security agreement". Section 9—105.

. . .

§ 9—206. Agreement Not to Assert Defenses Against Assignee; Modification of Sales Warranties Where Security Agreement Exists

(1) Subject to any statute or decision which establishes a different rule for buyers or lessees of consumer goods, an agreement by a buyer or lessee that he will not assert against an assignee any claim or defense which he may have against the seller or lessor is enforceable by an assignee who takes his assignment for value, in good faith and without notice of a claim or defense, except as to defenses of a type which may be asserted against a holder in due course of a negotiable instrument under the Article on Commercial Paper (Article 3). A buyer who as part of one transaction signs both a negotiable instrument and a security agreement makes such an agreement. . . .

Definitional Cross References:

"Agreement". Section 1—201.
"Consumer goods". Section 9—109.
"Good faith". Section 1—201.
"Holder". Section 1—201.

. . .

"Notice". Section 1—201.

. . .

"Security agreement". Section 9—105.

. . .

"Value". Section 1—201.

. . .

PART 3

RIGHTS OF THIRD PARTIES; PERFECTED AND UNPERFECTED SECURITY INTERESTS; RULES OF PRIORITY

. . .

§ 9—318. Defenses Against Assignee; Modification of Contract After Notification of Assignment; Term Prohibiting Assignment Ineffective; Identification and Proof of Assignment

(1) Unless an account debtor has made an enforceable agreement not to assert defenses or claims arising out of a sale as provided in Section 9—206 the rights of an assignee are subject to

    (a) all the terms of the contract between the account debtor and assignor and any defense or claim arising therefrom; and

    (b) any other defense or claim of the account debtor against the assignor which accrues before the account debtor receives notification of the assignment.

(2) So far as the right to payment or a part thereof under an assigned contract has not been fully earned by performance, and notwithstanding notification of the assignment, any modification of or

substitution for the contract made in good faith and in accordance with reasonable commercial standards is effective against an assignee unless the account debtor has otherwise agreed but the assignee acquires corresponding rights under the modified or substituted contract. The assignment may provide that such modification or substitution is a breach by the assignor.

(3) The account debtor is authorized to pay the assignor until the account debtor receives notification that the amount due or to become due has been assigned and that payment is to be made to the assignee. A notification which does not reasonably identify the rights assigned is ineffective. If requested by the account debtor, the assignee must seasonably furnish reasonable proof that the assignment has been made and unless he does so the account debtor may pay the assignor.

(4) A term in any contract between an account debtor and an assignor is ineffective if it prohibits assignment of an account or prohibits creation of a security interest in a general intangible for money due or to become due or requires the account debtor's consent to such assignment or security interest.[a]

Definitional Cross References:

"Account". Section 9—106.
"Account debtor". Section 9—105.
"Agreement". Section 1—201.
"Contract". Section 1—201.
"Good faith". Section 1—201.
"Party". Section 1—201.
"Receives" notification. Section 1—201.
"Rights". Section 1—201.
"Sale". Sections 2—106 . . .
"Seasonably". Section 1—204.
"Term". Section 1—201.

a. In 1972 the sponsors of the UCC proposed amendments to the previous Official Text—that of 1962. By all odds the most extensive amendments were made in Article 9, and they did not leave section 9–318 untouched. However, the principal change there may fairly be called editorial in character. (One that cannot was an alteration in subsection (4) so as to add the material about a general intangible and about a requirement of the debtor's consent.)

The editorial changes are reflected in subsection (2) by the "not fully earned" passage, and in subsection (3) by the phrase "amount due or to become due." Unlike the current Official Text, the 1962 version contained a definition of "contract right," which embraced most payment rights "not yet earned by performance."

In that version the definition of "account" seems to have been restricted to *earned* payment rights; the thought was that a contract right (usually) turns into an account when an executory contract is performed on the payee's side. The revisers considered that the expression "contract right" could be dispensed with. By broadening the definition of account they simplified some parts of Article 9. But in section 9–318 the distinction had to be reintroduced. In subsection (2) that was accomplished by putting a qualification on the term "assigned contract;" and in subsection (3) where the word "account" had been used it was deleted in favor of "amount due or to become due."

By 1992 the 1972 amendments had been enacted in all states except Vermont.

RESTATEMENT OF THE LAW, SECOND, OF CONTRACTS

(Selected Sections)

COMPILERS' NOTE

The American Law Institute was formed in 1923 as the outgrowth of a "Committee on the Establishment of a Permanent Organization for the Improvement of the Law." Its members were to be 400 practitioners, judges and law professors. (There are now about 2,000.) The idea of the Institute, and of "restating" the law, was broached by Professor William Draper Lewis and fostered by Elihu Root and others. The Carnegie Corporation contributed some quarter of a million dollars toward work on the original Restatement, comprising nine subjects, which was completed by 1944. Contracts was one of the first three subjects upon which the Institute began work, and the Restatement of Contracts was completed in 1932. Professor Samuel W. Williston acted as Reporter, with responsibility for preparing drafts. (Professor Arthur L. Corbin served as Reporter for the Chapter on Remedies.) Other experts in the subject were formed into a Committee of Advisers who conferred with the Reporter over the whole period in producing drafts for submission to the Council of the Institute. The plan was "that the drafts of the different chapters submitted to the Council shall be the product of the committee composed of the Reporter and his advisers; that these drafts after discussion and amendment by the Council and before revision shall be submitted as tentative drafts for criticism and suggestion with a view to their improvement to the annual meetings of the Institute and to bar associations and the profession generally." Restatement of Contracts, Introduction, p. x. Final promulgation depended on approval of the text by both the Council and the full meeting of Institute members. The same procedure was followed in making revisions and in preparing the Restatement Second.

In 1962 the Institute initiated the preparation of the Restatement, Second, of Contracts, parts of which are reproduced here. Professor Robert Braucher served as Reporter until his appointment to the Supreme Judicial Court of Massachusetts in 1971; he was succeeded by Professor Farnsworth. The work was completed in 1980.

As originally conceived, the first Restatement was to be accompanied by treatises citing and discussing case authority, but experience proved that group production of such volumes was not feasible. As they stand, the Restatements consist of sections stating rules or principles (the so-called black letter), each followed by one or more comments with illustrations, and in the Restatement Second also by Reporters'

Notes in which supporting authorities are collected. (Reproduced here are the black letter of selected sections, omitting comments, illustrations and notes.) An eminent critic of the Restatement of Contracts immediately questioned the value of "black-letter Principles" not supported by discussion and analysis. "The Institute," he wrote, "seems constantly to be seeking the force of a statute without statutory enactment." Clark, The Restatement of the Law of Contracts, 42 Yale L.J. 643, 654 (1933). Other assaults on the Restatement, and more sympathetic appraisals, have produced a rich literature on the subject. Selections from these materials are contained in J. Honnold, The Life of the Law, Chapter 4 (1964). As courts and scholars began to deploy the rules, they gained in concreteness and resonance. The process of supplementation has been gradual, and will doubtless continue to be so. It was long ago described as follows: "From the austerity of the Contracts Restatement to the varied forms and expanded substance of the current Restatement has been an evolutional process. Introductory Notes, Special Notes, Statutory Notes, Rationale Comments, Historical Comments and Monographs—all these have crept into the picture without much fanfare of trumpets." Leach, The Restatements As They Were in the Beginning, Are Now, and Perhaps Henceforth Shall Be, 23 A.B.A.J. 517, 519 (1937). On occasion a legislature has given statutory backing to one or more provisions of the Restatement.[a] For example, in dealing with a problem of tort law (products liability), the Oregon legislature referred to certain comments in the Restatement Second of that subject, and declared: "It is the intent of the Legislative Assembly that the rule stated in [part of the statute] shall be construed in accordance with" those comments.[b] But the directive force of Restatement language is generally not so great. To what measure of authority is the Restatement entitled, then, in the courts?

This general question can have only a general answer. The Supreme Court of Oregon has emphasized the difference between statutory and Restatement texts: [c]

> Although this court frequently quotes sections of the Restatements of the American Law Institute, it does not literally "adopt" them in the manner of a legislature enacting, for instance, a draft prepared by the Commissioners on Uniform State Laws, such as the Residential Landlord and Tenant Act. In the nature of common law, such

a. From the Virgin Islands Code (Title 1, § 4): "The rules of the common law, as expressed in the restatements of the law approved by the American Law Institute, and to the extent not so expressed, as generally understood and applied in the United States, shall be the rules of decision in the courts of the Virgin Islands in cases to which they apply, in the absence of local laws to the contrary." In 1974 this directive gave some discomfort to the court in a case concerning the now-dated Restate-

ment of Restitution. Judge Young wrote: "I cannot ignore the fact that the Restatement was written in 1937 and should not be applied without some consideration of more recent developments." James v. Bailey, 370 F.Supp. 469, 472 (D.V.I.). See also Benjamin v. Cleburne Truck & Body Sales, Inc., 424 F.Supp. 1294 (D.V.I.1976).

b. Or. Laws 1979, c. 866, § 2(3).

c. Brewer v. Erwin, 600 P.2d 398, 410 n. 12 (Or.1979).

quotations in opinions are no more than shorthand expressions of the court's view that the analysis summarized in the Restatement corresponds to Oregon law applicable to the facts of the case before the court. They do not enact the exact phrasing of the Restatement rule, complete with comments, illustrations, and caveats. Such quotations should not be relied on in briefs as if they committed his court or lower courts to track every detail of the Restatement analysis in other cases. The Restatements themselves purport to be just that, "restatements" of law found in other sources, although at times they candidly report that the law is in flux and offer a formula preferred on policy grounds.

There is agreement among those who applaud the Restatement and those who depreciate it about the persuasiveness of an *ideal* restatement of the law. "A restatement, then, can have no other authority than as the product of men learned in the subject who have studied and deliberated over it. It needs no other, and what could be higher?" Clark, op. cit. supra, p. 655. Judge Herbert Goodrich, for many years Director of the Institute, explained:

> If an advocate thinks the Restatement was wrong as applied to his case, he can urge the court not to follow it, but to apply some other rule. If the court agrees, it will do so, but it will so do with the knowledge that the rule which it rejects has been written by the people who by training and reputation are supposed to be eminently learned in the particular subject and that the specialist's conclusions have been discussed and defended before a body of very able critics. The presumption is in favor of the Restatement. . . . Yet it can be overthrown and that fact leaves Restatement acceptance to persuasion. It is common law "persuasive authority" with a high degree of persuasion.

Restatement and Codification, David D. Field Centenary Essays 241, 244–45 (1949).

The Restatement Second. To a substantial extent the Restatement Second reflects the thought of two men in particular: Professor Corbin and Professor Llewellyn, both of whom shared attitudes toward law sometimes described as "legal realism." [d] Professor Corbin prepared a critical review of the original Restatement, which "has been the basis for much of the work on the revision." [e] He served also as consultant for the Restatement Second in its early stages. Professor Llewellyn's efforts affected the revision less directly, largely through the impact of his contributions to the Uniform Commercial Code.

In restating the law of contracts for the second half of the century, an obvious difficulty arose from the fact that large tracts of the subject had recently been occupied by legislation such as the Code and certain

d. For symposia devoted to the Restatement Second, see 81 Colum.L.Rev. 1 (1981) and 67 Cornell L.Rev. 631 (1982).

e. Braucher, Formation of Contract and the Second Restatement, 78 Yale L.J. 598 (1969).

consumer-protection statutes. Indeed, the worth of the enterprise was questioned on the ground of an apparently diminishing importance of common law doctrine. In response, Professor Braucher made this claim: "The effort to restate the law of contracts in modern terms highlights the reliance of private autonomy in an era of expanding government activity. . . . Freedom of contract, refined and redefined in response to social change, has power as it always had." [f]

A continuing theme of controversy about the Restatements is the wisdom or unwisdom of departing from rules derived from existing precedents, in the interest of a more just and more convenient regime of law. The Oregon opinion quoted above refers to a section of the Torts Restatement as a "bold sally." Notwithstanding that, the section has gained widespread adherence. An example from the first Restatement of Contracts was the formulation of the doctrine of promissory estoppel, in section 90.

[f.] Id. at 615–16. For another comment by Professor Braucher, see Offer and Acceptance in the Second Restatement, 74 Yale L.J. 302 (1964).

RESTATEMENT (SECOND) OF CONTRACTS [a]

Table of Contents

CHAPTER 1. MEANING OF TERMS

CHAPTER 2. FORMATION OF CONTRACTS— PARTIES AND CAPACITY

CHAPTER 3. FORMATION OF CONTRACTS— MUTUAL ASSENT

TOPIC 1. IN GENERAL

TOPIC 2. MANIFESTATION OF ASSENT IN GENERAL

TOPIC 3. MAKING OF OFFERS

TOPIC 4. DURATION OF THE OFFEREE'S POWER OF ACCEPTANCE

CHAPTER 1. MEANING OF TERMS

§ 1. Contract Defined

A contract is a promise or a set of promises for the breach of which the law gives a remedy, or the performance of which the law in some way recognizes as a duty.

CHAPTER 2. FORMATION OF CONTRACTS—PARTIES AND CAPACITY

§ 14. Infants

Unless a statute provides otherwise, a natural person has the capacity to incur only voidable contractual duties until the beginning of the day before the person's eighteenth birthday.

§ 15. Mental Illness or Defect

(1) A person incurs only voidable contractual duties by entering into a transaction if by reason of mental illness or defect

    (a) he is unable to understand in a reasonable manner the nature and consequences of the transaction, or

    (b) he is unable to act in a reasonable manner in relation to the transaction and the other party has reason to know of his condition.

(2) Where the contract is made on fair terms and the other party is without knowledge of the mental illness or defect, the power of avoidance under Subsection (1) terminates to the extent that the contract has been so performed in whole or in part or the circumstances have so changed that avoidance would be unjust. In such a case a court may grant relief on such equitable terms as justice requires.

CHAPTER 3. FORMATION OF CONTRACTS—MUTUAL ASSENT

TOPIC 1. IN GENERAL

§ 17. Requirement of a Bargain

(1) Except as stated in Subsection (2), the formation of a contract requires a bargain in which there is a manifestation of mutual assent to the exchange and a consideration.

(2) Whether or not there is a bargain a contract may be formed under special rules applicable to formal contracts or under the rules stated in §§ 82–94.

TOPIC 2. MANIFESTATION OF ASSENT IN GENERAL

§ 20. Effect of Misunderstanding

(1) There is no manifestation of mutual assent to an exchange if the parties attach materially different meanings to their manifestations and

    (a) neither party knows or has reason to know the meaning attached by the other; or

    (b) each party knows or each party has reason to know the meaning attached by the other.

(2) The manifestations of the parties are operative in accordance with the meaning attached to them by one of the parties if

    (a) that party does not know of any different meaning attached by the other, and the other knows the meaning attached by the first party; or

    (b) that party has no reason to know of any different meaning attached by the other, and the other has reason to know the meaning attached by the first party.

TOPIC 3. MAKING OF OFFERS

§ 24. Offer Defined

An offer is the manifestation of willingness to enter into a bargain, so made as to justify another person in understanding that his assent to that bargain is invited and will conclude it.

§ 26. Preliminary Negotiations

A manifestation of willingness to enter into a bargain is not an offer if the person to whom it is addressed knows or has reason to know that the person making it does not intend to conclude a bargain until he has made a further manifestation of assent.

§ 27. Existence of Contract Where Written Memorial Is Contemplated

Manifestations of assent that are in themselves sufficient to conclude a contract will not be prevented from so operating by the fact that the parties also manifest an intention to prepare and adopt a written memorial thereof; but the circumstances may show that the agreements are preliminary negotiations.

§ 30. Form of Acceptance Invited

(1) An offer may invite or require acceptance to be made by an affirmative answer in words, or by performing or refraining from

performing a specified act, or may empower the offeree to make a selection of terms in his acceptance.

(2) Unless otherwise indicated by the language or the circumstances, an offer invites acceptance in any manner and by any medium reasonable in the circumstances.

§ 32. Invitation of Promise or Performance

In case of doubt an offer is interpreted as inviting the offeree to accept either by promising to perform what the offer requests or by rendering the performance, as the offeree chooses.

§ 33. Certainty

(1) Even though a manifestation of intention is intended to be understood as an offer, it cannot be accepted so as to form a contract unless the terms of the contract are reasonably certain.

(2) The terms of a contract are reasonably certain if they provide a basis for determining the existence of a breach and for giving an appropriate remedy.

(3) The fact that one or more terms of a proposed bargain are left open or uncertain may show that a manifestation of intention is not intended to be understood as an offer or as an acceptance.

TOPIC 4. DURATION OF THE OFFEREE'S POWER OF ACCEPTANCE

§ 36. Methods of Termination of the Power of Acceptance

(1) An offeree's power of acceptance may be terminated by

    (a) rejection or counter-offer by the offeree, or

    (b) lapse of time, or

    (c) revocation by the offeror, or

    (d) death or incapacity of the offeror or offeree.

(2) In addition, an offeree's power of acceptance is terminated by the non-occurrence of any condition of acceptance under the terms of the offer.

§ 37. Termination of Power of Acceptance Under Option Contract

Notwithstanding §§ 38–49, the power of acceptance under an option contract is not terminated by rejection or counter-offer, by revocation, or by death or incapacity of the offeror, unless the requirements are met for the discharge of a contractual duty.

§ 38. Rejection

(1) An offeree's power of acceptance is terminated by his rejection of the offer, unless the offeror has manifested a contrary intention.

(2) A manifestation of intention not to accept an offer is a rejection unless the offeree manifests an intention to take it under further advisement.

§ 39. Counter–Offers

(1) A counter-offer is an offer made by an offeree to his offeror relating to the same matter as the original offer and proposing a substituted bargain differing from that proposed by the original offer.

(2) An offeree's power of acceptance is terminated by his making of a counter-offer, unless the offeror has manifested a contrary intention or unless the counter-offer manifests a contrary intention of the offeree.

§ 40. Time When Rejection or Counter–Offer Terminates the Power of Acceptance

Rejection or counter-offer by mail or telegram does not terminate the power of acceptance until received by the offeror, but limits the power so that a letter or telegram of acceptance started after the sending of an otherwise effective rejection or counter-offer is only a counter-offer unless the acceptance is received by the offeror before he receives the rejection or counter-offer.

§ 42. Revocation by Communication From Offeror Received by Offeree

An offeree's power of acceptance is terminated when the offeree receives from the offeror a manifestation of an intention not to enter into the proposed contract.

§ 43. Indirect Communication of Revocation

An offeree's power of acceptance is terminated when the offeror takes definite action inconsistent with an intention to enter into the proposed contract and the offeree acquires reliable information to that effect.

§ 45. Option Contract Created by Part Performance or Tender

(1) Where an offer invites an offeree to accept by rendering a performance and does not invite a promissory acceptance, an option contract is created when the offeree tenders or begins the invited performance or tenders a beginning of it.

(2) The offeror's duty of performance under any option contract so created is conditional on completion or tender of the invited performance in accordance with the terms of the offer.

§ 46. Revocation of General Offer

Where an offer is made by advertisement in a newspaper or other general notification to the public or to a number of persons whose identity is unknown to the offeror, the offeree's power of acceptance is terminated when a notice of termination is given publicity by advertisement or other general notification equal to that given to the offer and no better means of notification is reasonably available.

§ 48. Death or Incapacity of Offeror or Offeree

An offeree's power of acceptance is terminated when the offeree or offeror dies or is deprived of legal capacity to enter into the proposed contract.

TOPIC 5.   ACCEPTANCE OF OFFERS

§ 50. Acceptance of Offer Defined; Acceptance by Performance; Acceptance by Promise

(1) Acceptance of an offer is a manifestation of assent to the terms thereof made by the offeree in a manner invited or required by the offer.

(2) Acceptance by performance requires that at least part of what the offer requests be performed or tendered and includes acceptance by a performance which operates as a return promise.

(3) Acceptance by a promise requires that the offeree complete every act essential to the making of the promise.

§ 51. Effect of Part Performance Without Knowledge of Offer

Unless the offeror manifests a contrary intention, an offeree who learns of an offer after he has rendered part of the performance requested by the offer may accept by completing the requested performance.

§ 52. Who May Accept an Offer

An offer can be accepted only by a person whom it invites to furnish the consideration.

§ 53. Acceptance by Performance; Manifestation of Intention Not to Accept

(1) An offer can be accepted by the rendering of a performance only if the offer invites such an acceptance.

(2) Except as stated in § 69, the rendering of a performance does not constitute an acceptance if within a reasonable time the offeree exercises reasonable diligence to notify the offeror of non-acceptance.

(3) Where an offer of a promise invites acceptance by performance and does not invite a promissory acceptance, the rendering of the

invited performance does not constitute an acceptance if before the offeror performs his promise the offeree manifests an intention not to accept.

§ 54. Acceptance by Performance; Necessity of Notification to Offeror

(1) Where an offer invites an offeree to accept by rendering a performance, no notification is necessary to make such an acceptance effective unless the offer requests such a notification.

(2) If an offeree who accepts by rendering a performance has reason to know that the offeror has no adequate means of learning of the performance with reasonable promptness and certainty, the contractual duty of the offeror is discharged unless

> (a) the offeree exercises reasonable diligence to notify the offeror of acceptance, or
>
> (b) the offeror learns of the performance within a reasonable time, or
>
> (c) the offer indicates that notification of acceptance is not required.

§ 56. Acceptance by Promise; Necessity of Notification to Offeror

Except as stated in § 69 or where the offer manifests a contrary intention, it is essential to an acceptance by promise either that the offeree exercise reasonable diligence to notify the offeror of acceptance or that the offeror receive the acceptance seasonably.

§ 58. Necessity of Acceptance Complying With Terms of Offer

An acceptance must comply with the requirements of the offer as to the promise to be made or the performance to be rendered.

§ 59. Purported Acceptance Which Adds Qualifications

A reply to an offer which purports to accept it but is conditional on the offeror's assent to terms additional to or different from those offered is not an acceptance but is a counter-offer.

§ 60. Acceptance of Offer Which States Place, Time or Manner of Acceptance

If an offer prescribes the place, time or manner of acceptance its terms in this respect must be complied with in order to create a contract. If an offer merely suggests a permitted place, time or manner of acceptance, another method of acceptance is not precluded.

§ 61. Acceptance Which Requests Change of Terms

An acceptance which requests a change or addition to the terms of the offer is not thereby invalidated unless the acceptance is made to depend on an assent to the changed or added terms.

§ 62. Effect of Performance by Offeree Where Offer Invites Either Performance or Promise

(1) Where an offer invites an offeree to choose between acceptance by promise and acceptance by performance, the tender or beginning of the invited performance or a tender of a beginning of it is an acceptance by performance.

(2) Such an acceptance operates as a promise to render complete performance.

§ 63. Time When Acceptance Takes Effect

Unless the offer provides otherwise,

    (a) an acceptance made in a manner and by a medium invited by an offer is operative and completes the manifestation of mutual assent as soon as put out of the offeree's possession, without regard to whether it ever reaches the offeror; but

    (b) an acceptance under an option contract is not operative until received by the offeror.

§ 69. Acceptance by Silence or Exercise of Dominion

(1) Where an offeree fails to reply to an offer, his silence and inaction operate as an acceptance in the following cases only:

    (a) Where an offeree takes the benefit of offered services with reasonable opportunity to reject them and reason to know that they were offered with the expectation of compensation.

    (b) Where the offeror has stated or given the offeree reason to understand that assent may be manifested by silence or inaction, and the offeree in remaining silent and inactive intends to accept the offer.

    (c) Where because of previous dealings or otherwise, it is reasonable that the offeree should notify the offeror if he does not intend to accept.

(2) An offeree who does any act inconsistent with the offeror's ownership of offered property is bound in accordance with the offered terms unless they are manifestly unreasonable. But if the act is wrongful as against the offeror it is an acceptance only if ratified by him.

CHAPTER 4. FORMATION OF CONTRACTS—CONSIDERATION

TOPIC 1. THE REQUIREMENT OF CONSIDERATION

§ 71. Requirement of Exchange; Types of Exchange

(1) To constitute consideration, a performance or a return promise must be bargained for.

(2) A performance or return promise is bargained for if it is sought by the promisor in exchange for his promise and is given by the promisee in exchange for that promise.

(3) The performance may consist of

    (a) an act other than a promise, or

    (b) a forbearance, or

    (c) the creation, modification, or destruction of a legal relation.

(4) The performance or return promise may be given to the promisor or to some other person. It may be given by the promisee or by some other person.

§ 73. Performance of Legal Duty

Performance of a legal duty owed to a promisor which is neither doubtful nor the subject of honest dispute is not consideration; but a similar performance is consideration if it differs from what was required by the duty in a way which reflects more than a pretense of bargain.

§ 74. Settlement of Claims

(1) Forbearance to assert or the surrender of a claim or defense which proves to be invalid is not consideration unless

    (a) the claim or defense is in fact doubtful because of uncertainty as to the facts or the law, or

    (b) the forbearing or surrendering party believes that the claim or defense may be fairly determined to be valid.

(2) The execution of a written instrument surrendering a claim or defense by one who is under no duty to execute it is consideration if the execution of the written instrument is bargained for even though he is not asserting the claim or defense and believes that no valid claim or defense exists.

109

§ 77. Illusory and Alternative Promises

A promise or apparent promise is not consideration if by its terms the promisor or purported promisor reserves a choice of alternative performances unless

   (a)   each of the alternative performances would have been consideration if it alone had been bargained for; or

   (b)   one of the alternative performances would have been consideration and there is or appears to the parties to be a substantial possibility that before the promisor exercises his choice events may eliminate the alternatives which would not have been consideration.

§ 79. Adequacy of Consideration; Mutuality of Obligation

If the requirement of consideration is met, there is no additional requirement of

   (a)   a gain, advantage, or benefit to the promisor or a loss, disadvantage, or detriment to the promisee; or

   (b)   equivalence in the values exchanged; or

   (c)   "mutuality of obligation."

§ 81. Consideration as Motive or Inducing Cause

(1) The fact that what is bargained for does not of itself induce the making of a promise does not prevent it from being consideration for the promise.

(2) The fact that a promise does not of itself induce a performance or return promise does not prevent the performance or return promise from being consideration for the promise.

TOPIC 2. CONTRACTS WITHOUT CONSIDERATION

§ 82. Promise to Pay Indebtedness; Effect on the Statute of Limitations

(1) A promise to pay all or part of an antecedent contractual or quasi-contractual indebtedness owed by the promisor is binding if the indebtedness is still enforceable or would be except for the effect of a statute of limitations.

(2) The following facts operate as such a promise unless other facts indicate a different intention:

   (a)   A voluntary acknowledgment to the obligee, admitting the present existence of the antecedent indebtedness; or

   (b)   A voluntary transfer of money, a negotiable instrument, or other thing by the obligor to the obligee, made as interest on or part payment of or collateral security for the antecedent indebtedness; or

    (c) A statement to the obligee that the statute of limitations will not be pleaded as a defense.

§ 83. Promise to Pay Indebtedness Discharged in Bankruptcy

An express promise to pay all or part of an indebtedness of the promisor, discharged or dischargeable in bankruptcy proceedings begun before the promise is made, is binding.

§ 84. Promise to Perform a Duty in Spite of Non-occurrence of a Condition

(1) Except as stated in Subsection (2), a promise to perform all or part of a conditional duty under an antecedent contract in spite of the non-occurrence of the condition is binding, whether the promise is made before or after the time for the condition to occur, unless

    (a) occurrence of the condition was a material part of the agreed exchange for the performance of the duty and the promisee was under no duty that it occur; or

    (b) uncertainty of the occurrence of the condition was an element of the risk assumed by the promisor.

(2) If such a promise is made before the time for the occurrence of the condition has expired and the condition is within the control of the promisee or a beneficiary, the promisor can make his duty again subject to the condition by notifying the promisee or beneficiary of his intention to do so if

    (a) the notification is received while there is still a reasonable time to cause the condition to occur under the antecedent terms or an extension given by the promisor; and

    (b) reinstatement of the requirement of the condition is not unjust because of a material change of position by the promisee or beneficiary; and

    (c) the promise is not binding apart from the rule stated in Subsection (1).

§ 86. Promise for Benefit Received

(1) A promise made in recognition of a benefit previously received by the promisor from the promisee is binding to the extent necessary to prevent injustice.

(2) A promise is not binding under Subsection (1)

    (a) if the promisee conferred the benefit as a gift or for other reasons the promisor has not been unjustly enriched; or

    (b) to the extent that its value is disproportionate to the benefit.

§ 87. Option Contract

(1) An offer is binding as an option contract if it

(a) is in writing and signed by the offeror, recites a purported consideration for the making of the offer, and proposes an exchange on fair terms within a reasonable time; or

(b) is made irrevocable by statute.

(2) An offer which the offeror should reasonably expect to induce action or forbearance of a substantial character on the part of the offeree before acceptance and which does induce such action or forbearance is binding as an option contract to the extent necessary to avoid injustice.

§ 89. Modification of Executory Contract

A promise modifying a duty under a contract not fully performed on either side is binding

(a) if the modification is fair and equitable in view of circumstances not anticipated by the parties when the contract was made; or

(b) to the extent provided by statute; or

(c) to the extent that justice requires enforcement in view of material change of position in reliance on the promise.

§ 90. Promise Reasonably Inducing Action or Forbearance

(1) A promise which the promisor should reasonably expect to induce action or forbearance on the part of the promisee or a third person and which does induce such action or forbearance is binding if injustice can be avoided only by enforcement of the promise. The remedy granted for breach may be limited as justice requires.

(2) A charitable subscription or a marriage settlement is binding under Subsection (1) without proof that the promise induced action or forbearance.

CHAPTER 5. THE STATUTE OF FRAUDS

TOPIC 6. SATISFACTION OF THE STATUTE BY A MEMORANDUM

§ 131. General Requisites of a Memorandum

Unless additional requirements are prescribed by the particular statute, a contract within the Statute of Frauds is enforceable if it is evidenced by any writing, signed by or on behalf of the party to be charged, which

(a) reasonably identifies the subject matter of the contract,

   (b) is sufficient to indicate that a contract with respect thereto has been made between the parties or offered by the signer to the other party, and

   (c) states with reasonable certainty the essential terms of the unperformed promises in the contract.

TOPIC 8. CONSEQUENCES OF NON–COMPLIANCE

§ 139. Enforcement by Virtue of Action in Reliance

(1) A promise which the promisor should reasonably expect to induce action or forbearance on the part of the promisee or a third person and which does induce the action or forbearance is enforceable notwithstanding the Statute of Frauds if injustice can be avoided only by enforcement of the promise. The remedy granted for breach is to be limited as justice requires.

(2) In determining whether injustice can be avoided only by enforcement of the promise, the following circumstances are significant:

   (a) the availability and adequacy of other remedies, particularly cancellation and restitution;

   (b) the definite and substantial character of the action or forbearance in relation to the remedy sought;

   (c) the extent to which the action or forbearance corroborates evidence of the making and terms of the promise, or the making and terms are otherwise established by clear and convincing evidence;

   (d) the reasonableness of the action or forbearance;

   (e) the extent to which the action or forbearance was foreseeable by the promisor.

CHAPTER 6. MISTAKE

§ 152. When Mistake of Both Parties Makes a Contract Voidable

(1) Where a mistake of both parties at the time a contract was made as to a basic assumption on which the contract was made has a material effect on the agreed exchange of performances, the contract is voidable by the adversely affected party unless he bears the risk of the mistake under the rule stated in § 154.

(2) In determining whether the mistake has a material effect on the agreed exchange of performances, account is taken of any relief by way of reformation, restitution, or otherwise.

§ 153. When Mistake of One Party Makes a Contract Voidable

Where a mistake of one party at the time a contract was made as to a basic assumption on which he made the contract has a material effect on the agreed exchange of performances that is adverse to him, the contract is voidable by him if he does not bear the risk of the mistake under the rule stated in § 154, and

    (a) the effect of the mistake is such that enforcement of the contract would be unconscionable, or

    (b) the other party had reason to know of the mistake or his fault caused the mistake.

§ 154. When a Party Bears the Risk of a Mistake

A party bears the risk of a mistake when

    (a) The risk is allocated to him by agreement of the parties, or

    (b) he is aware, at the time the contract is made, that he has only limited knowledge with respect to the facts to which the mistake relates but treats his limited knowledge as sufficient, or

    (c) the risk is allocated to him by the court on the ground that it is reasonable in the circumstances to do so.

§ 157. Effect of Fault of Party Seeking Relief

A mistaken party's fault in failing to know or discover the facts before making the contract does not bar him from avoidance or reformation under the rules stated in this Chapter, unless his fault amounts to a failure to act in good faith and in accordance with reasonable standards of fair dealing.

§ 158. Relief Including Restitution

(1) In any case governed by the rules stated in this Chapter, either party may have a claim for relief including restitution under the rules stated in §§ 240 and 376.

(2) In any case governed by the rules stated in this Chapter, if those rules together with the rules stated in Chapter 16 will not avoid injustice, the court may grant relief on such terms as justice requires including protection of the parties' reliance interest.

CHAPTER 7. MISREPRESENTATION, DURESS AND UNDUE INFLUENCE

TOPIC 1. MISREPRESENTATION

§ 161. When Non-disclosure Is Equivalent to an Assertion

A person's non-disclosure of a fact known to him is equivalent to an assertion that the fact does not exist in the following cases only:

(a) where he knows that disclosure of the fact is necessary to prevent some previous assertion from being a misrepresentation or from being fraudulent or material.

(b) where he knows that disclosure of the fact would correct a mistake of the other party as to a basic assumption on which that party is making the contract and if non-disclosure of the fact amounts to a failure to act in good faith and in accordance with reasonable standards of fair dealing.

(c) where he knows that disclosure of the fact would correct a mistake of the other party as to the contents or effect of a writing, evidencing or embodying an agreement in whole or in part.

(d) where the other person is entitled to know the fact because of a relation of trust and confidence between them.

§ 162. When a Misrepresentation Is Fraudulent or Material

(1) A misrepresentation is fraudulent if the maker intends his assertion to induce a party to manifest his assent and the maker

(a) knows or believes that the assertion is not in accord with the facts, or

(b) does not have the confidence that he states or implies in the truth of the assertion, or

(c) knows that he does not have the basis that he states or implies for the assertion.

(2) A misrepresentation is material if it would be likely to induce a reasonable person to manifest his assent, or if the maker knows that it would be likely to induce the recipient to do so.

§ 163. When a Misrepresentation Prevents Formation of a Contract

If a misrepresentation as to the character or essential terms of a proposed contract induces conduct that appears to be a manifestation of assent by one who neither knows nor has reasonable opportunity to know of the character or essential terms of the proposed contract, his conduct is not effective as a manifestation of assent.

§ 164. When a Misrepresentation Makes a Contract Voidable

(1) If a party's manifestation of assent is induced by either a fraudulent or a material misrepresentation by the other party upon which the recipient is justified in relying, the contract is voidable by the recipient.

(2) If a party's manifestation of assent is induced by either a fraudulent or a material misrepresentation by one who is not a party to the transaction upon which the recipient is justified in relying, the

contract is voidable by the recipient, unless the other party to the transaction in good faith and without reason to know of the misrepresentation either gives value or relies materially on the transaction.

§ 168. Reliance on Assertions of Opinion

(1) An assertion is one of opinion if it expresses only a belief, without certainty, as to the existence of a fact or expresses only a judgment as to quality, value, authenticity, or similar matters.

(2) If it is reasonable to do so, the recipient of an assertion of a person's opinion as to facts not disclosed and not otherwise known to the recipient may properly interpret it as an assertion

> (a) that the facts known to that person are not incompatible with his opinion, or
>
> (b) that he knows facts sufficient to justify him in forming it.

§ 169. When Reliance on an Assertion of Opinion Is Not Justified

To the extent that an assertion is one of opinion only, the recipient is not justified in relying on it unless the recipient

> (a) stands in such a relation of trust and confidence to the person whose opinion is asserted that the recipient is reasonable in relying on it, or
>
> (b) reasonably believes that, as compared with himself, the person whose opinion is asserted has special skill, judgment or objectivity with respect to the subject matter, or
>
> (c) is for some other special reason particularly susceptible to a misrepresentation of the type involved.

TOPIC 2. DURESS AND UNDUE INFLUENCE

§ 175. When Duress by Threat Makes a Contract Voidable

(1) If a party's manifestation of assent is induced by an improper threat by the other party that leaves the victim no reasonable alternative, the contract is voidable by the victim.

(2) If a party's manifestation of assent is induced by one who is not a party to the transaction, the contract is voidable by the victim unless the other party to the transaction in good faith and without reason to know of the duress either gives value or relies materially on the transaction.

§ 176. When a Threat Is Improper

(1) A threat is improper if

> (a) what is threatened is a crime or a tort, or the threat itself would be a crime or a tort if it resulted in obtaining property,

    (b)   what is threatened is a criminal prosecution,

    (c)   what is threatened is the use of civil process and the threat is made in bad faith, or

    (d)   the threat is a breach of the duty of good faith and fair dealing under a contract with the recipient.

(2) A threat is improper if the resulting exchange is not on fair terms, and

    (a)   the threatened act would harm the recipient and would not significantly benefit the party making the threat,

    (b)   the effectiveness of the threat in inducing the manifestation of assent is significantly increased by prior unfair dealing by the party making the threat, or

    (c)   what is threatened is otherwise a use of power for illegitimate ends.

§ 177. When Undue Influence Makes a Contract Voidable

(1) Undue influence is unfair persuasion of a party who is under the domination of the person exercising the persuasion or who by virtue of the relation between them is justified in assuming that that person will not act in a manner inconsistent with his welfare.

(2) If a party's manifestation of assent is induced by undue influence by the other party, the contract is voidable by the victim.

(3) If a party's manifestation of assent is induced by one who is not a party to the transaction, the contract is voidable by the victim unless the other party to the transaction in good faith and without reason to know of the undue influence either gives value or relies materially on the transaction.

CHAPTER 8. UNENFORCEABILITY ON GROUNDS OF PUBLIC POLICY

TOPIC 1. UNENFORCEABILITY IN GENERAL

§ 178. When a Term Is Unenforceable on Grounds of Public Policy

(1) A promise or other term of an agreement is unenforceable on grounds of public policy if legislation provides that it is unenforceable or the interest in its enforcement is clearly outweighed in the circumstances by a public policy against the enforcement of such terms.

(2) In weighing the interest in the enforcement of a term, account is taken of

    (a)   the parties' justified expectations,

    (b)   any forfeiture that would result if enforcement were denied, and

(c) any special public interest in the enforcement of the particular term.

(3) In weighing a public policy against enforcement of a term,
account is taken of

(a) the strength of that policy as manifested by legislation or
judicial decisions,

(b) the likelihood that a refusal to enforce the term will
further that policy,

(c) the seriousness of any misconduct involved and the extent
to which it was deliberate, and

(d) the directness of the connection between that misconduct
and the term.

§ 181. Effect of Failure to Comply With Licensing or Similar Requirement

If a party is prohibited from doing an act because of his failure to
comply with a licensing, registration or similar requirement, a promise
in consideration of his doing that act or of his promise to do it is
unenforceable on grounds of public policy if

(a) the requirement has a regulatory purpose, and

(b) the interest in the enforcement of the promise is clearly
outweighed by the public policy behind the requirement.

TOPIC 2. RESTRAINT OF TRADE

§ 187. Non-ancillary Restraints on Competition

A promise to refrain from competition that imposes a restraint that
is not ancillary to an otherwise valid transaction or relationship is
unreasonably in restraint of trade.

§ 188. Ancillary Restraints on Competition

(1) A promise to refrain from competition that imposes a restraint
that is ancillary to an otherwise valid transaction or relationship is
unreasonably in restraint of trade if

(a) the restraint is greater than is needed to protect the
promisee's legitimate interest, or

(b) the promisee's need is outweighed by the hardship to the
promisor and the likely injury to the public.

(2) Promises imposing restraints that are ancillary to a valid transaction or relationship include the following:

(a) a promise by the seller of a business not to compete with
the buyer in such a way as to injure the value of the
business sold;

    (b) a promise by an employee or other agent not to compete with his employer or other principal;

    (c) a promise by a partner not to compete with the partnership.

CHAPTER 9. THE SCOPE OF CONTRACTUAL OBLIGATIONS

TOPIC 1. THE MEANING OF AGREEMENTS

§ 201. Whose Meaning Prevails

(1) Where the parties have attached the same meaning to a promise or agreement or a term thereof, it is interpreted in accordance with that meaning.

(2) Where the parties have attached different meanings to a promise or agreement or a term thereof, it is interpreted in accordance with the meaning attached by one of them if at the time the agreement was made

    (a) that party did not know of any different meaning attached by the other, and the other knew the meaning attached by the first party; or

    (b) that party had no reason to know of any different meaning attached by the other, and the other had reason to know the meaning attached by the first party.

(3) Except as stated in this Section, neither party is bound by the meaning attached by the other, even though the result may be a failure of mutual assent.

§ 202. Rules in Aid of Interpretation

(1) Words and other conduct are interpreted in the light of all the circumstances, and if the principal purpose of the parties is ascertainable it is given great weight.

(2) A writing is interpreted as a whole, and all writings that are part of the same transaction are interpreted together.

(3) Unless a different intention is manifested,

    (a) where language has a generally prevailing meaning, it is interpreted in accordance with that meaning;

    (b) technical terms and words of art are given their technical meaning when used in a transaction within their technical field.

(4) Where an agreement involves repeated occasions for performance by either party with knowledge of the nature of the performance and opportunity for objection to it by the other, any course of perform-

119

ance accepted or acquiesced in without objection is given great weight in the interpretation of the agreement.

(5) Wherever reasonable, the manifestations of intention of the parties to a promise or agreement are interpreted as consistent with each other and with any relevant course of performance, course of dealing, or usage of trade.

§ 203. Standards of Preference in Interpretation

In the interpretation of a promise or agreement or a term thereof, the following standards of preference are generally applicable:

(a) an interpretation which gives a reasonable, lawful, and effective meaning to all the terms is preferred to an interpretation which leaves a part unreasonable, unlawful, or of no effect;

(b) express terms are given greater weight than course of performance, course of dealing, and usage of trade, course of performance is given greater weight than course of dealing or usage of trade, and course of dealing is given greater weight than usage of trade;

(c) specific terms and exact terms are given greater weight than general language;

(d) separately negotiated or added terms are given greater weight than standardized terms or other terms not separately negotiated.

§ 204. Supplying an Omitted Essential Term

When the parties to a bargain sufficiently defined to be a contract have not agreed with respect to a term which is essential to a determination of their rights and duties, a term which is reasonable in the circumstances is supplied by the court.

TOPIC 2. CONSIDERATIONS OF FAIRNESS AND THE PUBLIC INTEREST

§ 205. Duty of Good Faith and Fair Dealing

Every contract imposes upon each party a duty of good faith and fair dealing in its performance and its enforcement.

§ 208. Unconscionable Contract or Term

If a contract or term thereof is unconscionable at the time the contract is made a court may refuse to enforce the contract, or may enforce the remainder of the contract without the unconscionable term, or may so limit the application of any unconscionable term as to avoid any unconscionable result.

TOPIC 3. EFFECT OF ADOPTION OF A WRITING

§ 209. Integrated Agreements

(1) An integrated agreement is a writing or writings constituting a final expression of one or more terms of an agreement.

(2) Whether there is an integrated agreement is to be determined by the court as a question preliminary to determination of a question of interpretation or to application of the parol evidence rule.

(3) Where the parties reduce an agreement to a writing which in view of its completeness and specificity reasonably appears to be a complete agreement, it is taken to be an integrated agreement unless it is established by other evidence that the writing did not constitute a final expression.

§ 210. Completely and Partially Integrated Agreements

(1) A completely integrated agreement is an integrated agreement adopted by the parties as a complete and exclusive statement of the terms of the agreement.

(2) A partially integrated agreement is an integrated agreement other than a completely integrated agreement.

(3) Whether an agreement is completely or partially integrated is to be determined by the court as a question preliminary to determination of a question of interpretation or to application of the parol evidence rule.

§ 211. Standardized Agreements

(1) Except as stated in Subsection (3), where a party to an agreement signs or otherwise manifests assent to a writing and has reason to believe that like writings are regularly used to embody terms of agreements of the same type, he adopts the writing as an integrated agreement with respect to the terms included in the writing.

(2) Such a writing is interpreted wherever reasonable as treating alike all those similarly situated, without regard to their knowledge or understanding of the standard terms of the writing.

(3) Where the other party has reason to believe that the party manifesting such assent would not do so if he knew that the writing contained a particular term, the term is not part of the agreement.

§ 213. Effect of Integrated Agreement on Prior Agreements (Parol Evidence Rule)

(1) A binding integrated agreement discharges prior agreements to the extent that it is inconsistent with them.

(2) A binding completely integrated agreement discharges prior agreements to the extent that they are within its scope.

(3) An integrated agreement that is not binding or that is voidable and avoided does not discharge a prior agreement. But an integrated agreement, even though not binding, may be effective to render inoperative a term which would have been part of the agreement if it had not been integrated.

§ 214. Evidence of Prior or Contemporaneous Agreements and Negotiations

Agreements and negotiations prior to or contemporaneous with the adoption of a writing are admissible in evidence to establish

    (a) that the writing is or is not an integrated agreement;

    (b) that the integrated agreement, if any, is completely or partially integrated;

    (c) the meaning of the writing, whether or not integrated;

    (d) illegality, fraud, duress, mistake, lack of consideration, or other invalidating cause;

    (e) ground for granting or denying rescission, reformation, specific performance, or other remedy.

§ 215. Contradiction of Integrated Terms

Except as stated in the preceding Section, where there is a binding agreement, either completely or partially integrated, evidence of prior or contemporaneous agreements or negotiations is not admissible in evidence to contradict a term of the writing.

§ 216. Consistent Additional Terms

(1) Evidence of a consistent additional term is admissible to supplement an integrated agreement unless the court finds that the agreement was completely integrated.

(2) An agreement is not completely integrated if the writing omits a consistent additional agreed term which is

    (a) agreed to for separate consideration, or

    (b) such a term as in the circumstances might naturally be omitted from the writing.

§ 217. Integrated Agreement Subject to Oral Requirement of a Condition

Where the parties to a written agreement agree orally that performance of the agreement is subject to the occurrence of a stated condition, the agreement is not integrated with respect to the oral condition.

TOPIC 5. CONDITIONS AND SIMILAR EVENTS

§ 224. Condition Defined

A condition is an event, not certain to occur, which must occur, unless its non-occurrence is excused, before performance under a contract becomes due.

§ 225. Effects of the Non-occurrence of a Condition

(1) Performance of a duty subject to a condition cannot become due unless the condition occurs or its non-occurrence is excused.

(2) Unless it has been excused, the non-occurrence of a condition discharges the duty when the condition can no longer occur.

(3) Non-occurrence of a condition is not a breach by a party unless he is under a duty that the condition occur.

§ 227. Standards of Preference With Regard to Conditions

(1) In resolving doubts as to whether an event is made a condition of an obligor's duty, and as to the nature of such an event, an interpretation is preferred that will reduce the obligee's risk of forfeiture, unless the event is within the obligee's control or the circumstances indicate that he has assumed the risk.

(2) Unless the contract is of a type under which only one party generally undertakes duties, when it is doubtful whether

     (a) a duty is imposed on an obligee that an event occur, or

     (b) the event is made a condition of the obligor's duty, or

     (c) the event is made a condition of the obligor's duty and a duty is imposed on the obligee that the event occur,

the first interpretation is preferred if the event is within the obligee's control.

(3) In case of doubt, an interpretation under which an event is a condition of an obligor's duty is preferred over an interpretation under which the non-occurrence of the event is a ground for discharge of that duty after it has become a duty to perform.

§ 228. Satisfaction of the Obligor as a Condition

When it is a condition of an obligor's duty that he be satisfied with respect to the obligee's performance or with respect to something else, and it is practicable to determine whether a reasonable person in the position of the obligor would be satisfied, an interpretation is preferred under which the condition occurs if such a reasonable person in the position of the obligor would be satisfied.

§ 229. Excuse of a Condition to Avoid Forfeiture

To the extent that the non-occurrence of a condition would cause disproportionate forfeiture, a court may excuse the non-occurrence of that condition unless its occurrence was a material part of the agreed exchange.

CHAPTER 10. PERFORMANCE AND NON–PERFORMANCE

TOPIC 1. PERFORMANCES TO BE EXCHANGED UNDER AN EXCHANGE OF PROMISES

§ 234. Order of Performances

(1) Where all or part of the performances to be exchanged under an exchange of promises can be rendered simultaneously, they are to that extent due simultaneously, unless the language or the circumstances indicate the contrary.

(2) Except to the extent stated in Subsection (1), where the performance of only one party under such an exchange requires a period of time, his performance is due at an earlier time than that of the other party, unless the language or the circumstances indicate the contrary.

TOPIC 2. EFFECT OF PERFORMANCE AND NON–PERFORMANCE

§ 236. Claims for Damages for Total and for Partial Breach

(1) A claim for damages for total breach is one for damages based on all of the injured party's remaining rights to performance.

(2) A claim for damages for partial breach is one for damages based on only part of the injured party's remaining rights to performance.

§ 237. Effect on Other Party's Duties of a Failure to Render Performance

Except as stated in § 240, it is a condition of each party's remaining duties to render performances to be exchanged under an exchange of promises that there be no uncured material failure by the other party to render any such performance due at an earlier time.

§ 238. Effect on Other Party's Duties of a Failure to Offer Performance

Where all or part of the performances to be exchanged under an exchange of promises are due simultaneously, it is a condition of each party's duties to render such performance that the other party either render or, with manifested present ability to do so, offer performance of his part of the simultaneous exchange.

§ 240. Part Performances as Agreed Equivalents

If the performances to be exchanged under an exchange of promises can be apportioned into corresponding pairs of part performances so that the parts of each pair are properly regarded as agreed equivalents, a party's performance of his part of such a pair has the same effect on the other's duties to render performance of the agreed equivalent as it would have if only that pair of performances had been promised.

§ 241. Circumstances Significant in Determining Whether a Failure Is Material

In determining whether a failure to render or to offer performance is material, the following circumstances are significant:

    (a) the extent to which the injured party will be deprived of the benefit which he reasonably expected;

    (b) the extent to which the injured party can be adequately compensated for the part of that benefit of which he will be deprived;

    (c) the extent to which the party failing to perform or to offer to perform will suffer forfeiture;

    (d) the likelihood that the party failing to perform or to offer to perform will cure his failure, taking account of all the circumstances including any reasonable assurances;

    (e) the extent to which the behavior of the party failing to perform or to offer to perform comports with standards of good faith and fair dealing.

§ 242. Circumstances Significant in Determining When Remaining Duties Are Discharged

In determining the time after which a party's uncured material failure to render or to offer performance discharges the other party's remaining duties to render performance under the rules stated in §§ 237 and 238, the following circumstances are significant:

    (a) those stated in § 241;

    (b) the extent to which it reasonably appears to the injured party that delay may prevent or hinder him in making reasonable substitute arrangements;

    (c) the extent to which the agreement provides for performance without delay, but a material failure to perform or to offer to perform on a stated day does not of itself discharge the other party's remaining duties unless the circumstances, including the language of the agreement, indicate that performance or an offer to perform by that day is important.

§ 243. Effect of a Breach by Non-performance as Giving Rise to a Claim for Damages for Total Breach

(1) With respect to performances to be exchanged under an exchange of promises, a breach by non-performance gives rise to a claim for damages for total breach only if it discharges the injured party's remaining duties to render such performance, other than a duty to render an agreed equivalent under § 240.

(2) Except as stated in Subsection (3), a breach by nonperformance accompanied or followed by a repudiation gives rise to a claim for damages for total breach.

(3) Where at the time of the breach the only remaining duties of performance are those of the party in breach and are for the payment of money in installments not related to one another, his breach by non-performance as to less than the whole, whether or not accompanied or followed by a repudiation, does not give rise to a claim for damages for total breach.

(4) In any case other than those stated in the preceding subsections, a breach by non-performance gives rise to a claim for total breach only if it so substantially impairs the value of the contract to the injured party at the time of the breach that it is just in the circumstances to allow him to recover damages based on all his remaining rights to performance.

§ 248. Effect of Insufficient Reason for Rejection as Excusing the Non-occurrence of a Condition

Where a party rejecting a defective performance or offer of performance gives an insufficient reason for rejection, the non-occurrence of a condition of his duty is excused only if he knew or had reason to know of that non-occurrence and then only to the extent that the giving of an insufficient reason substantially contributes to a failure by the other party to cure.

TOPIC 3. EFFECT OF PROSPECTIVE NON–PERFORMANCE

§ 250. When a Statement or an Act Is a Repudiation

A repudiation is

    (a) a statement by the obligor to the obligee indicating that the obligor will commit a breach that would of itself give the obligee a claim for damages for total breach under § 243, or

    (b) a voluntary affirmative act which renders the obligor unable or apparently unable to perform without such a breach.

§ 251. When a Failure to Give Assurance May Be Treated as a Repudiation

(1) Where reasonable grounds arise to believe that the obligor will commit a breach by non-performance that would of itself give the obligee a claim for damages for total breach under § 243, the obligee may demand adequate assurance of due performance and may, if reasonable, suspend any performance for which he has not already received the agreed exchange until he receives such assurance.

(2) The obligee may treat as a repudiation the obligor's failure to provide within a reasonable time such assurance of due performance as is adequate in the circumstances of the particular case.

§ 253. Effect of a Repudiation as a Breach and on Other Party's Duties

(1) Where an obligor repudiates a duty before he has committed a breach by non-performance and before he has received all of the agreed exchange for it, his repudiation alone gives rise to a claim for damages for total breach.

(2) Where performances are to be exchanged under an exchange of promises, one party's repudiation of a duty to render performance discharges the other party's remaining duties to render performance.

§ 256. Nullification of Repudiation or Basis for Repudiation

(1) The effect of a statement as constituting a repudiation under § 250 or the basis for a repudiation under § 251 is nullified by a retraction of the statement if notification of the retraction comes to the attention of the injured party before he materially changes his position in reliance on the repudiation or indicates to the other party that he considers the repudiation to be final.

(2) The effect of events other than a statement as constituting a repudiation under § 250 or the basis for a repudiation under § 251 is nullified if, to the knowledge of the injured party, those events have ceased to exist before he materially changes his position in reliance on the repudiation or indicates to the other party that he considers the repudiation to be final.

CHAPTER 11. IMPRACTICABILITY OF PERFORMANCE AND FRUSTRATION OF PURPOSE

§ 261. Discharge by Supervening Impracticability

Where, after a contract is made, a party's performance is made impracticable without his fault by the occurrence of an event the non-occurrence of which was a basic assumption on which the contract was made, his duty to render that performance is discharged, unless the language or the circumstances indicate the contrary.

§ 265. Discharge by Supervening Frustration

Where, after a contract is made, a party's principal purpose is substantially frustrated without his fault by the occurrence of an event the non-occurrence of which was a basic assumption on which the contract was made, his remaining duties to render performance are discharged, unless the language or the circumstances indicate the contrary.

§ 272. Relief Including Restitution

(1) In any case governed by the rules stated in this Chapter, either party may have a claim for relief including restitution under the rules stated in §§ 240 and 377.

(2) In any case governed by the rules stated in this Chapter, if those rules together with the rules stated in Chapter 16 will not avoid injustice, the court may grant relief on such terms as justice requires including protection of the parties' reliance interests.

CHAPTER 14.   CONTRACT BENEFICIARIES

§ 302. Intended and Incidental Beneficiaries

(1) Unless otherwise agreed between promisor and promisee, a beneficiary of a promise is an intended beneficiary if recognition of a right to performance in the beneficiary is appropriate to effectuate the intention of the parties and either

> (a) the performance of the promise will satisfy an obligation of the promisee to pay money to the beneficiary; or
>
> (b) the circumstances indicate that the promisee intends to give the beneficiary the benefit of the promised performance.

(2) An incidental beneficiary is a beneficiary who is not an intended beneficiary.

§ 309. Defenses Against the Beneficiary

(1) A promise creates no duty to a beneficiary unless a contract is formed between the promisor and the promisee; and if a contract is voidable or unenforceable at the time of its formation the right of any beneficiary is subject to the infirmity.

(2) If a contract ceases to be binding in whole or in part because of impracticability, public policy, non-occurrence of a condition, or present or prospective failure of performance, the right of any beneficiary is to that extent discharged or modified.

(3) Except as stated in Subsections (1) and (2) and in § 311 or as provided by the contract, the right of any beneficiary against the promisor is not subject to the promisor's claims or defenses against the promisee or to the promisee's claims or defenses against the beneficiary.

(4) A beneficiary's right against the promisor is subject to any claim or defense arising from his own conduct or agreement.

§ 311. Variation of a Duty to a Beneficiary

(1) Discharge or modification of a duty to an intended beneficiary by conduct of the promisee or by a subsequent agreement between promisor and promisee is ineffective if a term of the promise creating the duty so provides.

(2) In the absence of such a term, the promisor and promisee retain power to discharge or modify the duty by subsequent agreement.

(3) Such a power terminates when the beneficiary, before he receives notification of the discharge or modification, materially changes his position in justifiable reliance on the promise or brings suit on it or manifests assent to it at the request of the promisor or promisee.

(4) If the promisee receives consideration for an attempted discharge or modification of the promisor's duty which is ineffective against the beneficiary, the beneficiary can assert a right to the consideration so received. The promisor's duty is discharged to the extent of the amount received by the beneficiary.

§ 313. Government Contracts

(1) The rules stated in this Chapter apply to contracts with a government or governmental agency except to the extent that application would contravene the policy of the law authorizing the contract or prescribing remedies for its breach.

(2) In particular, a promisor who contracts with a government or governmental agency to do an act for or render a service to the public is not subject to contractual liability to a member of the public for consequential damages resulting from performance or failure to perform unless

    (a) the terms of the promise provide for such liability; or

    (b) the promisee is subject to liability to the member of the public for the damages and a direct action against the promisor is consistent with the terms of the contract and with the policy of the law authorizing the contract and prescribing remedies for its breach.

CHAPTER 15. ASSIGNMENT AND DELEGATION

TOPIC 1. WHAT CAN BE ASSIGNED OR DELEGATED

§ 317. Assignment of a Right

(1) An assignment of a right is a manifestation of the assignor's intention to transfer it by virtue of which the assignor's right to performance by the obligor is extinguished in whole or in part and the assignee acquires a right to such performance.

(2) A contractual right can be assigned unless

   (a) the substitution of a right of the assignee for the right of the assignor would materially change the duty of the obligor, or materially increase the burden or risk imposed on him by his contract, or materially impair his chance of obtaining return performance, or materially reduce its value to him, or

   (b) the assignment is forbidden by statute or is otherwise inoperative on grounds of public policy, or

   (c) assignment is validly precluded by contract.

§ 318. Delegation of Performance of Duty

(1) An obligor can properly delegate the performance of his duty to another unless the delegation is contrary to public policy or the terms of his promise.

(2) Unless otherwise agreed, a promise requires performance by a particular person only to the extent that the obligee has a substantial interest in having that person perform or control the acts promised.

(3) Unless the obligee agrees otherwise, neither delegation of performance nor a contract to assume the duty made with the obligor by the person delegated discharges any duty or liability of the delegating obligor.

§ 322. Contractual Prohibition of Assignment

(1) Unless the circumstances indicate the contrary, a contract term prohibiting assignment of "the contract" bars only the delegation to an assignee of the performance by the assignor of a duty or condition.

(2) A contract term prohibiting assignment of rights under the contract, unless a different intention is manifested,

   (a) does not forbid assignment of a right to damages for breach of the whole contract or a right arising out of the assignor's due performance of his entire obligation;

(b) gives the obligor a right to damages for breach of the terms forbidding assignment but does not render the assignment ineffective;

(c) is for the benefit of the obligor, and does not prevent the assignee from acquiring rights against the assignor or the obligor from discharging his duty as if there were no such prohibition.

TOPIC 4. EFFECT ON THE OBLIGOR'S DUTY

§ 336. Defenses Against an Assignee

(1) By an assignment the assignee acquires a right against the obligor only to the extent that the obligor is under a duty to the assignor; and if the right of the assignor would be voidable by the obligor or unenforceable against him if no assignment had been made, the right of the assignee is subject to the infirmity.

(2) The right of an assignee is subject to any defense or claim of the obligor which accrues before the obligor receives notification of the assignment, but not to defenses or claims which accrue thereafter except as stated in this Section or as provided by statute.

(3) Where the right of an assignor is subject to discharge or modification in whole or in part by impossibility, illegality, non-occurrence of a condition, or present or prospective failure of performance by an obligee, the right of the assignee is to that extent subject to discharge or modification even after the obligor receives notification of the assignment.

(4) An assignee's right against the obligor is subject to any defense or claim arising from his conduct or to which he was subject as a party or a prior assignee because he had notice.

CHAPTER 16. REMEDIES

TOPIC 2. ENFORCEMENT BY AWARD OF DAMAGES

§ 347. Measure of Damages in General

Subject to the limitations stated in §§ 350–53, the injured party has a right to damages based on his expectation interest as measured by

(a) the loss in the value to him of the other party's performance caused by its failure or deficiency, plus

(b) any other loss, including incidental or consequential loss, caused by the breach, less

(c) any cost or other loss that he has avoided by not having to perform.

131

§ 348. Alternatives to Loss in Value of Performance

(1) If a breach delays the use of property and the loss in value to the injured party is not proved with reasonable certainty, he may recover damages based on the rental value of the property or on interest on the value of the property.

(2) If a breach results in defective or unfinished construction and the loss in value to the injured party is not proved with sufficient certainty, he may recover damages based on

> (a) the diminution in the market price of the property caused by the breach, or
>
> (b) the reasonable cost of completing performance or of remedying the defects if that cost is not clearly disproportionate to the probable loss in value to him.

(3) If a breach is of a promise conditioned on a fortuitous event and it is uncertain whether the event would have occurred had there been no breach, the injured party may recover damages based on the value of the conditional right at the time of breach.

§ 349. Damages Based on Reliance Interest

As an alternative to the measure of damages stated in § 347, the injured party has a right to damages based on his reliance interest, including expenditures made in preparation for performance or in performance, less any loss that the party in breach can prove with reasonable certainty the injured party would have suffered had the contract been performed.

§ 350. Avoidability as a Limitation on Damages

(1) Except as stated in Subsection (2), damages are not recoverable for loss that the injured party could have avoided without undue risk, burden or humiliation.

(2) The injured party is not precluded from recovery by the rule stated in Subsection (1) to the extent that he has made reasonable but unsuccessful efforts to avoid loss.

§ 351. Unforeseeability and Related Limitations on Damages

(1) Damages are not recoverable for loss that the party in breach did not have reason to foresee as a probable result of the breach when the contract was made.

(2) Loss may be foreseeable as a probable result of a breach because it follows from the breach

> (a) in the ordinary course of events, or
>
> (b) as a result of special circumstances beyond the ordinary course of events, that the party in breach had reason to know.

(3) A court may limit damages for foreseeable loss by excluding recovery for loss of profits, by allowing recovery only for loss incurred in reliance, or otherwise if it concludes that in the circumstances justice so requires in order to avoid disproportionate compensation.

§ 352. Uncertainty as a Limitation on Damages

Damages are not recoverable for loss beyond an amount that the evidence permits to be established with reasonable certainty.

§ 353. Loss Due to Emotional Disturbance

Recovery for emotional disturbance will be excluded unless the breach also caused bodily harm or the contract or the breach is of such a kind that serious emotional disturbance was a particularly likely result.

§ 355. Punitive Damages

Punitive damages are not recoverable for a breach of contract unless the conduct constituting the breach is also a tort for which punitive damages are recoverable.

TOPIC 4. RESTITUTION

§ 370. Requirement That Benefit Be Conferred

A party is entitled to restitution under the rules stated in this Restatement only to the extent that he has conferred a benefit on the other party by way of part performance or reliance.

§ 371. Measure of Restitution Interest

If a sum of money is awarded to protect a party's restitution interest, it may as justice requires be measured by either

    (a) the reasonable value to the other party of what he received in terms of what it would have cost him to obtain it from a person in the claimant's position, or

    (b) the extent to which the other party's property has been increased in value or his other interests advanced.

§ 373. Restitution When Other Party Is in Breach

(1) Subject to the rule stated in Subsection (2), on a breach by non-performance that gives rise to a claim for damages for total breach or on a repudiation, the injured party is entitled to restitution for any benefit that he has conferred on the other party by way of part performance or reliance.

(2) The injured party has no right to restitution if he has performed all of his duties under the contract and no performance by the

other party remains due other than payment of a definite sum of money for that performance.

§ 374. Restitution in Favor of Party in Breach

(1) Subject to the rule stated in Subsection (2), if a party justifiably refuses to perform on the ground that his remaining duties of performance have been discharged by the other party's breach, the party in breach is entitled to restitution for any benefit that he has conferred by way of part performance or reliance in excess of the loss that he has caused by his own breach.

(2) To the extent that, under the manifested assent of the parties, a party's performance is to be retained in the case of breach, that party is not entitled to restitution if the value of the performance as liquidated damages is reasonable in the light of the anticipated or actual loss caused by the breach and the difficulties of proof of loss.

§ 376. Restitution When Contract Is Voidable

A party who has avoided a contract on the ground of lack of capacity, mistake, misrepresentation, duress, undue influence or abuse of a fiduciary relation is entitled to restitution for any benefit that he has conferred on the other party by way of part performance or reliance.

§ 377. Restitution in Cases of Impracticability, Frustration, Non-occurrence of Condition or Disclaimer by Beneficiary

A party whose duty of performance does not arise or is discharged as a result of impracticability of performance, frustration of purpose, non-occurrence of a condition or disclaimer by a beneficiary is entitled to restitution for any benefit that he has conferred on the other party by way of part performance or reliance.

UNITED NATIONS CONVENTION ON CONTRACTS FOR THE INTERNATIONAL SALE OF GOODS

COMPILERS' NOTE

Since January 1, 1988 American exporters and importers have been subject to the Convention on Contracts for the International Sale of Goods (CISG). With respect to transactions within its scope, it displaces much of Article 2, Sales, of the Uniform Commercial Code—including, for example, the requirements of the statute of frauds (CISG 11).[a]

The Convention "applies to contracts for the sale of goods between parties whose places of business are in different States . . . when the States are Contracting States" (CISG 1).[b] The Convention preserves the autonomy of the parties by allowing them to "exclude the application of this Convention or . . . derogate from or vary the effect of any of its provisions" (CISG 6). The Convention does not displace rules of national law that relate to "the validity of the contract or of any of its provisions or of any usages." (CISG 4(a)).[c]

Work on the Convention began in the 1930s when the Institute for the Unification of Private Law in Rome, then under the auspices of the League of Nations, set up a drafting committee of European scholars to work on a uniform law for international sales. By the outbreak of the Second World War, the committee had prepared a first draft, solicited comments from governments, and prepared a revised draft taking account of these comments.

After the War the Dutch Government appointed a commission to do further work, solicited comments from governments and, in 1964, convened a diplomatic conference at The Hague. The conference approved a uniform law on the international sale of goods (ULIS) and a shorter companion uniform law on the formation of contracts for the international sale of goods.

a. The United States did not make the declaration described in CISG 12.

b. In this context "States" means nations and "Contracting" means adopting. The United States did not accept CISG 1(b), which would have given the Convention a broader application.

c. For a definitive treatment of the Convention, see J. Honnold, Uniform Law for International Sales under the 1980 U.N. Convention (1982). For a more critical analysis by authors from many countries, see C. Bianca, M. Bonell *et al.*, Commentary on the International Sales Law: The 1980 Vienna Convention (1987). For shorter appraisals, see Farnsworth, The Vienna Convention: An International Law for the Sale of Goods, in Private Investors Abroad—Problems and Solutions in International Business in 1983 121 (Southwestern Legal Foundation 1983); Rosett, Critical Reflections on the United Nations Convention on the International Sale of Goods, 45 Ohio St.L.J. 265 (1984).

Although the United States had quickly put together a delegation to The Hague to consider a draft prepared by a group of exclusively European scholars, that delegation's influence was not pervasive enough to produce a final text that justified United States ratification.[d] Nevertheless, ULIS did receive eight adoptions by other countries, enough for it to take effect.

Even before ULIS had taken effect, however, efforts were afoot under United Nations auspices to produce a revised international sales law that would be more widely acceptable. In 1966, the United Nations General Assembly established the United Nations Commission on International Trade Law (UNCITRAL). The Commission has "for its object the promotion of the progressive harmonization and unification of the law of international trade." Its thirty-six members include common law as well as civil law countries, developing as well as industrialized countries, and countries with centrally planned economics as well as those with free-market economies.

In 1969, UNCITRAL appointed a fourteen-member Working Group on Sales to consider what changes in ULIS would make it more acceptable to countries of varied legal, social, and economic systems. The United States was an active member of this Working Group from its inception. In 1977 UNCITRAL revised and approved a text of CISG prepared by the Working Group on Sales, and in 1978 it integrated into CISG additional provisions on formation and interpretation. In 1980, the United Nations held in Vienna a diplomatic conference to propose a final text of CISG. After five weeks of intensive effort by the sixty-two countries represented, CISG—often referred to as "the Vienna Convention"—was adopted.

The final product of this half-century of work consists of eighty-eight substantive articles (what we in the United States would call "sections") plus thirteen more articles on effective date, reservations, and the like. Only the eighty-eight substantive articles are set out below. CISG took effect following adoption by ten countries.[e]

d. The traditional scheme for international unification results in a multilateral treaty, put in final form at a diplomatic conference and then adopted by ratification or accession. One important difference between this scheme and that used for unification within the United States is that a country ratifying or acceding to a treaty cannot make changes in its text, except for a few variations that the diplomatic conference has allowed countries to make by means of reservations.

e. The Convention has been ratified by Argentina, Australia, Austria, Bulgaria, Belarus, Canada, Chile, China, Czechoslovakia, Denmark, Egypt, Finland, France, Germany, Guinea, Hungary, Iraq, Italy, Lesotho, Mexico, Netherlands, Norway, Romania, Russia, Spain, Syria, Sweden, Switzerland, Ukraine, United States, Yugoslavia, Zambia.

CONVENTION ON CONTRACTS FOR THE INTERNATIONAL SALE OF GOODS

THE STATES PARTIES TO THIS CONVENTION,

Bearing in mind the broad objectives in the resolutions adopted by the sixth special session of the General Assembly of the United Nations on the establishment of a New International Economic Order,

Considering that the development of international trade on the basis of equality and mutual benefit is an important element in promoting friendly relations among States,

Being of the opinion that the adoption of uniform rules which govern contracts for the international sale of goods and take into account the different social, economic and legal systems would contribute to the removal of legal barriers in international trade and promote the development of international trade,

Have agreed as follows:

Part I. Sphere of application and general provisions

CHAPTER I. SPHERE OF APPLICATION

Article 1

(1) This Convention applies to contracts of sale of goods between parties whose places of business are in different States:

    (a) When the States are Contracting States; or

    (b) When the rules of private international law lead to the application of the law of a Contracting State.

(2) The fact that the parties have their places of business in different States is to be disregarded whenever this fact does not appear either from the contract or from any dealings between, or from information disclosed by, the parties at any time before or at the conclusion of the contract.

(3) Neither the nationality of the parties nor the civil or commercial character of the parties or of the contract is to be taken into consideration in determining the application of this Convention.

Article 2

This Convention does not apply to sales:

    (a) Of goods bought for personal, family or household use, unless the seller, at any time before or at the conclusion of

137

the contract, neither knew nor ought to have known that the goods were bought for any such use;

(b) By auction;

(c) On execution or otherwise by authority of law;

(d) Of stocks, shares, investment securities, negotiable instruments or money;

(e) Of ships, vessels, hovercraft or aircraft;

(f) Of electricity.

Article 3

(1) Contracts for the supply of goods to be manufactured or produced are to be considered sales unless the party who order the goods undertakes to supply a substantial part of the materials necessary for such manufacture or production.

(2) This Convention does not apply to contracts in which the preponderant part of the obligations of the party who furnishes the goods consists in the supply of labour or other services.

Article 4

This Convention governs only the formation of the contract of sale and the rights and obligations of the seller and the buyer arising from such a contract. In particular, except as otherwise expressly provided in this Convention, it is not concerned with:

(a) The validity of the contract or of any of its provisions or of any usage;

(b) The effect which the contract may have on the property in the goods sold.

Article 5

This Convention does not apply to the liability of the seller for death or personal injury caused by the goods to any person.

Article 6

The parties may exclude the application of this Convention or, subject to article 12, derogate from or vary the effect of any of its provisions.

CHAPTER II. GENERAL PROVISIONS

Article 7

(1) In the interpretation of this Convention, regard is to be had to its international character and to the need to promote uniformity in its application and the observance of good faith in international trade.

(2) Questions concerning matters governed by this Convention which are not expressly settled in it are to be settled in conformity with the general principles on which it is based or, in the absence of such principles, in conformity with the law applicable by virtue of the rules of private international law.

Article 8

(1) For the purposes of this Convention statements made by and other conduct of a party are to be interpreted according to his intent where the other party knew or could not have been unaware what that intent was.

(2) If the preceding paragraph is not applicable, statements made by and other conduct of a party are to be interpreted according to the understanding that a reasonable person of the same kind as the other party would have had in the same circumstances.

(3) In determining the intent of a party or the understanding a reasonable person would have had, due consideration is to be given to all relevant circumstances of the case including the negotiations, any practices which the parties have established between themselves, usages and any subsequent conduct of the parties.

Article 9

(1) The parties are bound by any usages to which they have agreed and by any practices which they have established between themselves.

(2) The parties are considered, unless otherwise agreed, to have impliedly made applicable to their contract or its formation a usage of which the parties knew or ought to have known and which in international trade is widely known to, and regularly observed by, parties to contracts of the type involved in the particular trade concerned.

Article 10

For the purposes of this Convention:

    (a) If a party has more than one place of business, the place of business is that which has the closest relationship to the contract and its performance, having regard to the circumstances known to or contemplated by the parties at any time before or at the conclusion of the contract;

    (b) If a party does not have a place of business, reference is to be made to his habitual residence.

Article 11

A Contract of sale need not be concluded in or evidenced by writing and is not subject to any other requirement as to form. It may be proved by any means, including witnesses.

Article 12

Any provision of article 11, article 29 or Part II of this Convention that allows a contract of sale or its modification or termination by agreement or any offer, acceptance or other indication of intention to be made in any form other than in writing does not apply where any party has his place of business in a Contracting State which has made a declaration under article 96 of this Convention. The parties may not derogate from or vary the effect of this article.

Article 13

For the purposes of this Convention "writing" includes telegram and telex.

Part II. Formation of the contract

Article 14

(1) A proposal for concluding a contract addressed to one or more specific persons constitutes an offer if it is sufficiently definite and indicates the intention of the offeror to be bound in case of acceptance. A proposal is sufficiently definite if it indicates the goods and expressly or implicitly fixes or makes provision for determining the quantity and the price.

(2) A proposal other than one addressed to one or more specific persons is to be considered merely as an invitation to make offers, unless the contrary is clearly indicated by the person making the proposal.

Article 15

(1) An offer becomes effective when it reaches the offeree.

(2) An offer, even if it is irrevocable, may be withdrawn if the withdrawal reaches the offeree before or at the same time as the offer.

Article 16

(1) Until a contract is concluded an offer may be revoked if the revocation reaches the offeree before he has dispatched an acceptance.

(2) However, an offer cannot be revoked:

    (a) If it indicates, whether by stating a fixed time for acceptance or otherwise, that it is irrevocable; or

    (b) If it was reasonable for the offeree to rely on the offer as being irrevocable and the offeree has acted in reliance on the offer.

Article 17

An offer, even if it is irrevocable, is terminated when a rejection reaches the offeror.

Article 18

(1) A statement made by or other conduct of the offeree indicating assent to an offer is an acceptance. Silence or inactivity does not in itself amount to acceptance.

(2) An acceptance of an offer becomes effective at the moment the indication of assent reaches the offeror. An acceptance is not effective if the indication of assent does not reach the offeror within the time he has fixed or, if no time is fixed, within a reasonable time, due account being taken of the circumstances of the transaction, including the rapidity of the means of communication employed by the offeror. An oral offer must be accepted immediately unless the circumstances indicate otherwise.

(3) However, if, by virtue of the offer or as a result of practices which the parties have established between themselves or of usage, the offeree may indicate assent by performing an act, such as one relating to the dispatch of the goods or payment of the price, without notice to the offeror, the acceptance is effective at the moment the act is performed, provided that the act is performed within the period of time laid down in the preceding paragraph.

Article 19

(1) A reply to an offer which purports to be an acceptance but contains additions, limitations or other modifications is a rejection of the offer and constitutes a counter-offer.

(2) However, a reply to an offer which purports to be an acceptance but contains additional or different terms which do not materially alter the terms of the offer constitutes an acceptance, unless the offeror, without undue delay, objects orally to the discrepancy or dispatches a notice to that effect. If he does not so object, the terms of the contract are the terms of the offer with the modifications contained in the acceptance.

(3) Additional or different terms relating, among other things, to the price, payment, quality and quantity of the goods, place and time of delivery, extent of one party's liability to the other or the settlement of disputes are considered to alter the terms of the offer materially.

Article 20

(1) A period of time for acceptance fixed by the offeror in a telegram or a letter begins to run from the moment the telegram is

141

handed in for dispatch or from the date shown on the letter or, if no such date is shown, from the date shown on the envelope. A period of time for acceptance fixed by the offeror by telephone, telex or other means of instantaneous communication, begins to run from the moment that the offer reaches the offeree.

(2) Official holidays or non-business days occurring during the period for acceptance are included in calculating the period. However, if a notice of acceptance cannot be delivered at the address of the offeror on the last day of the period because that day falls on an official holiday or a non-business day at the place of business of the offeror, the period is extended until the first business day which follows.

Article 21

(1) A late acceptance is nevertheless effective as an acceptance if without delay the offeror orally so informs the offeree or dispatches a notice to that effect.

(2) If a letter or other writing containing a late acceptance shows that it has been sent in such circumstances that if its transmission had been normal it would have reached the offeror in due time, the late acceptance is effective as an acceptance unless, without delay, the offeror orally informs the offeree that he considers his offer as having lapsed or dispatches a notice to that effect.

Article 22

An acceptance may be withdrawn if the withdrawal reaches the offeror before or at the same time as the acceptance would have become effective.

Article 23

A contract is concluded at the moment when an acceptance of an offer becomes effective in accordance with the provisions of this Convention.

Article 24

For the purposes of this Part of the Convention, an offer, declaration of acceptance or any other indication of intention "reaches" the addressee when it is made orally to him or delivered by any other means to him personally, to his place of business or mailing address or, if he does not have a place of business or mailing address, to his habitual residence.

Part III. Sale of goods

CHAPTER I. GENERAL PROVISIONS

Article 25

A breach of contract committed by one of the parties is fundamental if it results in such detriment to the other party as substantially to deprive him of what he is entitled to expect under the contract, unless the party in breach did not foresee, and a reasonable person of the same kind in the same circumstances would not have foreseen, such a result.

Article 26

A declaration of avoidance of the contract is effective only if made by notice to the other party.

Article 27

Unless otherwise expressly provided in this Part of the Convention, if any notice, request or other communication is given or made by a party in accordance with this Part and by means appropriate in the circumstances, a delay or error in the transmission of the communication or its failure to arrive does not deprive that party of the right to rely on the communication.

Article 28

If, in accordance with the provisions of this Convention, one party is entitled to require performance of any obligation by the other party, a court is not bound to enter a judgment for specific performance unless the court would do so under its own law in respect of similar contracts of sale not governed by this Convention.

Article 29

(1) A contract may be modified or terminated by the mere agreement of the parties.

(2) A contract in writing which contains a provision requiring any modification or termination by agreement to be in writing may not be otherwise modified or terminated by agreement. However, a party may be precluded by his conduct from asserting such a provision to the extent that the other party has relied on that conduct.

CHAPTER II. OBLIGATIONS OF THE SELLER

Article 30

The seller must deliver the goods, hand over any documents relating to them and transfer the property in the goods, as required by the contract and this Convention.

143

Section I. Delivery of the goods and handing over of documents

Article 31

If the seller is not bound to deliver the goods at any other particular place, his obligation to deliver consists:

(a) If the contract of sale involves carriage of the goods—in handing the goods over to the first carrier for transmission to the buyer;

(b) If, in cases not within the preceding subparagraph, the contract relates to specific goods, or unidentified goods to be drawn from a specific stock or to be manufactured or produced, and at the time of the conclusion of the contract the parties knew that the goods were at, or were to be manufactured or produced at, a particular place—in placing the goods at the buyer's disposal at that place;

(c) In other cases—in placing the goods at the buyer's disposal at the place where the seller had his place of business at the time of the conclusion of the contract.

Article 32

(1) If the seller, in accordance with the contract or this Convention, hands the goods over to a carrier and if the goods are not clearly identified to the contract by markings on the goods, by shipping documents or otherwise, the seller must give the buyer notice of the consignment specifying the goods.

(2) If the seller is bound to arrange for carriage of the goods, he must make such contracts as are necessary for carriage to the place fixed by means of transportation appropriate in the circumstances and according to the usual terms for such transportation.

(3) If the seller is not bound to effect insurance in respect of the carriage of the goods, he must, at the buyer's request, provide him with all available information necessary to enable him to effect such insurance.

Article 33

The seller must deliver the goods:

(a) If a date is fixed by or determinable from the contract, on that date;

(b) If a period of time is fixed by or determinable from the contract, at any time within that period unless circumstances indicate that the buyer is to choose a date; or

(c) In any other case, within a reasonable time after the conclusion of the contract.

Article 34

If the seller is bound to hand over documents relating to the goods, he must hand them over at the time and place and in the form required by the contract. If the seller has handed over documents before that time, he may, up to that time, cure any lack of conformity in the documents, if the exercise of this right does not cause the buyer unreasonable inconvenience or unreasonable expense. However, the buyer retains any right to claim damages as provided for in this Convention.

Section II. Conformity of the goods and third party claims

Article 35

(1) The seller must deliver goods which are of the quantity, quality and description required by the contract and which are contained or packaged in the manner required by the contract.

(2) Except where the parties have agreed otherwise, the goods do not conform with the contract unless they:

(a) Are fit for the purposes for which goods of the same description would ordinarily be used;

(b) Are fit for any particular purpose expressly or impliedly made known to the seller at the time of the conclusion of the contract, except where the circumstances show that the buyer did not rely, or that it was unreasonable for him to rely, on the seller's skill and judgment;

(c) Possess the qualities of goods which the seller has held out to the buyer as a sample or model;

(d) Are contained or packaged in the manner usual for such goods or, where there is no such manner, in a manner adequate to preserve and protect the goods.

(3) The seller is not liable under subparagraphs (a) to (d) of the preceding paragraph for any lack of conformity of the goods if at the time of the conclusion of the contract the buyer knew or could not have been unaware of such lack of conformity.

Article 36

(1) The seller is liable in accordance with the contract and this Convention for any lack of conformity which exists at the time when the risk passes to the buyer, even though the lack of conformity becomes apparent only after that time.

145

(2) The seller is also liable for any lack of conformity which occurs after the time indicated in the preceding paragraph and which is due to a breach of any of his obligations, including a breach of any guarantee that for a period of time the goods will remain fit for their ordinary purpose or for some particular purpose or will retain specified qualities or characteristics.

Article 37

If the seller has delivered goods before the date for delivery, he may, up to that date, deliver any missing part or make up any deficiency in the quantity of the goods delivered, or deliver goods in replacement of any nonconforming goods delivered or remedy any lack of conformity in the goods delivered, provided that the exercise of this right does not cause the buyer unreasonable inconvenience or unreasonable expense. However, the buyer retains any right to claim damages as provided for in this Convention.

Article 38

(1) The buyer must examine the goods, or cause them to be examined, within as short a period as is practicable in the circumstances.

(2) If the contract involves carriage of the goods, examination may be deferred until after the goods have arrived at their destination.

(3) If the goods are redirected in transit or redispatched by the buyer without a reasonable opportunity for examination by him and at the time of the conclusion of the contract the seller knew or ought to have known of the possibility of such redirection or redispatch, examination may be deferred until after the goods have arrived at the new destination.

Article 39

(1) The buyer loses the right to rely on a lack of conformity of the goods if he does not give notice to the seller specifying the nature of the lack of conformity within a reasonable time after he has discovered it or ought to have discovered it.

(2) In any event, the buyer loses the right to rely on a lack of conformity of the goods if he does not give the seller notice thereof at the latest within a period of two years from the date on which the goods were actually handed over to the buyer, unless this time-limit is inconsistent with a contractual period of guarantee.

Article 40

The seller is not entitled to rely on the provisions of articles 38 and 39 if the lack of conformity relates to facts of which he knew or could not have been unaware and which he did not disclose to the buyer.

Article 41

The seller must deliver goods which are free from any right or claim of a third party, unless the buyer agreed to take the goods subject to that right or claim. However, if such right or claim is based on industrial property or other intellectual property, the seller's obligation is governed by article 42.

Article 42

(1) The seller must deliver goods which are free from any right or claim of a third party based on industrial property or other intellectual property, of which at the time of the conclusion of the contract the seller knew or could not have been unaware, provided that the right or claim is based on industrial property or other intellectual property:

   (a) Under the law of the State where the goods will be resold or otherwise used, if it was contemplated by the parties at the time of the conclusion of the contract that the goods would be resold or otherwise used in that State; or

   (b) In any other case, under the law of the State where the buyer has his place of business.

(2) The obligation of the seller under the preceding paragraph does not extend to cases where:

   (a) At the time of the conclusion of the contract the buyer knew or could not have been unaware of the right or claim; or

   (b) The right or claim results from the seller's compliance with technical drawings, designs, formulae or other such specifications furnished by the buyer.

Article 43

(1) The buyer loses the right to rely on the provisions of article 41 or article 42 if he does not give notice to the seller specifying the nature of the right or claim of the third party within a reasonable time after he has become aware or ought to have become aware of the right or claim.

(2) The seller is not entitled to rely on the provisions of the preceding paragraph if he knew of the right or claim of the third party and the nature of it.

Article 44

Notwithstanding the provisions of paragraph (1) of article 39 and paragraph (1) of article 43, the buyer may reduce the price in accordance with article 50 or claim damages, except for loss of profit, if he has a reasonable excuse for his failure to give the required notice.

Section III. Remedies for breach of contract by the seller

Article 45

(1) If the seller fails to perform any of his obligations under the contract or this Convention, the buyer may:

   (a) Exercise the rights provided in articles 46 to 52;

   (b) Claim damages as provided in articles 74 to 77.

(2) The buyer is not deprived of any right he may have to claim damages by exercising his right to other remedies.

(3) No period of grace may be granted to the seller by a court or arbitral tribunal when the buyer resorts to a remedy for breach of contract.

Article 46

(1) The buyer may require performance by the seller of his obligations unless the buyer has resorted to a remedy which is inconsistent with this requirement.

(2) If the goods do not conform with the contract, the buyer may require delivery of substitute goods only if the lack of conformity constitutes a fundamental breach of contract and a request for substitute goods is made either in conjunction with notice given under article 39 or within a reasonable time thereafter.

(3) If the goods do not conform with the contract, the buyer may require the seller to remedy the lack of conformity by repair, unless this is unreasonable having regard to all the circumstances. A request for repair must be made either in conjunction with notice given under article 39 or within a reasonable time thereafter.

Article 47

(1) The buyer may fix an additional period of time of reasonable length for performance by the seller of his obligations.

(2) Unless the buyer has received notice from the seller that he will not perform within the period so fixed, the buyer may not, during that period, resort to any remedy for breach of contract. However, the buyer is not deprived thereby of any right he may have to claim damages for delay in performance.

Article 48

(1) Subject to article 49, the seller may, even after the date for delivery, remedy at his own expense any failure to perform his obligations, if he can do so without unreasonable delay and without causing the buyer unreasonable inconvenience or uncertainty of reimbursement

by the seller of expenses advanced by the buyer. However, the buyer retains any right to claim damages as provided for in this Convention.

(2) If the seller requests the buyer to make known whether he will accept performance and the buyer does not comply with the request within a reasonable time, the seller may perform within the time indicated in his request. The buyer may not, during that period of time, resort to any remedy which is inconsistent with performance by the seller.

(3) A notice by the seller that he will perform within a specified period of time is assumed to include a request, under the preceding paragraph, that the buyer make known his decision.

(4) A request or notice by the seller under paragraph (2) or (3) of this article is not effective unless received by the buyer.

Article 49

(1) The buyer may declare the contract avoided:

(a) If the failure by the seller to perform any of his obligations under the contract or this Convention amounts to a fundamental breach of contract; or

(b) In case of non-delivery, if the seller does not deliver the goods within the additional period of time fixed by the buyer in accordance with paragraph (1) of article 47 or declares that he will not deliver within the period so fixed.

(2) However, in cases where the seller has delivered the goods, the buyer loses the right to declare the contract avoided unless he does so:

(a) In respect of late delivery, within a reasonable time after he has become aware that delivery has been made;

(b) In respect of any breach other than late delivery, within a reasonable time:

(i) After he knew or ought to have known of the breach;

(ii) After the expiration of any additional period of time fixed by the buyer in accordance with paragraph (1) of article 47, or after the seller has declared that he will not perform his obligations within such an additional period; or

(iii) After the expiration of any additional period of time indicated by the seller in accordance with paragraph (2) of article 48, or after the buyer has declared that he will not accept performance.

Article 50

If the goods do not conform with the contract and whether or not the price has already been paid, the buyer may reduce the price in the same proportion as the value that the goods actually delivered had at the time of the delivery bears to the value that conforming goods would have had at that time. However, if the seller remedies any failure to perform his obligations in accordance with article 37 or article 48 or if the buyer refuses to accept performance by the seller in accordance with those articles, the buyer may not reduce the price.

Article 51

(1) If the seller delivers only a part of the goods or if only a part of the goods delivered is in conformity with the contract, articles 46 to 50 apply in respect of the part which is missing or which does not conform.

(2) The buyer may declare the contract avoided in its entirety only if the failure to make delivery completely or in conformity with the contract amounts to a fundamental breach of the contract.

Article 52

(1) If the seller delivers the goods before the date fixed, the buyer may take delivery or refuse to take delivery.

(2) If the seller delivers a quantity of goods greater than that provided for in the contract, the buyer may take delivery or refuse to take delivery of the excess quantity. If the buyer takes delivery of all or part of the excess quantity, he must pay for it at the contract rate.

CHAPTER III. OBLIGATIONS OF THE BUYER

Article 53

The buyer must pay the price for the goods and take delivery of them as required by the contract and this Convention.

Section I. Payment of the price

Article 54

The buyer's obligation to pay the price includes taking such steps and complying with such formalities as may be required under the contract or any laws and regulations to enable payment to be made.

Article 55

Where a contract has been validly concluded but does not expressly or implicitly fix or make provision for determining the price, the parties are considered, in the absence of any indication to the contrary, to have impliedly made reference to the price generally charged at the time of the conclusion of the contract for such goods sold under comparable circumstances in the trade concerned.

Article 56

If the price is fixed according to the weight of the goods, in case of doubt it is to be determined by the net weight.

Article 57

(1) If the buyer is not bound to pay the price at any other particular place, he must pay it to the seller:

    (a) At the seller's place of business; or

    (b) If the payment is to be made against the handing over of the goods or of documents, at the place where the handing over takes place.

(2) The seller must bear any increase in the expenses incidental to payment which is caused by a change in his place of business subsequent to the conclusion of the contract.

Article 58

(1) If the buyer is not bound to pay the price at any other specific time, he must pay it when the seller places either the goods or documents controlling their disposition at the buyer's disposal in accordance with the contract and this Convention. The seller may make such payment a condition for handing over the goods or documents.

(2) If the contract involves carriage of the goods, the seller may dispatch the goods on terms whereby the goods, or documents controlling their disposition, will not be handed over to the buyer except against payment of the price.

(3) The buyer is not bound to pay the price until he has had an opportunity to examine the goods, unless the procedures for delivery or payment agreed upon by the parties are inconsistent with his having such an opportunity.

Article 59

The buyer must pay the price on the date fixed by or determinable from the contract and this Convention without the need for any request or compliance with any formality on the part of the seller.

Section II. Taking delivery

Article 60

The buyer's obligation to take delivery consists:

    (a) In doing all the acts which could reasonably be expected of him in order to enable the seller to make delivery; and

    (b) In taking over the goods.

Section III.   Remedies for breach of contract by the buyer

Article 61

(1) If the buyer fails to perform any of his obligations under the contract or this Convention, the seller may:

    (a)   Exercise the rights provided in articles 62 to 65;

    (b)   Claim damages as provided in articles 74 to 77.

(2) The seller is not deprived of any right he may have to claim damages by exercising his right to other remedies.

(3) No period of grace may be granted to the buyer by a court or arbitral tribunal when the seller resorts to a remedy for breach of contract.

Article 62

The seller may require the buyer to pay the price, take delivery or perform his other obligations, unless the seller has resorted to a remedy which is inconsistent with this requirement.

Article 63

(1) The seller may fix an additional period of time of reasonable length for performance by the buyer of his obligations.

(2) Unless the seller has received notice from the buyer that he will not perform within the period so fixed, the seller may not, during that period, resort to any remedy for breach of contract. However, the seller is not deprived thereby of any right he may have to claim damages for delay in performance.

Article 64

(1) The seller may declare the contract avoided:

    (a)   If the failure by the buyer to perform any of his obligations under the contract or this Convention amounts to a fundamental breach of contract; or

    (b)   If the buyer does not, within the additional period of time fixed by the seller in accordance with paragraph (1) of article 63, perform his obligation to pay the price or take delivery of the goods, or declares that he will not do so within the period so fixed.

(2) However, in cases where the buyer has paid the price, the seller loses the right to declare the contract avoided unless he does so:

    (a)   In respect of late performance by the buyer, before the seller has become aware that performance has been rendered; or

(b) In respect of any breach other than late performance by the buyer, within a reasonable time:

    (i) After the seller knew or ought to have known of the breach; or

    (ii) After the expiration of any additional period of time fixed by the seller in accordance with paragraph (1) of article 63, or after the buyer has declared that he will not perform his obligations within such an additional period.

Article 65

(1) If under the contract the buyer is to specify the form, measurement or other features of the goods and he fails to make such specification either on the date agreed upon or within a reasonable time after receipt of a request from the seller, the seller may, without prejudice to any other rights he may have, make the specification himself in accordance with the requirements of the buyer that may be known to him.

(2) If the seller makes the specification himself, he must inform the buyer of the details thereof and must fix a reasonable time within which the buyer may make a different specification. If, after receipt of such a communication, the buyer fails to do so within the time so fixed, the specification made by the seller is binding.

CHAPTER IV. PASSING OF RISK

Article 66

Loss of or damage to the goods after the risk has passed to the buyer does not discharge him from his obligation to pay the price, unless the loss or damage is due to an act or omission of the seller.

Article 67

(1) If the contract of sale involves carriage of the goods and the seller is not bound to hand them over at a particular place, the risk passes to the buyer when the goods are handed over to the first carrier for transmission to the buyer in accordance with the contract of sale. If the seller is bound to hand the goods over to a carrier at a particular place, the risk does not pass to the buyer until the goods are handed over to the carrier at that place. The fact that the seller is authorized to retain documents controlling the disposition of the goods does not affect the passage of the risk.

(2) Nevertheless, the risk does not pass to the buyer until the goods are clearly identified to the contract, whether by markings on the goods, by shipping documents, by notice given to the buyer or otherwise.

Article 68

The risk in respect of goods sold in transit passes to the buyer from the time of the conclusion of the contract. However, if the circumstances so indicate, the risk is assumed by the buyer from the time the goods were handed over to the carrier who issued the documents embodying the contract of carriage. Nevertheless, if at the time of the conclusion of the contract of sale the seller knew or ought to have known that the goods had been lost or damaged and did not disclose this to the buyer, the loss or damage is at the risk of the seller.

Article 69

(1) In cases not within articles 67 and 68, the risk passes to the buyer when he takes over the goods or, if he does not do so in due time, from the time when the goods are placed at his disposal he commits a breach of contract by failing to take delivery.

(2) However, if the buyer is bound to take over the goods at a place other than a place of business of the seller, the risk passes when delivery is due and the buyer is aware of the fact that the goods are placed at his disposal at that place.

(3) If the contract relates to goods not then identified, the goods are considered not to be placed at the disposal of the buyer until they are clearly identified to the contract.

Article 70

If the seller has committed a fundamental breach of contract, articles 67, 68, and 69 do not impair the remedies available to the buyer on account of the breach.

CHAPTER V. PROVISIONS COMMON TO THE OBLIGATIONS OF THE SELLER AND OF THE BUYER

Section I. Anticipatory breach and instalment contracts

Article 71

(1) A party may suspend the performance of his obligations if, after the conclusion of the contract, it becomes apparent that the other party will not perform a substantial part of his obligations as a result of:

(a) A serious deficiency in his ability to perform or in his creditworthiness; or

(b) His conduct in preparing to perform or in performing the contract.

(2) If the seller has already dispatched the goods before the grounds described in the preceding paragraph become evident, he may

prevent the handing over of the goods to the buyer even though the buyer holds a document which entitles him to obtain them. The present paragraph relates only to the rights in the goods as between the buyer and the seller.

(3) A party suspending performance, whether before or after dispatch of the goods, must immediately give notice of the suspension to the other party and must continue with performance if the other party provides adequate assurance of his performance.

Article 72

(1) If prior to the date for performance of the contract it is clear that one of the parties will commit a fundamental breach of contract, the other party may declare the contract avoided.

(2) If time allows, the party intending to declare the contract avoided must give reasonable notice to the other party in order to permit him to provide adequate assurance of his performance.

(3) The requirements of the preceding paragraph do not apply if the other party has declared that he will not perform his obligations.

Article 73

(1) In the case of a contract for delivery of goods by instalments, if the failure of one party to perform any of his obligations in respect of any instalment constitutes a fundamental breach of contract with respect to that instalment, the other party may declare the contract avoided with respect to that instalment.

(2) If one party's failure to perform any of his obligations in respect of any instalment gives the other party good grounds to conclude that a fundamental breach of contract will occur with respect to future instalments, he may declare the contract avoided for the future, provided that he does so within a reasonable time.

(3) A buyer who declares the contract avoided in respect of any delivery may, at the same time, declare it avoided in respect of deliveries already made or of future deliveries if, by reason of their interdependence, those deliveries could not be used for the purpose contemplated by the parties at the time of the conclusion of the contract.

Section II. Damages

Article 74

Damages for breach of contract by one party consist of a sum equal to the loss, including loss of profit, suffered by the other party as a consequence of the breach. Such damages may not exceed the loss which the party in breach foresaw or ought to have foreseen at the time of the conclusion of the contract, in the light of the facts and matters of which he then knew or ought to have known, as a possible consequence of the breach of contract.

Article 75

If the contract is avoided and if, in a reasonable manner and within a reasonable time after avoidance, the buyer has bought goods in replacement or the seller has resold the goods, the party claiming damages may recover the difference between the contract price and the price in the substitute transaction as well as any further damages recoverable under article 74.

Article 76

(1) If the contract is avoided and there is a current price for the goods, the party claiming damages may, if he has not made a purchase or resale under article 75, recover the difference between the price fixed by the contract and the current price at the time of avoidance as well as any further damages recoverable under article 74. If, however, the party claiming damages has avoided the contract after taking over the goods, the current price at the time of such taking over shall be applied instead of the current price at the time of avoidance.

(2) For the purposes of the preceding paragraph, the current price is the price prevailing at the place where delivery of the goods should have been made or, if there is no current price at that place, the price at such other place as serves as a reasonable substitute, making due allowance for differences in the cost of transporting the goods.

Article 77

A party who relies on a breach of contract must take such measures as are reasonable in the circumstances to mitigate the loss, including loss of profit, resulting from the breach. If he fails to take such measures, the party in breach may claim a reduction in the damages in the amount by which the loss should have been mitigated.

Section III. Interest

Article 78

If a party fails to pay the price or any other sum that is in arrears, the other party is entitled to interest on it, without prejudice to any claim for damages recoverable under article 74.

Section IV. Exemptions

Article 79

(1) A party is not liable for a failure to perform any of his obligations if he proves that the failure was due to an impediment beyond his control and that he could not reasonably be expected to have

taken the impediment into account at the time of the conclusion of the contract or to have avoided or overcome it or its consequences.

(2) If the party's failure is due to the failure by a third person whom he has engaged to perform the whole or a party of the contract, that party is exempt from liability only if:

    (a) He is exempt under the preceding paragraph; and

    (b) The person whom he has so engaged would be so exempt if the provisions of that paragraph were applied to him.

(3) The exemption provided by this article has effect for the period during which the impediment exists.

(4) The party who fails to perform must give notice to the other party of the impediment and its effect on his ability to perform. If the notice is not received by the other party within a reasonable time after the party who fails to perform knew or ought to have known of the impediment, he is liable for damages resulting from such non-receipt.

(5) Nothing in this article prevents either party from exercising any right other than to claim damages under this Convention.

Article 80

A party may not rely on a failure of the other party to perform, to the extent that such failure was caused by the first party's act or omission.

Section V. Effects of avoidance

Article 81

(1) Avoidance of the contract releases both parties from their obligations under it, subject to any damages which may be due. Avoidance does not affect any provision of the contract for the settlement of disputes or any other provision of the contract governing the rights and obligations of the parties consequent upon the avoidance of the contract.

(2) A party who has performed the contract either wholly or in part may claim restitution from the other party of whatever the first party has supplied or paid under the contract. If both parties are bound to make restitution, they must do so concurrently.

Article 82

(1) The buyer loses the right to declare the contract avoided or to require the seller to deliver substitute goods if it is impossible for him to make restitution of the goods substantially in the condition in which he received them.

(2) The preceding paragraph does not apply:

    (a) If the impossibility of making restitution of the goods or of making restitution of the goods substantially in the condition in which the buyer received them is not due to his act or omission;

    (b) If the goods or part of the goods have perished or deteriorated as a result of the examination provided for in article 38; or

    (c) If the goods or part of the goods have been sold in the normal course of business or have been consumed or transformed by the buyer in the course of normal use before he discovered or ought to have discovered the lack of conformity.

Article 83

A buyer who has lost the right to declare the contract avoided or to require the seller to deliver substitute goods in accordance with article 82 retains all other remedies under the contract and this Convention.

Article 84

(1) If the seller is bound to refund the price, he must also pay interest on it, from the date on which the price was paid.

(2) The buyer must account to the seller for all benefits which he has derived from the goods or part of them:

    (a) If he must make restitution of the goods or part of them; or

    (b) If it is impossible for him to make restitution of all or part of the goods or to make restitution of all or part of the goods substantially in the condition in which he received them, but he has nevertheless declared the contract avoided or required the seller to deliver substitute goods.

Section VI. Preservation of the goods

Article 85

If the buyer is in delay in taking delivery of the goods or, where payment of the price and delivery of the goods are to be made concurrently, if he fails to pay the price, and the seller is either in possession of the goods or otherwise able to control their disposition, the seller must take such steps as are reasonable in the circumstances to preserve them. He is entitled to retain them until he has been reimbursed his reasonable expenses by the buyer.

Article 86

(1) If the buyer has received the goods and intends to exercise any right under the contract or this Convention to reject them, he must take such steps to preserve them as are reasonable in the circumstances. He is entitled to retain them until he has been reimbursed his reasonable expenses by the seller.

(2) If goods dispatched to the buyer have been placed at his disposal at their destination and he exercises the right to reject them, he must take possession of them on behalf of the seller, provided that this can be done without payment of the price and without unreasonable inconvenience or unreasonable expense. This provision does not apply if the seller or a person authorized to take charge of the goods on his behalf is present at the destination. If the buyer takes possession of the goods under this paragraph, his rights and obligations are governed by the preceding paragraph.

Article 87

A party who is bound to take steps to preserve the goods may deposit them in a warehouse of a third person at the expense of the other party provided that the expense incurred is not unreasonable.

Article 88

(1) A party who is bound to preserve the goods in accordance with article 85 or 86 may sell them by any appropriate means if there has been an unreasonable delay by the other party in taking possession of the goods or in taking them back or in paying the price or the cost of preservation, provided that reasonable notice of the intention to sell has been given to the other party.

(2) If the goods are subject to rapid deterioration or their preservation would involve unreasonable expense, a party who is bound to preserve the goods in accordance with article 85 or 86 must take reasonable measures to sell them. To the extent possible he must give notice to the other party of this intention to sell.

(3) A party selling the goods has the right to retain out of the proceeds of sale an amount equal to the reasonable expenses of preserving the goods and of selling them. He must account to the other party for the balance.

SELECTED FORMS

Table of Contents

Acknowledgment

Thanks are due to the following, among others, for their willingness to permit reproduction of their standard forms: American Institute of Architects, American Textile Manufacturers Institute, Cocoa Merchants' Association of America, Inc., General Electric Company, National Football League, and North American Export Grain Association. In the process of reproduction some forms have been substantially reduced in size.

NFL PLAYER CONTRACT

THIS CONTRACT is between _____, hereinafter "Player,"
and _____, a _____
corporation (limited partnership) (partnership), hereinafter "Club," operating under the name of the _____
_____ as a member of the National Football League, hereinafter "League."
In consideration of the promises made by each to the other, Player and Club agree as follows:

1. TERM. This contract covers one football season, and will begin on the date of execution or April 1, 19__, whichever is later, and end on April 1, 19__, unless extended, terminated, or renewed as specified elsewhere in this contract.

2. EMPLOYMENT AND SERVICES. Club employs Player as a skilled football player. Player accepts such employment. He agrees to give his best efforts and loyalty to the Club, and to conduct himself on and off the field with appropriate recognition of the fact that the success of professional football depends largely on public respect for and approval of those associated with the game. Player will report promptly for and participate fully in Club's official pre-season training camp, all Club meetings and practice sessions, and all pre-season, regular-season and post-season football games scheduled for or by Club. If invited, Player will practice for and play in any all-star football game sponsored by the League. Player will not participate in any football game not sponsored by the League unless the game is first approved by the League.

3. OTHER ACTIVITIES. Without prior written consent of Club, Player will not play football or engage in activities related to football otherwise than for Club or engage in any activity other than football which may involve a significant risk of personal injury. Player represents that he has special, exceptional and unique knowledge, skill, ability, and experience as a football player, the loss of which cannot be estimated with any certainty and cannot be fairly or adequately compensated by damages. Player therefore agrees that Club will have the right, in addition to any other right which Club may possess, to enjoin Player by appropriate proceedings from playing football or engaging in football-related activities other than for Club or from engaging in any activity other than football which may involve a significant risk of personal injury.

4. PUBLICITY. Player grants to Club and League, separately and together, the authority to use his name and picture for publicity and promotional purposes in newspapers, magazines, motion pictures, game programs and roster manuals, broadcasts and telecasts, and all other publicity and advertising media, provided such publicity and promotion does not in itself constitute an endorsement by Player of a commercial product. Player will cooperate with the news media, and will participate upon request in reasonable promotional activities of Club and the League.

5. COMPENSATION. For performance of Player's services and all other promises of Player, Club will pay Player a yearly salary of $_____, payable as provided in Paragraph 6; such earned performance bonuses as may be called for in Paragraph 24 of or any attachment to this contract; Player's necessary traveling expenses from his residence to training camp; Player's reasonable board and lodging expenses during pre-season training and in connection with playing pre-season, regular-season, and post-season football games outside Club's home city; Player's necessary traveling expenses to and from pre-season, regular-season, and post-season football games outside Club's home city; Player's necessary traveling expenses to his residence if this contract is terminated by Club; and such additional compensation, benefits and reimbursement of expenses as may be called for in any collective bargaining agreement in existence during the term of this contract. (For purposes of this contract, a collective bargaining agreement will be deemed to be "in existence" during its stated term or during any period for which the parties to that agreement agree to extend it.)

6. PAYMENT. Unless this contract or any collective bargaining agreement in existence during the term of this contract specifically provides otherwise, Player will be paid as follows: If Player has not previously reported to any NFL club's official pre-season training camp in any year, he will be paid 100% of his yearly salary under this contract in equal weekly or bi-weekly installments over the course of the regular season period, commencing with the first regular season game played by club. If Player has previously reported to any NFL club's official pre-season training camp in any year, he will be paid 10% of his yearly salary under this contract in equal weekly installments over the course of the pre-season period, commencing with the end of the first week of Club's official pre-season training camp as designated for Player and ending one week prior to the first regular season game played by Club, and 90% of his yearly salary in equal weekly or bi-weekly installments over the course of the regular season period, commencing with the first regular season game played by Club. If this contract is executed or Player is activated after the start of Club's official pre-season training camp, the yearly salary payable to Player will be reduced proportionately and Player will be paid the weekly or bi-weekly portions of his yearly salary becoming due and payable after he is activated. If this contract is terminated after the start of Club's official pre-season training camp, the yearly salary payable to Player will be reduced proportionately and Player will be paid the weekly or bi-weekly portions of his yearly salary having become due and payable up to the time of termination (prorated daily if termination occurs before one week prior to the first regular season game played by Club).

7. DEDUCTIONS. Any advance made to Player will be repaid to Club, and any properly levied Club fine or Commissioner fine against Player will be paid, in cash on demand or by means of deductions from payments coming due to the Player under this contract, the amount of such deductions to be determined by Club unless this contract specifically provides otherwise.

PROFESSIONAL FOOTBALL PLAYER'S CONTRACT

8. PHYSICAL CONDITION. Player represents to Club that he is and will maintain himself in excellent physical condition. Player will undergo a complete physical examination by the Club physician upon Club request, during which physical examination Player agrees to make full and complete disclosure of any physical or mental condition known to him which might impair his performance under this contract and to respond fully and in good faith when questioned by the Club physician about such condition. If Player fails to establish or maintain his excellent physical condition to the satisfaction of the Club physician, or make the required full and complete disclosure and good faith responses to the Club physician, then Club may terminate this contract.

9. INJURY. If Player is injured in the performance of his services under this contract and promptly reports such injury to the Club physician or trainer, then Player will receive such medical and hospital care during the term of this contract as the Club physician may deem necessary, and, in accordance with Club's practice, will continue to receive his yearly salary for so long, during the season of injury only and for no subsequent period, as Player is physically unable to perform the services required of him by this contract because of such injury. If Player's injury in the performance of his services under this contract results in his death, the unpaid balance of his yearly salary for the season of injury will be paid to his stated beneficiary or, in the absence of a stated beneficiary, to his estate.

10. WORKMEN'S COMPENSATION. Any compensation paid to Player under this contract or under any collective bargaining agreement in existence during the term of this contract for a period during which he is entitled to workmen's compensation benefits by reason of temporary total, permanent total, temporary partial, or permanent partial disability will be deemed an advance payment of workmen's compensation benefits due Player, and Club will be entitled to be reimbursed the amount of such payment out of any award of workmen's compensation.

11. SKILL, PERFORMANCE AND CONDUCT. Player understands that he is competing with other players for a position on Club's roster within the applicable player limits. If at any time, in the sole judgment of Club, Player's skill or performance has been unsatisfactory as compared with that of other players competing for positions on Club's roster, or if Player has engaged in personal conduct reasonably judged by Club to adversely affect or reflect on Club, then Club may terminate this contract.

12. TERMINATION. The rights of termination set forth in this contract will be in addition to any other rights of termination allowed either party by law. Termination will be effective upon the giving of written notice, except that Player's death, other than as a result of injury incurred in the performance of his services under this contract, will automatically terminate this contract. If this contract is terminated by Club and either Player or Club so requests, Player will promptly undergo a complete physical examination by the Club physician.

13. INJURY GRIEVANCE. Unless a collective bargaining agreement in existence at the time of termination of this contract by Club provides otherwise, the following injury grievance procedure will apply: If Player believes that at the time of termination of this contract by Club he was physically unable to perform the services required of him by this contract because of an injury incurred in the performance of his services under this contract, Player may, within a reasonably brief time after examination by the Club physician, submit at his own expense to examination by a physician of his choice. If the opinion of Player's physician with respect to his physical ability to perform the services required of him by this contract is contrary to that of the Club's physician, the dispute will be submitted within a reasonable time to final and binding arbitration by an arbitrator selected by Club and Player or, if they are unable to agree, one selected by the League Commissioner on application by either party.

14. RULES. Player will comply with and be bound by all reasonable Club rules and regulations in effect during the term of this contract which are not inconsistent with the provisions of this contract or of any collective bargaining agreement in existence during the term of this contract. Player's attention is also called to the fact that the League functions with certain rules and procedures expressive of its operation as a joint venture among its member clubs and that these rules and practices may affect Player's relationship to the League and its member clubs independently of the provisions of this contract.

15. INTEGRITY OF GAME. Player recognizes the detriment to the League and professional football that would result from impairment of public confidence in the honest and orderly conduct of NFL games or the integrity and good character of NFL players. Player therefore acknowledges his awareness that if he accepts a bribe or agrees to throw or fix an NFL game; fails to promptly report a bribe offer or an attempt to throw or fix an NFL game; bets on an NFL game; knowingly associates with gamblers or gambling activity; uses or provides other players with stimulants or other drugs for the purpose of attempting to enhance on-field performance; or is guilty of any other form of conduct reasonably judged by the League Commissioner to be detrimental to the League or professional football, the Commissioner will have the right, but only after giving Player the opportunity for a hearing at which he may be represented by counsel of his choice, to fine Player in a reasonable amount; to suspend Player for a period certain or indefinitely; and/or to terminate this contract.

16. EXTENSION. If Player becomes a member of the Armed Forces of the United States or any other country, or retires from professional football as an active player, or otherwise fails or refuses to perform his services under this contract, then this contract will be tolled between the date of Player's induction into the Armed Forces, or his retirement, or his failure or refusal to perform, and the later date of his return to professional football. During the period this contract is tolled, Player will not be entitled to any compensation or benefits. On Player's return to professional football, the term of this contract will be extended for a period of time equal to the number of seasons (to the nearest multiple of one) remaining at the time the contract was tolled. The right of renewal, if any, contained in this contract will remain in effect until the end of any such extended term.

17. RENEWAL. Unless this contract specifically provides otherwise, Club may, by sending written notice to Player on or before the April 1 expiration date referred to in Paragraph 1, renew this contract for a period of one year. The terms and conditions for the renewal year will be the same as those provided in this contract for the last preceding year, except that there will be no further right of renewal in Club and, unless this contract specifically provides otherwise, the rate of compensation for the renewal year will be 90% of the rate of compensation provided in this contract for the last preceding year. The phrase "rate of compensation" as used above means yearly salary, including deferred compensation, and any performance bonus, but excluding any

signing or reporting bonus. In order for Player to receive 90% of any performance bonus under this contract he must meet the previously established conditions of that bonus during the renewal year.

18. ASSIGNMENT. Unless this contract specifically provides otherwise, Club may assign this contract and Player's services under this contract to any successor to Club's franchise or to any other Club in the League. Player will report to the assignee club promptly upon being informed of the assignment of his contract and will faithfully perform his services under this contract. The assignee club will pay Player's necessary traveling expenses in reporting to it and will faithfully perform this contract with Player.

19. FILING. This contract will be valid and binding upon Player and Club immediately upon execution. A copy of this contract, including any attachment to it, will be filed by Club with the League Commissioner within 10 days after execution. The Commissioner will have the right to disapprove this contract on reasonable grounds, including but not limited to an attempt by the parties to abridge or impair the rights of any other club, uncertainty or incompleteness in expression of the parties' respective rights and obligations, or conflict between the terms of this contract and any collective bargaining agreement then in existence. Approval will be automatic unless, within 10 days after receipt of this contract in his office, the Commissioner notifies the parties either of disapproval or of extension of this 10-day period for purposes of investigation or clarification pending his decision. On the receipt of notice of disapproval and termination, both parties will be relieved of their respective rights and obligations under this contract.

20. DISPUTES. Any dispute between Player and Club involving the interpretation or application of any provision of this contract will be submitted to final and binding arbitration in accordance with the procedure called for in any collective bargaining agreement in existence at the time the event giving rise to any such dispute occurs. If no collective bargaining agreement is in existence at such time, the dispute will be submitted within a reasonable time to the League Commissioner for final and binding arbitration by him, except as provided otherwise in Paragraph 13 of this contract.

21. NOTICE. Any notice, request, approval or consent under this contract will be sufficiently given if in writing and delivered in person or mailed (certified or first class) by one party to the other at the address set forth in this contract or to such other address as the recipient may subsequently have furnished in writing to the sender.

22. OTHER AGREEMENTS This contract, including any attachment to it, sets forth the entire agreement between Player and Club and cannot be modified or supplemented orally. Player and Club represent that no other agreement, oral or written, except as attached to or specifically incorporated in this contract, exists between them. The provisions of this contract will govern the relationship between Player and Club unless there are conflicting provisions in any collective bargaining agreement in existence during the term of this contract, in which case the provisions of the collective bargaining agreement will take precedence over conflicting provisions of this contract relating to the rights or obligations of either party.

23. LAW. This contract is made under and shall be governed by the laws of the State of _____.

24. SPECIAL PROVISIONS.

THIS CONTRACT is executed in five (5) copies. Player acknowledges that before signing this contract he was given the opportunity to seek advice from or be represented by persons of his own selection.

PLAYER _____

Home Address _____

_____

Telephone Number _____

Date _____

CLUB _____

By _____

Club Address _____

_____

Date _____   [E2230]

League Office Copy

PUBLISHING AGREEMENT

Name:

(the "Author") shall prepare and deliver to the
  (the "Publisher") a manuscript for a work entitled

(the "Work") or such other title as may be mutually agreeable to the Publisher and the Author, and the Publisher shall publish the Work, in accordance with and subject to the provisions of this Agreement dated   , 19

1 RIGHTS CONVEYED TO PUBLISHER AND PAYMENTS TO AUTHOR

a. Rights and Royalties. The Author grants and assigns exclusively to the Publisher the following rights, for which the Publisher shall pay to the Author the royalties indicated:

• • •

b. Other Matters Relating to Grant of Rights

• • •

c. Other Matters Relating to Royalties and Payments

• • •

(2) *Advances.* The Publisher shall pay the Author, or the Author's duly authorized representative, an advance of $, which shall be a charge against all sums accruing to the Author under this Agreement, payable to the Author as follows:

• • •

2 MANUSCRIPT PREPARATION AND DELIVERY

a. The Author shall prepare and deliver to the Publisher on or before   ,19   , two complete, clean copies of a manuscript for the Work in double-spaced typewritten form on 8½- by 11-inch or metric size A4 sheets or as may otherwise be specified by the Publisher. The manuscript for the Work must be acceptable to the Publisher in both form and content for publication. It shall be between   and   words in length and shall include such materials as the Publisher may reasonably specify for the Work, including but not limited to copy for the title page, table of contents, index, tables, and bibliographies, and copy for drawings, illustrations, and charts. The Author shall supply these in finished form to the Publisher within a reasonable time after the delivery of the completed manuscript; if the Author shall fail to do so, the Publisher may supply them and charge the expense to the Author.

b. The Author shall obtain, without expense to the Publisher, written permission to include in the Work any copyrighted material which is not in the public domain as well as any other material for which permission is necessary in connection with the Author's warranty in Section 3 of this Agreement. These permissions must be consistent with the rights granted to the Publisher in this Agreement so that they may cover all the uses to

BOOK PUBLISHER'S CONTRACT

which the material may eventually be put. The Author shall deliver to the Publisher a copy of all these permissions with the complete manuscript.

c. If the Work or any subdivision of it contains a significant portion of material taken from documents prepared and published by the United States government and therefore not subject to copyright, the Author shall notify the Publisher in writing of the existence and location of all such material in the Work.

d. If the Author fails to deliver the complete manuscript within 90 days after the delivery date specified in this Agreement, or if the Author fails or refuses to perform any correction or revision of the manuscript within the time or as otherwise specified by the Publisher, the Publisher shall have the right in its discretion: (1) to give the Author written notice of its intention to terminate this Agreement, in which event the Author shall promptly reimburse the Publisher for all sums advanced to the Author against royalties under this Agreement, and upon such reimbursement this Agreement shall terminate; or (2) to make such other arrangements in connection with this Agreement as the Publisher deems advisable to complete, correct, or revise the manuscript, in which event the reasonable cost of such arrangements may be charged against any sums accruing to the Author under this Agreement.

e. If requested by the Publisher, the Author shall correct proof of the Work and return it promptly to the Publisher. If the Author makes or causes to be made any alterations in the type, illustrations, or film which are not typographical, drafting, or Publisher's errors and which exceed 15 percent of the original cost of composition and artwork independent of the cost of these Author's alterations, the cost of the excess alterations shall be charged against any sums accruing to the Author under this Agreement.

f. The Author shall retain one copy of the manuscript submitted to the Publisher until the Work is published. The Publisher shall have no liability of any kind to the Author by reason of the loss, destruction, or mutilation of the manuscript delivered to the Publisher. This provision shall also be applicable to the original artwork, illustrations, and photographs, unless such loss, destruction, or mutilation is covered by insurance of the Publisher, in which case the Author shall look only to the insurance carrier for replacement or reimbursement.

3 AUTHOR'S WARRANTY

a. The Author represents and warrants to the Publisher that the Author has full power and authority to enter into this Agreement and to grant the rights granted in this Agreement; that the Work is original except for material in the public domain and those excerpts from other works as may be included with the written permission of the copyright owners; that the Work does not contain any libelous or obscene material or injurious formulas, recipes, or instructions; that it does not infringe any trade name, trademark, or copyright; and that it does not invade or violate any right of privacy, personal or proprietary right, or other common law or statutory right.

b. The Author agrees to indemnify the Publisher and its licensees and assignees under this Agreement and hold them harmless from any and all losses, damages, liabilities, costs, charges, and expenses, including reasonable attorneys' fees, arising out of any breach of any of the Author's representations and warranties contained in this Agreement or third-party claims relating to the matters covered by the representations and warranties in this Section 3, which are finally sustained in a court of original jurisdiction. If any action or proceeding is brought against the Publisher with respect to the matters covered by the representations and warranties in this Section 3, the Publisher shall have the right, in its sole discretion, to select counsel to defend against this action or proceeding. In addition to other remedies available to the Publisher, the Publisher may charge the amount of these losses, damages, liabilities, costs, charges, and expenses against any sums accruing to the Author under this Agreement or any other agreement currently existing between Author and Publisher.

c. If there is an infringement of any rights granted to the Publisher or rights which the Publisher is authorized to license or in which the Publisher is to share in the proceeds, the Publisher shall have the right, in its sole discretion, to select counsel to bring an action to enforce those rights, and the Author and the Publisher shall have the right to participate jointly in the action. If both participate, they shall share equally the expenses of and any sums recovered in the action, except that if the Author retains separate legal counsel, the Author shall be solely responsible for the legal expenses of the Author's counsel. If either party declines to participate in the action, the other may proceed, and the party maintaining the action shall bear all expenses and shall retain all sums recovered.

The provisions of this Section 3 shall survive any termination of this Agreement.

4 COMPETING WORKS

While this Agreement is in effect, the Author shall not, without the prior written consent of the Publisher, write, edit, print, or publish, or cause to be written, edited, printed, or published, any other edition of the Work, whether revised, supplemented, corrected, enlarged, abridged, or otherwise, or any other work of a nature which might interfere with or injure the sales of the Work or any grant of rights or licenses permitted under this Agreement by the Publisher, or permit the use of the Author's name or likeness in connection with any such work.

5 PUBLICATION OF THE WORK

After giving written notice to the Author that it has accepted the Work for publication, the Publisher shall within 12 months of written acceptance of the manuscript publish the Work at its own expense and in such style and manner and with such trademarks, service marks, and imprints of Publisher, and sell the Work at such prices, as it shall deem suitable. The Publisher shall publish the Work with a copyright notice and register the Work in accordance with the United States copyright laws in the name of the Publisher or Author as the Author may elect.

6 AUTHOR'S COPIES

The Publisher shall give the Author ten copies of the Work upon publication, free of charge, and sell to the Author as many additional copies as the Author may wish for personal use and not for resale, at a discount of 40 percent of the Publisher's then list price, f.o.b. the Publisher's warehouse.

7 DISCONTINUANCE OF PUBLICATION

a. When in the judgment of the Publisher the demand for the Work is no longer sufficient to warrant its continued publication, the Publisher shall have the right to discontinue the publication and declare the Work out of print, in which event the Author shall be so advised in writing.

b. If the Work is not for sale in at least one edition (including any revised edition or reprint edition) published by the Publisher or under license from the Publisher and, within eight months after written demand by the Author, the Publisher or its licensee fails to offer it again for sale, then this Agreement shall term inate and all rights granted to the Publisher in it shall revert to the Author (except for material prepared by or obtained at the expense of the Publisher which shall remain the property of the Publisher).

c. The termination of this Agreement under this Section 7 or otherwise shall be subject to (1) any license, contract, or option granted to third parties by the Publisher before the termination and the Publisher's right to its share of the proceeds from these agreements after the termination and (2) the Publisher's continuing right to sell all remaining bound copies and sheets of the Work and all derivative works which are on hand at the time of termination.

8 RIGHTS OF REFUSAL

a. Other Rights. The Author grants the Publisher the "right of first refusal" to exercise or license any dramatization, video, audiovisual, and commercial rights in the Work to the extent that any of these rights have not been granted to the Publisher. The Author shall not enter into an agreement with another party relating to such rights upon terms equal to or less favorable than the last offered by the Publisher.

b. **Author's Next Work.** The Author grants to the Publisher the "right of first refusal" to publish the Author's next full-length book and shall submit the manuscript for it to the Publisher before submitting it to any other publisher. In no case shall the Publisher be required to exercise this option before publication or within three months following publication of the Work. The Author shall not enter into a contract for the publication of this next work with any publisher upon terms less favorable than any offered by the Publisher.

9 AGENT
The Author hereby authorizes as agent:

• • •

10 OTHER MATTERS
a. Assignments. No assignment of this Agreement, voluntary or by operation of law, shall be binding upon either of the parties without the prior written consent of the other, provided, however, that the Author may assign or transfer any sums due or to become due under this Agreement without the Publisher's consent.

b. **Law to Govern.** This Agreement shall be interpreted and governed by the laws of the State of New York and the United States of America.

c. **Bankruptcy.** In the event of bankruptcy, receivership, or liquidation of the Publisher, this Agreement shall terminate without further procedure and all rights granted in this Agreement to the Publisher by the Author shall revert to the Author.

d. **Notices.** Any written notice required under any of the provisions of this Agreement shall be deemed to have been properly served by delivery in person or by first-class mail, postage prepaid, to the last known address.

e. **Binding Agreement.** This Agreement shall be binding upon the parties signing it and on all their heirs, personal representatives, successors, and permitted assignees.

f. **Complete Agreement.** This Agreement constitutes the complete understanding of the parties and supersedes all prior agreements of the parties relating to the Work. No amendment or waiver of any provision of this Agreement shall be valid unless in writing and signed by all parties affected by the amendment or waiver.

11 SUPPLEMENTARY PROVISIONS (IF ANY)

By _____

_____   _____
TAX OR SOCIAL SECURITY NUMBER   AUTHOR

_____
CITIZENSHIP

Worth Street
Textile Market Rules

Approved and Promulgated by

American Textile Manufacturers Institute, Inc.

Knitted Textile Association

Textile Distributors Association, Inc.

Standard Textile Salesnote

Revision of July 1, 1986

This present revision is effective with respect to any contract of subsequent date, which incorporates the Standard Textile Salesnote by reference, expressly giving notice that it provides for arbitration of disputes.

Arbitration

(a) Any controversy or claim arising out of or relating to this contract, or the interpretation or breach thereof, including any modification or extension thereof, shall be settled by arbitration in the City of New York in accordance with the rules then obtaining of the General Arbitration Council of the Textile and Apparel Industries, a division of the American Arbitration Association or its successor.

(b) Arbitrators shall be bound by the terms and conditions of this contract and shall have no power to alter or in rendering their award to depart from any express provision of this contract, and their failure to observe this limitation shall constitute grounds for vacating their award.

(c) The fees and expenses of such arbitration proceedings, including reasonable counsel fees, may be allocated between the parties or charged to any one of the parties by the arbitrators as part of their award.

Jurisdiction

The parties consent to the jurisdiction of the Supreme Court of the State of New York or the United States District Court for the Southern District of New York for all purposes relating to this contract, whether in connection with arbitration or otherwise. The parties consent that any process or notice of motion or other application to either of said courts, and any paper in connection with such proceedings may be served within or outside of the State of New York by certified mail or registered mail or by personal service or by such other manner as may be permissible under the rules of the applicable court or arbitration tribunal.

[E2231]

STANDARD TEXTILE SALESNOTE

Assortments

If buyer does not furnish specifications for assortments, patterns or other particulars within the time specified or, if not specified, within five (5) business days after Seller's demand in writing therefore, or forty-five (45) days prior to the initial delivery date, whichever is earlier, Seller may at its option either (1) treat the contract as substantially breached and claim damages for such breach, or (2) hold the goods for Buyer's account and invoice the Buyer therefore at finished goods contract price, in which case the Seller shall be deemed to have fully performed and to be entitled to payment from the Buyer and risk shall be upon the Buyer when goods are so set aside and invoiced. If Seller permits the Buyer to complete assortments or specifications subsequent to the time required hereunder, Seller may delay delivery for such period of time as may be then reasonably necessary.

Warranties

Seller warrants that merchandise delivered shall conform with the description on the face of the contract between the parties.

Buyer agrees that the Seller makes no warranty in fact or in law that the merchandise which is the subject of this sale is suitable for any particular use or purpose and that the suitability of the merchandise for any use is the sole responsibility of the Buyer.

Seller shall not be liable for normal manufacturing, processing or finishing defects nor for customary variations from quantities or specifications. Whether the goods are first quality shall be determined in accordance with the applicable quality standards of the Worth Street Textile Market Rules.

However, performance and other physical or chemical characteristics of the merchandise are not guaranteed unless and except to such extent as is otherwise specifically provided herein or in any other writing signed by the seller.

Deliveries

(a) Unless otherwise expressly provided herein, any shipment or tender made within fifteen (15) days after any date specified for delivery shall constitute timely delivery hereunder.

(b) Delivery to a carrier, or in the absence of shipping instructions, the mailing of a covering invoice after completion of manufacture shall constitute good delivery or tender of delivery, subject to Seller's right of stoppage in transit, and subject to Seller's security interest therein as elsewhere herein provided. Goods invoiced and held by the Seller for whatever reason shall be at Buyer's risk.

(c) In the event that delivery under this contract is prevented or delayed by strikes, lockouts, embargoes, force majeure or act of God, or any cause or circumstance not limited to the above, which is beyond the Seller's reasonable control, Seller shall not be held liable for the consequences thereof. [E2232]

Credit and Payment

(a) In case any invoice shall not be paid when due or upon Buyer's breach or default with respect to any term or condition of this or any other contract with Seller, all sums owing under this and other contracts between Buyer and Seller, shall at the option of Seller or its factor, at once become due irrespective of the terms of sale, and the Seller may defer delivery under this and such other contracts until such sums shall be paid and for a reasonable time thereafter. If the total amount due or to become due under the contracts between the Buyer and Seller exceeds the credit limit for Buyer, which may be fixed or varied from time to time at and in accordance with the sole discretion and opinion of Seller, or its factor, Buyer agrees to pay cash before delivery or anticipate payment for any future shipment in excess of such credit limit. Upon failure by Buyer to make any such payment within five (5) days after demand in writing, Seller shall have the option to cancel this and other contracts between Buyer and Seller or to sell all or part of the merchandise undelivered thereunder without notice, at public or private sale, holding Buyer responsible for any deficiency, or to bill Buyer as of the date of such demand for all or any part of the merchandise undelivered thereunder on terms of cash before delivery. Approval or credit for one delivery or more shall not be deemed a waiver of this provision.

(b) Any property of the Buyer, at any time in Seller's possession, including but not limited to merchandise paid for by the Buyer, shall be deemed held as security (with a security interest therein granted by Buyer to Seller) for Buyer's obligation under this and any other contract with the Seller. Such property, to the extent of the value thereof, may be applied by the Seller as a credit against such obligations of the Buyer, or such property or any part thereof may be sold by the Seller at public or private sale with the proceeds thereof applied as a credit against such obligations of the Buyer.

Claims

If Buyer claims goods are defective, they must be promptly and properly offered to Seller for examination. If Buyer fails to make such goods available for examination, Buyer shall not be entitled to make any claim with respect to such goods. Seller may within fifteen (15) days after such examination replace any merchandise which is found to be not in accordance with the contract, and in such event no claim may be made by Buyer. Buyer may cancel only that portion of the order pertaining to goods found to be defective in quality and not replaced by Seller.

With respect to greige goods, claims for patent defects are barred unless made in writing within twenty (20) days of discovery or within ninety (90) days after the date dyeing instructions were first issued for all or part of the goods by the Buyer, or within six (6) months after the Seller's invoice date, whichever is earliest. Buyer may make no claim for any quantity of greige goods with patent defects which have already been cut or otherwise processed beyond dyeing and finishing.   [E2233]

With respect to dyed or finished goods, claims for patent defects are barred unless made in writing within twenty (20) days after discovery or within sixty (60) days from shipment by the Seller or ninety (90) days from Seller's invoice date, whichever is earliest, but prior to the cutting or processing of the goods beyond the original condition as shipped by the Seller.

Claims for greige or finished goods with latent defects are barred unless made in writing within twenty (20) days after discovery, or ninety (90) days after shipment of the goods by the Seller to the Buyer, or within nine (9) months after the Seller's invoice date, whichever is the earliest.

The limit of liability of Seller for late delivery or nondelivery or any other breach shall be the difference, if any, between the contract price and the fair market price on the contract date of delivery of the goods delivered or to be delivered. In no event shall Buyer be entitled to claim any consequential damages or any other damages of any nature whatsoever, and in no instances shall damages include profit on contemplated use or profit of any description. Without limiting the foregoing, if Buyer exports the goods, Seller shall not be liable whatsoever for freight charges outside of the continental United States, or for customs duties, or for insurance or for forwarding costs or any other costs connected with the export of the goods.

Amendments

This contract cannot be changed, modified, amended, canceled or discharged in whole or in part unless so done in writing and signed by the party to be charged therewith.

Applicable Law

The laws of the State of New York shall apply to this contract and shall control its interpretation.

[The Salesnote is accompanied by many pages of standardized Specifications, Definitions and Trade Customs, and Quality Standards.]

[E2234]

Amended 7/86

STANDARD CONTRACT 2-A

of

THE COCOA MERCHANTS' ASSOCIATION OF AMERICA, Inc.

New York, N. Y.

Covering F.O.B. Terms for Shipments to the United States

CONTRACT NO.

Messrs.

We confirm having bought from you (through the Intermediary of)
sold to

SUBJECT TO THE RULES AND CONDITIONS HEREIN, AND ON THE REVERSE SIDE, UNLESS NEGATED BY SPECIFIC AGREEMENT HEREIN

1—Quantity:

2—Description: cocoa beans, usual good quality of the season at time of shipment.

3—Quality: Quality on arrival to be Crop Cocoa, usual good quality.

4—Destination:

5—Price: , F.O.B. ocean carrying steamer at

6—Shipment: per direct steamer and/or steamers during
indirect

from

Seller guarantees to engage freight and ship by first class steamer(s) to destination at freight rate ruling at time of shipment not exceeding rate quoted in the
Conference Tariff. permitted).
Partial shipments not permitted (in lots of not less than

The word *Shipment* shall mean shipment by steamer and/or steamers, motor ship and/or motor ships.
Immediate Shipment shall mean shipment within 15 calendar days from date of contract.
Prompt Shipment shall mean shipment within 30 calendar days from date of contract.
Direct Shipment shall mean shipment not involving transshipment.
Indirect Shipment shall mean shipment involving transshipment.
The date of on board Bill of Lading shall be proof of shipment.

6A—Containers: If this Contract covers a sale of cocoa beans, shipment in containers shall not be allowed without buyer's consent.

COMMODITY IMPORTER'S STANDARD FORM

7—Declaration: Each Bill of Lading from origin and/or Ship's Delivery Order shall be treated as a separate contract.

To be communicated to Buyer, as soon as known by Seller, direct or through Seller's Agent, by cable if overseas, by telephone if within the United States or Canada and confirmed in writing, with name of steamer, quantity, grade, contract date, port of shipment and destination.

Seller shall be entitled to declare a shipment against this contract, ship lost or not lost.

Declarations shall be binding upon Seller and Buyer and cannot be changed except by mutual consent. Declarations are subject to cable error.

8—Insurance: Buyer to effect Marine and War Risk Insurance for his account.

9—Weights and Franchise: Net   weights.

If contract on basis of net shipping weights, any loss or weight exceeding   % of the net shipping weight is for account of Seller.

Claims for excess loss in weight accompanied by certified official weights and tares shall be submitted and settled promptly.

If contract on basis of net delivered weights, any variation from net invoice weight to be adjusted at contract price.

Provisional invoices, if any, shall be on the basis of   % of shipping weights.

Final invoice shall be established promptly upon determination of final outturn weights.

Claims and final invoices to be established on the basis of the landed net weights of full, sound bags but applied to the whole parcel. Cocoa to be weighed within 15 working days after completion of discharge of the vessel or release by U. S. Government, whichever occurs latest.

10—Payment: In the event of the steamer becoming a casualty, payment shall be made by Buyer for full invoice value, net shipping weights, against usual shipping documents on presentation.

11—Special and Other Conditions:

SELLER   · B U Y E R

Signature   Signature

(Please sign and return)

ACCEPTED:

173

12—Quality: Cocoa to be equal to contract description; however, bona fide shipments inferior thereto, provided within the standards of the U.S. Government, shall be accepted by the Buyer subject to an allowance to be fixed, if necessary, by arbitration in New York as herein specified.
Claims for inferior quality must be made and arbitration samples, if required, drawn within fifteen working days after the cocoa is discharged from vessel or released by the U.S. Government, whichever occurs latest, and in any event prior to removal of cocoa from dock. Failing amicable adjustment, demand for arbitration—which may be submitted by cable—must be made not later than one month after such removal or release.
Cocoa shipped against this contract is guaranteed by Seller to pass inspection by and comply with the standards of the U.S. Government.
In the event, however, that a shipment is detained by the Government solely on account of infestation. Buyer shall promptly arrange for fumigation.
If the Government releases the shipment after such fumigation, the Buyer shall accept the cocoa, Seller paying all costs incurred in connection with fumigation. If the Government refuses release, Buyer may reject the cocoa and all costs incurred in connection with fumigation shall be paid by the Seller.
Where a shipment of cocoa against this contract is rejected by Buyer because

  (a) entry or release has been refused by U.S. Government, or
  (b) by mutual agreement or at arbitration

Seller shall, upon Buyer's demand, replace such cocoa within the contract period by delivery at destination specified herein, and/or shipment from origin or any intermediate point, within 30 days after either of the contingencies enumerated under (a) or (b) has been established, whichever is the later period. Buyer shall hold in custody such unacceptable cocoa for the account of Seller until replacement and/or reimbursement for payment made against such cocoa, plus freight, insurance, labor, cartage, storage, interest and other bona fide expenses incurred by Buyer, have been paid; and Seller agrees to effect reimbursement of the principal amount of these expenses immediately upon Buyer's demand.
In the event that Seller cannot make replacement, the contract shall be closed out as provided for under the heading "DEFAULTS".

13—Defaults: When either party to a contract claims that a default has occurred, then failing an amicable settlement, the dispute shall be referred to arbitration, and if it is decided that a default has occurred, the contract shall be closed out at a price and weight, which price shall be the estimated market value of the cocoa contracted for on the day the default has occurred or is established within the discretion of the arbitrators with a penalty of not less than one-half percent and not more than ten percent over the estimated market value of the shipment or delivery contracted for on the day on which the default occurs. The difference between contract price and the closing out price plus penalty and cost of arbitration as awarded to be paid in cash within fifteen days, and this payment shall constitute a final and complete settlement of all claims by either party in respect of the said contract.

14—Quantities and/or Weights: The words "about" or "more or less" when used to define quantities and/or weights contracted for, shall mean the nearest amount which Seller can fairly and reasonably deliver, but no excess or deficiency shall be greater than three percent. This leeway shall be void whenever a contract is liquidated by payment of difference between the purchase and sale prices, in lieu of shipment or tender.
Unless otherwise stipulated, a ton shall be 2,240 lbs. net. If metric tons are specified, a ton shall be 2,204.6 lbs. net.

15—Supervision: Seller may appoint a representative to supervise weighing and sampling and must state the name of such representative in the advice of shipment, but should Seller not name his representative or should his representative fail to be present, after having received due notice of time and place of weighing and sampling, weights certified and samples sealed by sworn weighers and samplers and provided by the Buyer shall be accepted by Seller.
Should Buyer fail to notify Seller's representative in accordance with this clause, shipping weights shall be accepted and no quality claim shall be admitted.

16—Duties, Taxes, Etc.: Any export duty or other tax imposed by the Government of the exporting country or political subdivision thereof or any levy imposed under the International cocoa Agreement is assumed and shall be paid by the Seller. Any import duty or other tax imposed by the U.S. Government or political subdivision thereof is assumed and shall be paid by the Buyer.
Unless otherwise stipulated, any charges incurred in landing, weighing and sampling shall be for account of Buyer.

17—Marking: Bags to be branded in English with the name of country of origin and otherwise to comply with laws and regulations of U.S. Government in effect at time of shipment, governing marking of import merchandise. Any expense incurred by failure to comply with these regulations to be borne by Seller.

17A—Shipping Documents: Unless mutually agreed otherwise by Seller and Buyer, usual shipping documents shall consist of a full set of clean on board ocean Bills of Lading and a shipper's invoice.

174

18—Force Majeure: Should shipment be prevented or delayed owing to prohibition of exports, fire, strikes, lockouts, riots, war, revolution or other cases of "Force Majeure" the time of shipment shall be extended by one month, but should the delay exceed one month the Buyer shall have the option of cancelling the contract for any quantity not shipped or of accepting the cocoa for shipment as soon as the cause for prevention or delay of shipment shall have been removed provided if such shipment be not effected within five months following the expiration date of the first month's extension the contract shall be automatically cancelled for any quantity not shipped; such option to be declared in writing as soon as the Seller announces his inability to ship within the extended period, or, at latest, seven days after the extended period has expired, a reasonable time being allowed for passing on such announcements. Contract void if the Buyer fails to declare such aforesaid option as hereinbefore provided. If required, Seller must produce conclusive evidence to establish his claim for extension.

19—Insolvency or Other Failure to Meet Engagements: In the event that

(a) Buyer shall fail to make any payment required hereunder within three (3) business days after its due date, or

(b) at any time prior to the completion of this contract, there shall be filed by or against either party hereto, in any court, a petition in bankruptcy or insolvency or for reorganization or for appointment of a receiver or trustee of all or a portion of such party's property, or

(c) at any time prior to completion of this contract, either party shall make an assignment for the benefit of creditors, then and in any one of such events, this contract shall be forthwith closed at the market price then current for similar goods for delivery at the time or times, or for shipment during the period or periods, provided for in this contract. Such market price shall be ascertained, at the option of the aggrieved party, by repurchase or resale or by arbitration, and the loss, if any, suffered by such aggrieved party shall be the measure of damages to which such party shall be entitled and which shall be payable within fifteen (15) days after such determination. Such aggrieved party shall not be required to reimburse the other party for any profit derived from any repurchase or resale made pursuant to this provision.

20—Assignment: This contract may not be assigned by either party without the prior written consent of the other party.

21—Successors: The covenants, conditions and agreements contained in this contract shall bind and inure to the benefit of the parties and their respective heirs, distributees, executors, administrators, successors and, except as otherwise provided herein, their assigns.

22—Arbitration: Any question, controversy, claim or dispute whatever arising out of, or under this contract, not adjusted by mutual agreement, shall be settled by arbitration in the City of New York, State of New York, under the auspices of and in accordance with the rules of THE COCOA MERCHANTS' ASSOCIATION OF AMERICA, INC. and judgment upon the award rendered may be entered in the Supreme Court of the State of New York in accordance with the provisions of the laws of the State of New York. The parties to this contract do hereby waive personal service of any papers, notices or process necessary or proper in connection with the foregoing. Such papers, notices or process may be served in accordance with the rules of THE COCOA MERCHANTS' ASSOCIATION OF AMERICA, INC. This contract is deemed made in New York and shall be construed pursuant to the laws of the State of New York.

NORTH AMERICAN EXPORT GRAIN ASSOCIATION, INC.

FREE ON BOARD EXPORT CONTRACT U.S.A./CANADA

NO. 2

Revised as of January 1, 1985

Contract No. _____

New York, N.Y. _____ 19 _____

1. **Sold by** _____

2. **Purchased by** _____

3. **Broker/Agent** _____

4. **Quantity**   in bulk, including dockage, 5% more or less at buyer's option, and at market price (per Clause 10) as follows: If the first delivery under this contract is for a quantity between contract minimum and contract maximum (both inclusive), no further deliveries shall be made. If this contract is to be executed by more than one vessel, the loading tolerance of 5% more or less shall apply on the difference between the mean contract quantity and the quantity that has been delivered on all prior vessels. Any delivery which falls within this difference, plus or minus 5%, shall complete the contract.

5. **Weight**   Quantity to be final at port of loading in accordance with customary weight certificates. 1,016 kilos shall be equal to 2,240 lbs.

COMMODITY EXPORTER'S STANDARD FORM

6. Commodity

_____

In accordance with the official grain standards of the United States or Canada, whichever applicable, in effect on the date of this contract.

7. Quality

Quality and condition to be final at port of loading in accordance with official inspection certificates.

In case of delivery at St. Lawrence ports, quality and condition to be final in accordance with Lake and/or loading ports official inspection certificates; Lake inspection certificates to be properly identified at ports of shipment.

Each party hereby authorizes the other party to request in both parties' names an appeal inspection under the U.S. Grain Standards Act at any time prior to or during the loading of the vessel, and whether or not such request was filed before commencement of loading. The cost of such appeal inspection, unless otherwise stipulated in this contract, shall be borne by the party requesting it.

Delivery of higher grades of grain of the same type and description is permissible. The commodity is not warranted free from defect, rendering same unmerchantable, which would not be apparent on reasonable examination, any statute or rule of law to the contrary notwithstanding.

8. Delivery

Delivery shall be made between _____ and _____ , both inclusive (the "delivery period"), at discharge end of loading spout, to buyer's tonnage in readiness to load, in accordance with custom of the port and subject to the elevator tariff to the extent that it does not conflict with the terms of this contract.

Buyer shall give vessel nominations ("preadvice") in accordance with Clause 15, in time for seller to receive minimum _____ days notice of probable readiness of tonnage and quantities required (the "preadvice period"). Buyer to keep seller informed of changes in expected date of vessel readiness.

Time for the preadvice shall be deemed to commence to count at 1200 noon, local time at place of receipt, on the business day of receipt by seller and shall be counted in consecutive periods of 24 hours.

Seller shall, if applicable, declare port and berth of loading within a reasonable time (but not later than _____ days) after receipt by seller of the preadvice, except that seller shall not be obligated to make such declaration earlier than (a) the 8th day prior to commencement of the delivery period for port declaration and (b) the 5th day prior to commencement of the delivery period for berth declaration.

The vessel shall not be prevented from filing and from taking its place in the vessel line-up at the designated port/berth during the preadvice period or before commencement of the delivery period, notwithstanding which, seller shall not be obliged to effect delivery to the vessel before the expiration of the preadvice period or before commencement of the delivery period. For the purposes of this contract a vessel shall be considered filed when it (a) has tendered valid notice of readiness to load to the charterer or his agent, at the port of loading, (b) has given written advice of such tender to the loading elevator, complete with all customarily required documents, such advice having been presented between the hours of 0900 and 1600 local time on a business day or between the hours of 0900 and 1200 noon on Saturday (provided not a holiday) and (c) is ready to receive grain in the compartments required for loading under this contract.

Buyer shall be allowed to make one substitution of a vessel, provided the substituting vessel is of the same type and approximately the same size and position. If the original or the substituting vessel is unable to lift the commodity by reason of the vessel having sunk or having suffered incapacitating physical damage, an additional substitution shall be made of a vessel of the same type and approximately the same size, and with a position agreeable to buyer and seller. Such agreement shall not be unreasonably withheld. The nomination of the substituting vessel shall be subject to the preadvice requirements of this clause, regardless of any preadvice previously given, unless the estimated time of arrival of the substituting vessel is the same as the estimated time of arrival of the original vessel when nominated. No substitution of vessels other than as provided in this clause shall be made. If this is a "named vessel" contract, no substitution other than after a casualty as described above shall be permitted.

Bills of lading and/or mate's receipts to be considered proof of date of delivery in the absence of evidence to the contrary. Any delivery in part fulfillment of this contract shall be considered as if made under a separate contract.

9. Days

In any month containing an odd number of days, the middle day shall be reckoned as belonging to both halves of the month.

10. Price

_____ per _____

free on board buyer's tonnage at _____

If this contract is for a flat price, any variance in quantity from the mean contract quantity shall be settled basis the FOB market value (as defined in paragraph (a) and (b) below).

If the contract price is to be established on an exchange of futures, futures shall be exchanged prior to delivery of the commodity or at least 5 calendar days prior to the last trading day of the applicable futures month, whichever is earlier, to the nearest 5,000 bushels of the mean contract quantity. If deliveries under this contract result in a variance from the mean contract quantity, there shall be another exchange of futures as soon as possible after the last date of loading to bring the resulting amount of futures exchanged to the nearest 5,000 bushels of the quantity delivered. All exchanges of futures shall be made within the range of prices prevailing on the futures market on the date of the exchange. The variance from the mean contract quantity shall be settled basis the market value of the premium (as defined in paragraph (a) and (b) below).

(a) The FOB (flat price) market value, or the market value of the premium, as the case may be, shall be that prevailing on the close of the appropriate market in the country of origin of the commodity on the last date of loading, if such be a business day, otherwise on the close of such market on the previous business day.

(b) In the event the parties do not agree on the market value by the time the shipping documents are ready to be transmitted to buyer, seller shall invoice the entire shipment provisionally at contract price. Thereafter, final invoice for the difference between contract price and market value shall be presented as soon as possible and payment shall be made immediately.

11. Payment

*(a) Net cash by irrevocable divisible letters of credit issued or confirmed by a prime U.S. bank in New York (or by mutual agreement), available by sight drafts accompanied by shipping documents per Clause 12 (or warehouse receipts if option (c) of Clause 18 is exercised). Such letters of credit, in a form acceptable to seller, shall be established not later than 5 days prior to the beginning of the delivery period, and shall be valid at least until the 30th day after expiration of the delivery period. Should delivery be delayed beyond the delivery period, buyer, if requested by seller, shall amend letters of credit accordingly and buyer shall increase the amount of the letter of credit to provide for carrying charges, if applicable. All bank charges shall be for buyer's account.

— or —

*(b) Net cash in U.S. Dollars, by telegraphic transfer to the bank designated by seller, against presentation of and in exchange for shipping documents per Clause 12 (or warehouse receipts if option (c) of Clause 18 is exercised). Such presentation shall be made in the city of _____

_____

All bank charges in connection with payment shall be for buyer's account.

— or —

*(c) _____

_____

*Delete paragraphs which are not applicable.

12. Shipping Documents

Payment to be made against bills of lading or mate's receipts (at seller's option), and weight and inspection certificates. However, if practicable, seller shall follow instructions of buyer in establishing bills of lading containing such clauses as buyer's/vessel's agents or owners usually endorse or attach. Buyer shall accept such bills of lading but seller assumes no responsibility for their correctness.

13. Notice of Delivery

Notice of delivery stating vessel's name, dates of bills of lading (or mate's receipts), quantities and qualities loaded (including percentage of dockage if applicable) shall be given or passed on by seller to buyer without undue delay. Notices of delivery shall be subject to correction of any errors.

14. Insurance

Marine and war risk (plus strikes, riots, civil commotions and mine risk) insurance, covering seller's/buyer's interests as they may appear, is to be covered by buyer with first-class approved companies and/or underwriters and to be confirmed by such companies and/or underwriters to seller at least 5 days prior to the expected readiness of the vessel. If this confirmation is not received by seller by such time, seller may place such insurance for buyer's account and at buyer's risk and expense.

15. Communications

All notices under this contract shall be given by letter, if delivered by hand on the day of writing, or by cable, telex or other method of rapid written communication. Any notice received after 1600 hours (local time at place of receipt) on a business day shall be deemed to have been

179

received on the following business day, except that for preadvice given and received by parties which are both located in the Continental United States and/or Canada, the reference herein to 1600 hours shall signify 1600 hours New York City time (E.S.T. or E.D.T., as in effect on date of receipt of the notice).

16. Circles

(a) For the purposes of this clause, a circle shall consist of a series of contracts in which each seller is also a buyer of a commodity of the same description and quality, for delivery at the same ports and with compatible delivery periods.

(b) If this contract forms part of a circle, each party may agree with the other parties in the circle to forego actual delivery and to participate in a clearing agreement for the settlement of contract price differences. Monies due and owed to parties in the circle shall be payable on the middle day of the contract delivery period.

(c) If a circle can be shown to exist but no clearing agreement has been reached by the 10th calendar day following the last day of the delivery period, actual delivery shall not be made and payment shall be made by each buyer to his seller of the excess of seller's invoice amount over the lowest invoice amount in the circle. Such payments shall be made promptly after the 10th calendar day following the last day of the delivery period.

(d) Should any party in a circle fail to make payment on the due date as required under paragraph (b) or (c) above for reasons cited in Clause 23 or for any other reason, payment shall be made between each buyer and his seller of the difference between the seller's invoice amount at contract price and the market value of the commodity on date of insolvency or default, as the case may be. Such payment shall be made latest on the 2nd business day after the due date under paragraph (b) or (c) above.

Payments already made under paragraph (b) or (c) above shall be refunded.

(e) All circle settlements shall be based on the mean contract quantity.

If a circle under paragraph (b), (c) or (d) above exists, Clause 21 shall not apply and Clauses 18 and 20 shall not be invoked.

Payments due on a non-business day shall be made not later than the following business day.

All payments made after the delivery period shall include carrying charges from the day following the last day of the delivery period, to the date of payment, at the rates stipulated in this contract. These carrying charges shall be settled individually between each buyer and his seller.

(f) The parties agree that any dispute arising out of the voluntary clearing agreement entered into in accordance with paragraph (b) above shall be subject to arbitration as to any party thereto. Such arbitration shall be conducted in accordance with the provisions of Clause 27.

17. U.S./Canadian Government Rules and Regulations

Buyer and seller agree to comply with the U.S. and Canadian regulatory prerequisites applicable to this contract, including, but not limited to, those governing any export subsidy, destination controls, government financing of agricultural commodities and the monitoring of export purchases and sales. Any losses, fines, penalties, expenses, costs or damages incurred as a result of failure to perform in accordance with this provision shall be borne by the party responsible for such failure.

18. Failure to Take Delivery

If vessel fails to file before the end of the delivery period, buyer shall be in breach of contract and seller shall carry the grain for buyer's account and risk as provided in Clause 19. In the event that buyer has not given vessel nominations conforming to the applicable provisions of Clause 8 by the 15th calendar day following the last day of the delivery period, or if the vessels having been nominated within such time, fail to file by the 35th calendar day following the last day of the delivery period, seller may, in his discretion: (a) continue to carry the commodity for buyer's account and risk, (b) declare buyer in default, or (c) tender to buyer proper warehouse receipts in a quantity equal to the mean quantity open under this contract, in exchange for which buyer shall pay at contract price plus accrued carrying charges, but less out-elevation and outbound weighing and inspection charges. Such tender of warehouse receipts shall be deemed due performance of the contract by seller.

SPECIAL PROVISIONS FOR CONTRACTS PROVIDING FOR DELIVERY AT ST. LAWRENCE, GREAT LAKES OR HUDSON BAY PORTS:

(1) Seller shall be barred from declaring option (b) above while the navigation in the designated delivery area is officially closed for the ice season, and for 20 days thereafter.

(2) However, if options (a), (b) and (c) above become available to seller only while the navigation is officially closed, the seller may declare option (b) during the first 10 days it becomes available to him; thereafter, he shall be barred from declaring it, until the 21st day after the official opening of navigation.

(3) If seller carries the grain into the new season for buyer's account, buyer shall have the right to nominate vessels per Clause 8, regardless of whether vessels were already nominated during the delivery period.

19. Carrying Charges

If the commodity is being carried for buyer's account and risk as provided in Clause 18, it is mutually agreed that carrying charges, consisting of storage, insurance and interest, shall accrue as follows:

(a) Storage and insurance from the day following the last date of the delivery period up to and including the dates of delivery (or if seller exercises option (b) or (c) of Clause 18, the date applicable thereto), both dates inclusive, at the following rates:

_____ U.S. cents per bushel per day

_____ U.S. cents per bushel per day

(b) Interest from the day following the last day of the delivery period up to and including the last day of delivery (or if seller exercises option (b) or (c) of Clause 18, the date applicable thereto), both dates inclusive, at the following rates:

_____
_____
_____

Carrying charges for the delivery completing this contract shall be computed on the mean contract quantity less the amounts previously delivered (if any), irrespective of whether or not buyer has availed himself of the loading tolerance option under Clause 4. It is further expressly agreed that carrying charges as provided herein are to be construed in the nature of liquidated damages and, as such, that no further proof of damages shall be required in substantiation thereof.

20. Strikes or Other Causes of Delay in Delivery

(a) This clause shall apply if delivery by seller of the commodity, or any part thereof, is prevented or delayed at the port(s) of delivery and/or elevator(s) of delivery or elsewhere, or if the forwarding of the commodity to such port(s) and/or elevator(s) is prevented, by reason of the causes enumerated in paragraph (b) below; PROVIDED that seller shall have sent notice to buyer not later than 2 business days after the date of commencement of the causes, or not later than 2 business days after the 1st day of the delivery period, whichever occurs later (except that subsequent sellers shall not be bound by these deadlines, provided they pass along the notice to their buyer, without delay); and PROVIDED further that seller shall, at buyer's request, furnish a certificate of the North American Export Grain Association, Inc., certifying the existence and the duration of the causes. Such certificate shall be final.

(b) The causes of delay and/or prevention ("causes") referred to in paragraph (a) above shall be:
(1) Riots, strikes, lockouts, interruptions in or stoppages of the normal course of labor,
(2) Embargoes or exceptional impediments to transportation,
(3) Action by Federal, State or local government or authority.

(c) The obligation of seller to make delivery shall be suspended while the causes are in effect, until the termination of the causes and/or the resumption of work after the termination of the causes, whichever is later. Seller shall not be responsible for further delays after resumption of work (whether such termination or resumption of work occurs prior to, during or after the delivery period) except that, if a vessel nominated under this contract is not loaded in the proper rotation but is bypassed by vessels (other than liners) which had filed after the vessel nominated under this contract, seller shall pay to buyer damages equal to the actual working time lost (weather working days, Saturdays, Sundays and holidays excluded) to buyer's vessel during the loading of the bypassing vessels, at the demurrage rate in the Charter Party for the vessel nominated under this contract.
If the Charter Party of the vessel under this contract does not indicate a demurrage rate, the damages are to be calculated at a reasonable demurrage rate predicated on the then current market, to be agreed upon amicably or to be determined by arbitration.

(d) (1) If the causes commence before or during the delivery period and terminate during or after delivery period, then the delivery period shall be deemed to be extended by a number of days equivalent to the period starting with the commencement of the causes or the commencement of the delivery period, whichever is later, and ending with the termination of the causes, and/or the resumption of work after the termination of the causes, whichever is later.
(2) If the causes commence during the additional time afforded to buyer under Clause 18 with respect to vessel nominations and filings, then the right of seller to exercise option (b) or (c) under Clause 18 shall be deemed to be delayed by a number of days equivalent to the period starting with the commencement of the causes and ending with the termination of the causes and/or the resumption of work after the termination of the causes, whichever is later.

(e) Carrying charges, if due under Clauses 18/19, shall begin to accrue on the day following the last day of the delivery period, as extended by paragraph (d) (1) above; however, if this clause becomes operative while carrying charges are already accruing, then such charges shall continue to accrue as they would in the absence of the causes.

21. Prohibition

In case of prohibition of export, blockade or hostilities or in case of any executive or legislative act done by or on behalf of the government of the country of origin or of the territory where the ports of shipment named herein are situate, restricting export, whether partially or otherwise, any such restriction shall be deemed by both parties to apply to this contract and to the extent of such total or partial restriction to prevent fulfillment and to that extent this contract or any unfulfilled portion thereof shall be cancelled without prejudice to seller's entitlement to carrying charges. Seller shall advise buyer without delay of the reasons therefor, and if required by buyer, seller shall provide certification of the North American Export Grain Association, Inc., as sufficient evidence for cancellation under this clause.

22. Default

In case of default by either party, the other party shall be at liberty, after giving notice, to resell or repurchase, as the case may be, without undue delay and the defaulting party shall make good the loss, if any, to the other party but the defaulting party shall not be entitled to any profit. If the non-defaulting party has not repurchased or resold the commodity by the 10th calendar day after the giving of notice of default, the market value on the said 10th day shall be used for settlement purposes. If such 10th day falls on a non-business day, the market value

182

on the previous business day shall govern. In the event of a default by buyer, the sale price under this contract shall automatically be increased by the value of carrying charges calculated up to the date of resale, or the 10th calendar day after the giving of notice of default, whichever is applicable.

23. Insolvency

Either party shall, at any time after sending notice, have the right to terminate this contract and to recover the loss (if any) in the event that:

(a) the other party suspends payment or commits an act of bankruptcy;

— or —

(b) reasonable grounds for insecurity having arisen with respect to the financial capacity of the other party to perform under this contract, and a written demand for adequate assurance of due performance having been made, such assurance is not received within a period of time not exceeding 5 days.

24. Construction

For the purposes of this contract, except as otherwise expressly provided or unless the context otherwise requires, plural terms include the singular.

25. Passage of Title

Anything in this contract to the contrary notwithstanding, seller shall retain title to the commodity until seller has been paid in full (per Clause 11), it being understood that risk of loss shall pass to buyer on delivery at discharge end of loading spout (per Clause 8).

26. Other Conditions

27. Arbitration

Buyer and seller expressly agree that any controversy or claim arising out of, in connection with or relating to this contract, or the interpretation, performance or breach thereof, shall be settled by arbitration in the City of New York before the American Arbitration Association, or its successors, pursuant to the Grain Arbitration Rules of the American Arbitration Association, as those Rules may be in effect at the time of such arbitration proceeding, which Rules are hereby deemed incorporated herein and made a part hereof, and under the laws of the State of New York. The arbitration award shall be final and binding on both parties and judgment upon such arbitration award may be entered in the Supreme Court of the State of New York or any other court having jurisdiction thereof. Buyer and seller hereby recognize and expressly consent to the jurisdiction over each of them of the American Arbitration Association or its successors, and of all the courts in the State of New York. Buyer and seller agree that this contract shall be deemed to have been made in New York State and be deemed to be performed there, any reference herein or elsewhere to the contrary notwithstanding.

BUYER

SELLER

183

GENERAL ELECTRIC COMPANY

CONDITIONS OF EXPORT SALE

NOTICE: THE OFFER, ORDER ACKNOWLEDGEMENT, ORDER ACCEPTANCE OR SALE OF ANY PRODUCTS COVERED HEREIN IS CONDITIONED UPON THE TERMS CONTAINED IN THIS INSTRUMENT. ANY ADDITIONAL OR DIFFERENT TERMS PROPOSED BY BUYER ARE OBJECTED TO AND WILL NOT BE BINDING UPON SELLER UNLESS SPECIFICALLY ASSENTED TO IN WRITING BY SELLER.

ARTICLE I - PRICES

Prices include the cost of (i) Seller's usual inspection and factory tests, (ii) Seller's usual packing (or containerizing, if applicable) for export, and (iii) freight by Seller's usual means to alongside vessel at the point of export designated by Seller (but not the cost of insurance, or charges for pier handling, marshaling, lighterage and heavy lifts). Insurance to cover the inland shipment shall be arranged by Seller at Buyer's expense if Seller is arranging for the export shipment pursuant to Article III.

ARTICLE II - DELIVERY, TITLE AND RISK OF LOSS

A. Except as stated in Paragraph B below, Seller shall deliver the Products to Buyer F.O.B. factory. Partial deliveries shall be permitted. Upon delivery, title to the Products and all risk of loss or damage shall pass to Buyer. Delivery times are approximate and are dependent upon prompt receipt by Seller of all material and information necessary to proceed with work without interruption.

B. If any part of the Products cannot be shipped from the point of inland shipment to alongside vessel when ready due to any cause referred to in Article V, Seller may place such Products in storage (which may be at the place of manufacture). In such event, (i) Seller shall notify Buyer of the placement of any Product in storage, (ii) Seller's delivery obligations shall be deemed fulfilled and title and all risk of loss or damage shall thereupon pass to Buyer, (iii) any amounts otherwise payable to Seller upon delivery shall be payable upon presentation of Seller's invoices therefor and its certification as to such cause, (iv) promptly upon submission of Seller's invoices, Buyer shall reimburse Seller for all expenses incurred by Seller, such as preparation for and placement into storage, handling, storage, inspection, preservation and insurance, and (v) when conditions permit and upon payment of all amounts due hereunder, Seller shall assist and cooperate with Buyer in any reasonable manner with respect to the removal of any Product which has been placed in storage.

ARTICLE III - EXPORT SHIPMENT

A. In the event Buyer wishes to arrange for export shipment, Buyer shall inform Seller by so indicating on the order. In the absence of such indication, or if Seller exercises its rights under Paragraph B of Article VI, Seller shall arrange for (i) export shipment to Buyer's country and (ii) marine warehouse-to-warehouse insurance (including war risk, if available). Buyer shall pay Seller for all fees and expenses, including, but not limited to, those covering preparation of consular documents, consular fees, ocean freight, storage, insurance and Seller's then current fee for such services. Notwithstanding any extension of credit to Buyer, all such charges shall be promptly reimbursed by Buyer in U.S. Dollars upon submission of Seller's invoices therefor.

B. In performing any of the foregoing services, Seller shall comply with any reasonable instructions of Buyer or, in the absence thereof, shall act according to its best judgment. In so acting on Buyer's behalf, neither Seller nor its agents shall be liable for negligence or for any special, consequential, incidental, indirect or exemplary damages to Buyer resulting therefrom.

ARTICLE IV - GOVERNMENTAL AUTHORIZATIONS

A. The party that arranges for export shipment (or Buyer's designated export agent) shall be responsible for the timely application in its own name for any required U.S.A. export license. Buyer shall be responsible for timely obtaining and maintaining any required import license, exchange permit or any other governmental authorization. Buyer and Seller shall assist each other when such help is reasonably possible. Seller shall not be liable if any authorization of any government is delayed, denied, revoked, restricted or not renewed, and Buyer shall not be relieved thereby of its obligations to pay Seller for its Products or any other charges which are the obligation of the Buyer hereunder.

B. All shipments hereunder shall at all times be subject to the export control laws and regulations of the U.S.A. and any amendments thereof. Buyer agrees that it shall not make any disposition of U.S.A.-origin Products purchased from Seller, by way of trans-shipment, re-export, diversion or otherwise, other than in and to the ultimate country of destination specified on Buyer's order or declared as the country of ultimate destination on Seller's invoices, except as said laws and regulations may expressly permit.

ARTICLE V - EXCUSABLE DELAYS

A. Seller shall not be liable for delays in delivery or failure to perform due directly or indirectly to (i) causes beyond Seller's reasonable control, (ii) acts of God, acts (including failure to act) of any governmental authority (de jure or de facto), wars (declared or undeclared), governmental priorities, port congestion, riots, revolutions, strikes or other labor disputes, fires, floods, sabotage, nuclear incidents, earthquakes, storms, epidemics, or (iii) inabilities due to causes beyond Seller's reason-

able control timely to obtain either necessary and proper labor, materials, components, facilities, energy, fuel, transportation, governmental authorizations or instructions, material or information required from Buyer. The foregoing shall apply even though any of such causes exists at the time of the order or occurs after Seller's performance of its obligations is delayed for other causes.

B. Seller shall notify Buyer of any delay or failure excused by this Article and shall specify the revised delivery date as soon as practicable. In the event of such delay, subject to Paragraph C of this Article, there shall be no termination and the time of delivery or of performance shall be extended for a period equal to the time lost by Seller by reason of the delay.

C. If delay excused by this Article extends for more than 60 days and the parties have not agreed upon a revised basis for continuing the work at the end of the delay, including adjustment of the price, then either party (except where delay is caused by Buyer, in which event only Seller), upon 30 days written notice, may terminate the order with respect to the unexecuted portion of the work, whereupon Buyer shall promptly pay Seller its termination charges determined in accordance with Seller's standard accounting practices upon submission of Seller's invoices therefor.

ARTICLE VI - PAYMENT

A. Payment shall be made in U.S. Dollars in New York as follows:

(i) On an order of fifteen thousand U.S. Dollars (U.S. $15,000) or under, payment shall be made simultaneously with the placing of the order where the laws of the Buyer's country permit.

(ii) On an order over fifteen thousand U.S. Dollars (U.S. $15,000), or if the laws of the Buyer's country forbid compliance with Paragraph (i) above, payment shall be made through a letter of credit to be established by Buyer at its expense. All costs, including any bank confirmation charges, relating to such letter of credit are for the account of the Buyer. All letters of credit shall be in favor of and acceptable to Seller, shall be consistent with the terms of this instrument, shall be maintained in sufficient amounts and for the period necessary to meet all payment obligations, shall be irrevocable and issued by, or confirmed by, a bank in New York acceptable to Seller within 15 days after acceptance of the order, shall permit partial deliveries and shall provide for pro rata payments upon presentation of Seller's invoices therefor and either Seller's certificate of delivery FOB factory or of delivery into storage with certification of cause therefor and for the payment of any charges for storage, export shipment, price adjustments, and cancellation or termination.

B. In the event that Seller agrees to any deviation from the cash or the letter of credit requirements set forth above, Seller reserves the right to arrange for export shipment of the Products.

C. If Buyer fails to fulfill any condition of its payment obligations, Seller may (i) withhold deliveries and suspend performance, or (ii) continue performance if Seller deems it reasonable to do so, or (iii) place the Products in storage pursuant to the provisions of Article II hereof. In any event, the costs incurred by Seller as a result of Buyer's non-fulfillment shall be payable by Buyer upon submission of Seller's invoices therefor. Seller shall be entitled to an extension of time for performance of its obligations equaling the period of Buyer's non-fulfillment whether or not Seller elects to suspend performance. If such non-fulfillment is not rectified by Buyer promptly upon notice thereof, Seller may cancel the agreement and Buyer shall pay Seller its charges for cancellation upon submission of Seller's invoices therefor.

ARTICLE VII - TAXES AND DUTIES

A. All U.S.A. taxes are included in the price except sales, use, excise, value-added and similar taxes which have been excluded based on the assumption that the transaction involves exportation. All rights to drawback of U.S.A. customs duties paid by Seller with respect to Products (or material or components thereof) belong to and shall remain in Seller. If Buyer arranges for export shipment, Buyer agrees to furnish without charge evidence of exportation or other evidence of tax or duty exemption acceptable to the taxing or customs authorities when requested by Seller, failing which, the amount of any U.S.A. taxes or duties imposed on Seller in connection with the transaction shall be promptly reimbursed in U.S. Dollars by Buyer to Seller upon submission of Seller's invoices therefor.

B. Any taxes (including income, stamp and turnover or value-added taxes), duties, fees, charges or assessments of any nature levied by any governmental authority other than of the U.S.A. in connection with this transaction, whether levied against Buyer, against Seller or its employees or against any of Seller's subcontractors or their employees, shall be the responsibility of the Buyer and shall be paid directly by Buyer to the governmental authority concerned. If Seller or its subcontractors, or the employees of either, are required to pay any such levies and/or fines, penalties, or assessments in the first instance, or as a result of Buyer's failure to comply with any applicable laws or regulations governing the payment of such levies by Buyer, the amount of any payments so made, plus the expense of currency conversion, shall be promptly reimbursed in U.S. Dollars by Buyer upon submission of Seller's invoices therefor.

GE 43-H (5-82)

MACHINERY EXPORTER'S STANDARD FORM

ARTICLE VIII - WARRANTIES

A. Seller warrants that Products manufactured by Seller shall be free from defects in material, workmanship and title, and shall be of the kind and quality specified or designated by Seller. Seller's obligations, set forth below, shall apply only to failures to meet the foregoing warranties (except as to title) occurring within fifteen (15) months from date of delivery pursuant to Article II of which Seller is given written notice within thirty (30) days of such occurrence and provided the Product or part thereof is made available to Seller as specified by Seller.

B. If any Product or part thereof fails to meet the foregoing warranties (except as to title), Seller shall repair same or, at its option, replace same, in either case F.O.B. factory, on the same basis as described in Article I. Any such failure shall not be cause for the extension of the duration of the warranty specified in this Article VIII. If such failure or defect cannot be corrected by Seller's reasonable efforts, the parties shall negotiate an equitable adjustment.

C. Seller's obligations under Paragraph B above shall not apply to any Product, or part thereof, which (i) is normally consumed in operation, or (ii) has a normal life inherently shorter than the warranty period specified in Paragraph A, or (iii) is not properly stored, installed, used, maintained or repaired or is modified other than pursuant to Seller's instructions or approval, or (iv) has been subjected to any other kind of misuse or detrimental exposure, or has been involved in an accident.

D. With respect to any Products not manufactured by Seller (except for integral parts of Seller's Products to which the warranties set forth above shall apply). Seller gives no warranty, and only the warranty, if any, given by the manufacturer shall apply.

E. Subject to Article X, this Article sets forth the exclusive remedies for claims based upon defects in or nonconformity of the Products, whether the claim is in contract, warranty, tort (including negligence) or otherwise. Except as set forth in Article IX, the foregoing warranties are in lieu of all other warranties, whether oral, written, express, implied or statutory. **NO IMPLIED OR STATUTORY WARRANTIES OF MERCHANTABILITY OR FITNESS FOR PARTICULAR PURPOSE SHALL APPLY.**

ARTICLE IX - PATENTS

A. Seller warrants that any Product (or part thereof) manufactured by Seller and furnished hereunder shall be free of any rightful claim of any third party for infringement of any U.S.A. patent. If Buyer notifies Seller promptly of the receipt of any claim that such Product infringes a U.S.A. patent and gives Seller information, assistance and exclusive authority to settle and defend such claim, Seller shall, at its own expense and option, either (i) settle or defend such claim or any suit or proceeding arising therefrom and pay all damages and costs awarded therein against Buyer, or (ii) procure for Buyer the right to continue using such Product, or (iii) modify the Product so that it becomes non-infringing, or (iv) replace the Product with a non-infringing product, or (v) remove the Product and refund the purchase price (less reasonable depreciation) and any transportation or installation costs which have been separately paid by Buyer. If, in any such suit arising from such claim, the continued use of the Product for the purpose intended is enjoined by any court of competent jurisdiction, Seller shall, at its option, take one or more of the actions under (ii), (iii), (iv) or (v) above. The foregoing states the entire liability of Seller for patent infringement of any Product and is subject to the limitation of total liability set forth in Article X.

B. The preceding paragraph shall not apply (i) to any Product (or part thereof) which is manufactured to Buyer's design or (ii) to the use of any Product (or any part thereof) furnished hereunder in conjunction with any other apparatus or material. As to any Product, part or use described in the preceding sentence, Seller assumes no liability whatsoever for patent infringement.

C. With respect to any Product (or part thereof) furnished hereunder which is not manufactured by Seller, only the patent indemnity of the manufacturer, if any, shall apply.

D. The patent warranty and indemnity obligations recited above are in lieu of all other patent warranties and indemnities whatsoever, whether oral, written, express, implied or statutory.

ARTICLE X - LIMITATIONS OF LIABILITY

A. The total liability of Seller, including its subcontractors or suppliers, on any and all claims, whether in contract, warranty, tort (including negligence or patent infringement) or otherwise, arising out of, connected with, or resulting from the performance or non-performance of any agreement resulting herefrom or from the manufacture, sale, delivery, resale, repair, replacement or use of any Product or the furnishing of any service, shall not exceed the price allocable to the Product or service which gives rise to the claim. Except as to title, any such liability shall terminate upon the expiration of the warranty period specified in Article VIII.

B. In no event, whether as a result of breach of contract, warranty, tort (including negligence or patent infringement) or otherwise, shall Seller, or its subcontractors or suppliers, be liable for any special, consequential, incidental, indirect or exemplary damages, including, but not limited to, loss of profit or revenues, loss of use of the Products or any associated equipment, cost of capital, cost of substitute goods, facilities, services or replacement power, downtime costs or claims of Buyer's customers for such damages. If Buyer transfers title to, or leases the Products sold hereunder to, or otherwise permits or suffers use by, any third party. Buyer shall obtain from such third party a provision affording Seller and its subcontractors and suppliers the protection of the preceding sentence.

C. If Seller furnishes Buyer with advice or other assistance which concerns any Product supplied hereunder or any system or equipment in which any such Product may be installed and which is not required by the terms of this instrument or pursuant to any agreement resulting herefrom, the furnishing of such advice or assistance shall not subject Seller to any liability, whether in contract, warranty, tort (including negligence or patent infringement) or otherwise.

ARTICLE XI - NUCLEAR USE

A. Products and services sold hereunder are not intended for application (and shall not be used) in connection with the use or handling of nuclear material or the construction or operation of a nuclear installation. Buyer warrants that it shall not use such Products or services for such purposes, or permit others to use such Products or services for such purposes, unless such use is agreed to in writing by Seller.

B. If, in breach of the foregoing, any such use occurs, Seller disclaims all liability for any nuclear or other damages, injury or contamination, and Buyer shall indemnify Seller against any such liability, whether as a result of breach of contract, warranty, tort (including negligence) or otherwise.

ARTICLE XII - GENERAL

A. Any Products furnished by Seller hereunder shall comply with federal, state and local laws and regulations of the U.S.A. applicable to the manufacture, packing, sale and shipment of such Products as of the date of Seller's quotation and shall comply with any amendments thereto which may have come into effect prior to the time such Products are furnished, provided that the price and, if necessary, delivery shall be equitably adjusted to compensate Seller for the effect of compliance with any such amendments. Seller shall not comply with any law, regulation or requirement which would subject Seller to criminal or civil penalties or loss of tax benefits under any federal, state or local law or regulation of the U.S.A., and the furnishing of any quotation or acknowledgement of any order does not constitute the furnishing of or an agreement to furnish any information which would subject Seller to any of the above mentioned penalties or loss of tax benefits. Seller shall not comply with any other law, regulation or requirement which would increase Seller's costs, unless there is an appropriate adjustment in price.

B. The delegation or assignment by Buyer of any or all of its duties or rights hereunder without Seller's prior written consent shall be void.

C. Any representation, understanding, proposal, agreement, warranty, course of dealing or trade usage not contained or referenced herein shall not be binding on Seller. No modification, amendment, rescission, waiver or other change shall be binding on Seller unless assented to in writing by Seller.

D. The validity, performance and all matters relating to the interpretation and effect of any agreement resulting herefrom and any amendment thereto shall be governed by the internal substantive law of the State of New York, U.S.A.

E. The provisions of any agreement resulting herefrom are for the benefit of the parties hereto and not for any other person except as specifically provided herein.

F. Unless otherwise specified by Seller, any quotation of Seller shall expire 30 days from the date of issuance and may be modified or withdrawn at any time prior to the date of Buyer's order.

G. Buyer may terminate an order only upon paying Seller its termination charges determined in accordance with Seller's standard accounting practices upon submission of Seller's invoices therefor. Termination of an order shall not relieve either party of any obligation arising out of work performed prior to termination.

H. As used throughout this instrument, (i) the term Product (or Products) is defined to include all equipment, materials, supplies, components, services, engineering, design and data, or other work which Seller has contracted to supply and (ii) the term Seller is defined to mean General Electric Company, U.S.A.

I. The invalidity, in whole or in part, of any Article or Paragraph thereof shall not affect the validity of the remainder of such Article or Paragraph or of any agreement resulting herefrom.

GENERAL ⓖⓔ ELECTRIC

185

SELECTED FORMS

CRABTREE FORD, Inc.

⚡ AMC
RENAULT
Jeep

D/B/A CRABTREE FORD, AMC, RENAULT, JEEP
1435 Boston Post Rd. **LARCHMONT, N.Y. 10538**
SALES (914) 834-7000
SERVICE (914) 834-7025
PARTS (914) 834-7010

16007

THIS AGREEMENT IS NOT BINDING UNLESS SIGNED BY THE SELLER AND THE BUYER

BUYER _____ SALESMAN _____

STREET _____ PHONE _____ BUS _____

CITY _____ STATE _____ ZIP _____

THE TRANSACTION

I ORDER AND AGREE TO PURCHASE FROM YOU, ON THE TERMS CONTAINED ON BOTH SIDES OF THIS AGREEMENT, THE FOLLOWING VEHICLE:
(READ OTHER SIDE)

THE VEHICLE

YEAR	☐ NEW	☐ USED	☐ DEMONSTRATOR	MAKE	MODEL	SERIES
TYPE	COLOR			TRIM	V.I.N.	
TO BE DELIVERED ON OR ABOUT:				MILEAGE	STOCK NO. (IF RESERVED)	

THE PRICE

VEHICLE PRICE	(+)	$					
TRANSPORTATION (IF NOT INCLUDED IN VEHICLE PRICE)	(+)						
FACTORY INSTALLED EQUIPMENT	(+)			PROTECTION PACKAGE	(+)		
				DEALER INSTALLED EQUIPMENT AND SERVICES	(+)		
LIEN HOLDER INFORMATION							
				TOTAL	$		

THE TRADE-IN

DESCRIPTION OF TRADE				LESS TRADE-IN CREDIT	(−)	
YEAR	MILEAGE	MAKE	MODEL	(BUYER SEE 1 AND 6(b) ON BACK		
PLATE NO.	EXP. DATE	COLOR	V.I.N.		$	
TRADE-IN IS CLEAR OF ALL LIENS EXCEPT:		AMOUNT OWED	$	CASH PRICE		

IF YOU AGREE TO ASSIST ME IN OBTAINING FINANCING FOR ANY PART OF THE PURCHASE PRICE, THIS ORDER SHALL NOT BE BINDING UPON YOU OR ME UNTIL ALL OF THE CREDIT TERMS ARE PRESENTED TO ME IN ACCORDANCE WITH REGULATION "Z" (TRUTH-IN-LENDING) AND ARE ACCEPTED BY ME. IF I DO NOT ACCEPT THE CREDIT TERMS WHEN PRESENTED, I MAY CANCEL THIS ORDER AND MY DEPOSIT WILL BE REFUNDED.

SPECIAL NOTICE TO CONSUMER
IF, UNDER THE LAW OF THE STATE OF NEW YORK CONTROLLING THE SALE OF USED MOTOR VEHICLES, YOU SHOULD BE ENTITLED TO A REFUND IN CONNECTION WITH THIS TRANSACTION, THE VALUE OF ANY VEHICLE YOU MAY HAVE TRADED-IN (IF THE SELLER CHOOSES NOT TO RETURN IT TO YOU) SHALL NOT BE THE VALUE LISTED IN THIS DOCUMENT. INSTEAD, THE VALUE WILL BE DETERMINED BASED ON THE NATIONAL AUTO DEALERS ASSOCIATION USED CAR GUIDE WHOLESALE VALUE OR OTHER GUIDE APPROVED BY THE COMMISSIONER OF MOTOR VEHICLES, AND ADJUSTED FOR MILEAGE, IMPROVEMENTS AND ANY MAJOR PHYSICAL OR MECHANICAL DEFECTS.

CONTRACTUAL DISCLOSURE STATEMENT FOR USED VEHICLE ONLY
"The information you see on the window form for this vehicle is part of this contract. Information on the window form overrides any contrary provisions in the contract of sale."

DEPOSITS ARE NON-REFUNDABLE ON ALL APPROVED DEALS.
**ALL BALANCES MUST BE PAID IN CASH
OR CERTIFIED CHECK ON DELIVERY.**

TAXES AND OTHER FEES

SALES TAX	%	(+)		
TITLE FEE $2.50	N.Y.S. INSPECTION	New Car $ 8.00 Used Car $15.00		
REGISTRATION FEE (ESTIMATE)	(+)			
Dealer's Fee for Obtaining Registration and/or Certificate of Title (Fee May Not Exceed $10)	(+)	10	00
	(+)		
TOTAL CASH PRICE DELIVERED	$		
LESS DEPOSIT CHECK NO. _____ SUBMITTED WITH ORDER	(−)		
PLUS BALANCE OWING ON TRADE-IN	(+)		
CASH DUE ON DELIVERY	$		

I have read the terms on the back of this agreement and have received a completed copy of this agreement.

BUYER'S SIGNATURE _____ DATE: _____

CO-BUYER'S SIGNATURE _____ DATE: _____

SELLER APPROVED BY: _____ DATE: _____

[E2235]

Reynolds + Reynolds LITHO IN U.S.A. D44240

SEE OTHER SIDE FOR ADDITIONAL TERMS

AUTOMOBILE PURCHASE ORDER
186

SELECTED FORMS

ADDITIONAL TERMS OF AGREEMENT

"I", "me", and "my" refer to the Buyer and Co-Buyer. "You" and "your" refer to the Seller.

I agree this order is subject to the following terms:

1. **Trade-in Credit May Change.** If I do not deliver the trade-in vehicle to you when this Agreement is signed, I agree, that at the time the trade-in vehicle is delivered to you, should the value of my trade-in be materially diminished as a result of physical damage, alteration or deterioration in mechanical condition other than normal wear and tear, YOU HAVE THE RIGHT TO REAPPRAISE THE VEHICLE AS A RESULT OF SUCH REAPPARAISAL. I UNDERSTAND THAT THE TRADE-IN ALLOWANCE ON MY VEHICLE MAY BE REDUCED AND THAT THIS WILL IN TURN INCREASE THE NET PRICE WHICH I WILL HAVE TO PAY FOR THE VEHICLE IF I DECIDE TO PURCHASE THE VEHICLE. If the trade-in credit is reduced and I am not satisfied, I understand that I can cancel this agreement IF the purchased vehicle has not been registered in my name or delivered to me or you have not accepted delivery of the trade-in vehicle.

2. **Trade-In; Buyer's Obligations.** At the time I deliver the trade-in vehicle to you, I promise to sign a Bill of Sale and a mileage certification statement and give you satisfactory proof that I own the vehicle. I warrant (guarantee) (a) that there are no liens on the trade-in vehicle and that I owe no one any money for the vehicle or repairs to the vehicle, except as may be shown on the face of this agreement; (b) that the trade-in vehicle does not have a welded or bent frame and that the motor block is not cracked, welded or repaired; and (c) that the vehicle has not been flood damaged or declared a total loss for insurance purposes; and (d) that emission control devices have not been altered and/or removed, and nothing has been removed from the trade, including all seat belts, that was originally seen. The engine and/or transmission has not been tampered with to pass your inspection.

3. **Buyer's Refusal to Purchase.** Unless this agreement is non-binding because you are arranging credit for me, I understand that the cash deposit I have given to you can be retained, in accordance with your refund policy, to offset your damages if I refuse to complete my purchase. I also understand that I may be responsible for any other damages which you may incur as a result of my failure to perform my obligations under the terms of this agreement.

4. **Delays in Delivery.** I understand that you shall not be liable for delays caused by the manufacturer, accidents, sureties, fires or other causes beyond your control. Provided you promptly place my order with the manufacturer and the manufacturer refuses to accept the order or fails to deliver the vehicle after accepting the order, upon your prompt notification and refund of my deposit, I will not hold you liable and this agreement shall be cancelled. Dealer shall honor deposit on stock unit for no longer than 24 hrs. after contract date at which time unit will be placed back into inventory and deposit forfeited.

5. **Disclaimer of Warranties.** I UNDERSTAND THAT YOU EXPRESSLY DISCLAIM ALL WARRANTIES, EXPRESS OR IMPLIED, INCLUDING ANY IMPLIED WARRANTY OF MERCHANTABILITY OR FITNESS FOR A PARTICULAR PURPOSE, AND THAT YOU NEITHER ASSUME NOR AUTHORIZE ANY OTHER PERSON TO ASSUME FOR YOU ANY LIABILITY IN CONNECTION WITH THE SALE OF THE VEHICLE, except as otherwise provided in writing by YOU in an attachment to this Agreement or in a document delivered to ME when the vehicle is delivered.

Limitation on Implied Warranties. Some States do not allow either (1) Limitations on how long an implied warranty lasts or (2) the exclusion or limitation of incidental or consequential damages, so these limitations may not apply.

6. **Price Changes.**

(a) THE TOTAL CASH PRICE DELIVERED LESS THE TRADE-IN ALLOWANCE SHOWN ON THE FRONT OF THIS AGREEMENT IS THE FINAL CONTRACT PRICE TO WHICH YOU AND I HAVE AGREED. AND, IF THE VEHICLE IS A NEW MOTOR VEHICLE, NO ADDITIONAL FEE OR CHARGE WILL BE IMPOSED OR COLLECTED DUE TO CHANGES IN THE MANUFACTURER'S LIST PRICE, OR CHANGES IN THE COST OF FREIGHT OR SERVICES PROVIDED BY YOU.

(b) A REDUCTION IN THE VALUE OF THE TRADE-IN MAY RESULT IN AN INCREASE IN THE CASH PRICE DELIVERED I WILL HAVE TO PAY AS PROVIDED IN PARAGRAPH 1 OF THIS AGREEMENT.

(c) IF THE BALANCE I OWE ON MY TRADE-IN AT THE TIME OF DELIVERY OF THE TRADE-IN TO YOU IS DIFFERENT THAN THE AMOUNT I HAVE TOLD YOU AND WHICH AMOUNT IS SHOWN ON THE FRONT OF THIS AGREEMENT, THEN THE CASH PRICE DELIVERED OF THE VEHICLE I AM PURCHASING SHALL CHANGE ACCORDINGLY.

(d) IF THE REGISTRATION FEE VARIES FROM THE AMOUNT YOU HAVE ESTIMATED ON THE FRONT OF THIS AGREEMENT, THEN THE CASH PRICE DELIVERED SHALL CHANGE ACCORDINGLY.

(e) I AGREE THAT I WILL PAY THE FINAL CASH PRICE DELIVERED AS SHOWN ON THE FRONT OF THIS AGREEMENT. IF THERE HAVE BEEN ANY CHANGES IN THE TOTAL CASH PRICE DELIVERED FOR REASONS STATED IN THIS PARAGRAPH 6 THEN I WILL PAY THE CASH PRICE DELIVERED AS CHANGED BY ANY SUCH ADJUSTMENT. MY PAYMENT WILL BE EITHER IN CASH, BANK, OR CERTIFIED CHECK AT THE TIME OF DELIVERY OF THE VEHICLE I HAVE PURCHASED.

7. **Change of Design.** I understand that the manufacturer has the right to change the design of the vehicle, its chassis, accessories or any parts at any time without notice to YOU or ME. In the event of such a change by the manufacturer, YOU shall have no duty to ME except to deliver the vehicle as made by the manufacturer.

8. **No Other Agreements.** There are no understandings or agreements between you and me other than those set forth in this Agreement and attachments to this Agreement, if there are any such attachments.

9. **New York Law Applies.** You and I agree that this Agreement is governed by New York State Law.

WET 5551
[E2236]

187

RETAIL INSTALMENT CONTRACT

Meaning Of Some Words: In this Contract, the words "I," "me," "we," and "my" mean anyone signing this Contract as a Buyer. The words "you" and "your" mean the Seller, or, after the Seller transfers its rights under this Contract, anyone having those rights.

ANNUAL PERCENTAGE RATE The cost of my credit as a yearly rate.	FINANCE CHARGE The dollar amount the credit will cost me.	Amount Financed The amount of credit provided to me or on my behalf.	Total of Payments The amount I will have paid after I have made all scheduled payments.	Total Sale Price The total cost of my purchase on credit, including my downpayment of $ 2,500.00
14.55 %	$ 1,989.66	$ 8,290.50	$ 10,280.16	$ 12,780.16

My Payment Schedule will be: e means estimate

No. of Payments	Amount of Payments	When Payments Are Due
36	$ 285.56	Monthly, beginning June 15 , 1988
	$ N/A	

Security: I am giving a security interest in the motor vehicle being purchased.
Filing Fees: $ 5.00 Non-Filing Insurance: $ N/A
Late Charge: If a payment is late more than 10 days, I will be charged 5% of the payment.
Prepayment: If I pay off early, I will not have to pay a penalty.
My contract documents will have any additional information about nonpayment, default, any required repayment in full before the scheduled date, and prepayment refunds and penalties.

In this Contract
you are
the Seller. **L. Stanton Auto Sales, Inc., 1 Main Street, Buffalo, NY**

This Contract is between Seller and Buyer. All disclosures have been made by Seller. Seller intends to assign this Contract to the Assignee named below.

Name Address Zip Code

We are
the Buyer(s), **Beryl Buyer, 12 West Street, Elmira, NY   14502**

If there is more than one Buyer, each of us will be obligated separately and together, for all sums due you and the performance of all agreements as provided in this Contract.

Name(s) Address Zip Code

Description of Vehicle: (See Insurance Requirements section)

Acct. No. 13-428729
Date August 17 , 19 88

N/U	Year and Make	Series	Body Style	No. Cyl.	Truck Ton Capacity	Serial Number
	1988 Thunderwagen		2 door	4		A 1234567898

Equipped with [X] A.T. [X] P.S. [X] AM-FM Radio Other **Breakdown Insurance, Flashy**
[X] A.C. [ ] P.B. [ ] P.W. **Accessory Group**

I have traded-in the following vehicle:

Year and Make	Series	Gross	Still Owing	Net Trade-In
1984 Citron		$ 2,600.00	$ 650.00	= $ 1,950.00

Net Trade-In $ 1,950.00 Cash Downpayment + $ 550.00 Total Downpayment = $ 2,500.00

Property Insurance: I am required to obtain and maintain insurance on the Vehicle, BUT I MAY CHOOSE THE AGENT OR BROKER OF MY CHOICE.
Automobile Physical Damage Insurance: [X] Comprehensive $ 100-300M ; [X] $200 Deductible Collision $ 10,000.00 ;
[X] Towing and Labor; [ ] Other (Describe) _____ $ _____
If obtained through you, the cost of this insurance is $ 650.00 for 12 months, beginning on the date of this Contract. This insurance will be provided through us only if the premium is included in the Amount Financed shown at right.

Agent: _____

Liability insurance coverage for bodily injury and property damage is not included or provided for in this Contract.

Vendor's Single Interest Insurance: If this box is checked [ ] you require Vendor's Single Interest Insurance. I may choose the person through whom Vendor's Single Interest Insurance is to be obtained. This insurance is for the sole protection of the Assignee and my interest is not covered. If obtained through you, the cost of such insurance is $ N/A

Promise to Pay: I agree to pay you the Total Sale Price for the Vehicle by making the total Downpayment on or before the date of this Contract and paying you the Amount Financed plus credit service charge (called "interest" in this Contract) in the number and amount of monthly payments shown in the Payment Schedule. Payments are due on or before the same day of each month as the first payment date. Payments must be made at any office of:

ACE BANK (the "Assignee")

Itemization of Amount Financed

Cash Price $· 9,375.00
Total Downpayment - $ 2,500.00
Unpaid Balance of Cash Price 1 = $ 6,875.00
To Credit Insurance Company 2 + $ 300.00
To Property Insurance Company 3 + $ 650.00
To Public Officials 4 + $ 5.00
To Dir. & NYS Insp. Fees 5 + $ 15.00
To Sales Tax 6 + $ 445.00
To _____ 7 + $ N/A
Amount Financed (1 thru 7) = $ 8,290.50

REQUEST AND SCHEDULE FOR GROUP CREDIT INSURANCE

I understand that Group Credit Life Insurance and Group Credit Accident and Health Insurance are voluntary and are not required to obtain this loan. I further understand that I may select another insurer to provide this coverage.
If I choose to become insured, I understand that insurance will be provided in accordance with the certificate of group insurance that will be given to me. I also reserve the right to terminate my coverage at any time by notifying you in writing. The cost of insurance for the entire term of this loan is shown below.

[X] I WANT optional Group Credit Life Insurance. $ 125.00 Insured Buyer's present age 29
[ ] WE WANT optional Group Credit Joint Life Insurance. $ _____
[X] I WANT optional Group Credit Accident and Health Insurance. $ 175.00

Signature of Buyer *Beryl Buyer* Signature of Co-Buyer (For Joint Life Only) _____

Insurer: **DEUCE INS. CO.** Max. Amt. of Ins.: 30,000.00

Collateral: As Collateral for this Contract (to protect you if I don't pay), I give you a security interest in the Vehicle being purchased. A security interest means that if one of the events of default occurs you can take the Vehicle and under certain circumstances sell it, as is more fully explained in the Right to Demand Payment in Full and the Right to Repossess sections on the back of this Contract. "Vehicle" shall include tires, parts, equipment, replacement parts or additions to the Vehicle or any vehicle insurance refunds or any insurance proceeds resulting from loss or damage to the Vehicle. If I default (see "Right to Demand Payment in Full" section), you have the right to apply any sums that I have on deposit with you and any group insurance refunds which you receive against any balance that I owe.

I AGREE THAT THE PROVISIONS ON THE BACK ARE PART OF THIS CONTRACT. (Continued on reverse side.)

NOTICE TO THE BUYER: 1. Do not sign this Agreement before you read it or if it contains any blank space. 2. You are entitled to a completely filled in copy of this Agreement. 3. Under the law, you have the right to pay off in advance the full amount due. If you do so, you may, depending on the nature of the credit service charge, either: (a) prepay without penalty, or (b) under certain circumstances obtain a rebate of the credit service charge. 4. According to law you have the privilege of purchasing the insurance on the motor vehicle provided for in this Contract from an agent or broker of your own selection.

Seller agrees to this Contract, including the terms and conditions on back, and assigns it to the Assignee named in accordance with the first Assignment printed on the reverse side, unless otherwise marked.

I HAVE RECEIVED A COPY OF THIS CONTRACT SIGNED BY THE SELLER. RETAIL INSTALMENT CONTRACT

Seller **L. Stanton Auto Sales, Inc.** Buyer *Beryl Buyer*
(Firm Name)
By *Linda Stanton* Co-Buyer _____

BANCONSUMER FORM NY 220-SLC (Rev. 6/86) NOTICE: SEE REVERSE SIDE FOR IMPORTANT INFORMATION. ORIGINAL ©1986 BANCONSUMER SERVICE, INC. (E2237)

AUTOMOBILE RETAIL INSTALLMENT SALE CONTRACT

How The Finance Charge Is Figured: The Finance Charge, which consists only of interest, has been computed upon the basis that I will pay all instalments on the scheduled due dates. If any instalment is received later than the scheduled due date, I will be obligated to pay such additional amounts as may become payable by reason of the accrual of interest calculated daily upon the unpaid balance of the Amount Financed. In the event that any instalment is made in advance of the scheduled due date, the interest charges will be reduced accordingly. The amount of this decrease or increase will be reflected in the final payment. I shall have the right to prepay the unpaid principal balance in full or in part at any time provided that payments are first applied to accrued interest as of the date of prepayment.

How Payment In Advance Of Credit Insurance Is Figured: If I pay all amounts owing under this Contract in advance, I will receive a refund for Group Credit Insurance premiums calculated by a formula approved by the Insurance Department.

Late Charge: If I fail to pay any instalment for more than 10 days from the date it is due, I will pay a late charge of 5% of the unpaid instalment.

Collection Costs: If you hire an attorney to bring a lawsuit to collect any amount owing under this Contract, I will pay you attorney's fees up to 15% of the amount then due plus court costs or such lesser amounts as the court allows.

Insurance Requirements: I agree at all times to keep the Vehicle insured with comprehensive, fire and theft, and a minimum amount of deductible collision insurance satisfactory to you, endorsed to protect you with a licensed insurance company. If I fail to insure my Vehicle, you may do so and I agree to pay the cost. I agree that any insurance moneys payable by reason of damage to or loss of the Vehicle shall be paid directly and solely to you and may be used to pay my debt to you. If the Vehicle is lost or damaged, you can use the insurance proceeds (money) to replace or repair it, or to repay any amounts I owe you, and I agree that, if necessary, you can settle any insurance claims or sign any insurance checks on my behalf. I agree that loss, damage to or destruction of the Vehicle shall not affect my duty to make the payments under this Contract.

Payment After All Amounts Owing Become Immediately Due: Under certain circumstances, you can declare all amounts owing under this Contract immediately due. If you do and all amounts owing are paid or you sue for them and obtain a judgment, you will calculate what I owe as if I were going to pay in advance.

Right to Demand Payment in Full: Upon the following events of default, you can require that the entire balance of my loan be paid at once, without prior notice or demand if:
1. I do not pay an instalment on time; or
2. I break one of my promises under this Contract; or
3. I have made any false or misleading statement on this Contract and/or credit application; or
4. Your name does not appear as the only "lienholder" (claim) on any certificate of title issued now or in the future; or
5. The Vehicle is lost or damaged without adequate insurance coverage; or sold, or given away, or seized; or
6. I file bankruptcy or if any proceeding is instituted to seek relief from my debts; or
7. I die or become legally unable to manage my affairs; or
8. Something else happens that you reasonably feel affects my ability to pay the remaining instalments when due.

Right to Repossess: You can repossess (take) the Vehicle if one of the events of default (listed in the Right to Demand Payment in Full section) occurs. After my default, I will deliver the Vehicle upon your request or you can enter the premises where it is kept and take it yourself (as permitted by law) and you need not notify me before you do this. You can sell the Vehicle after repossession and apply the proceeds to the balance of what I owe after deducting your reasonable repossession, storage, repair, preparation for sale and selling expenses. You will send me 7 days' notice by mail of any sale of the Vehicle. I can still recover the Vehicle before you sell it by paying any amounts past due under this Contract and any charges you are legally entitled to.
To recover any articles I claim were contained in the Collateral but were contained in the Vehicle, I must notify you in writing within 7 days after repossession. Failure to claim and take possession of these items promptly will be an abandonment of them.
If the sale doesn't cover all that I owe, I will be responsible for the amount still owed. If there is any surplus money it will be refunded to me.

Care of Vehicle: I agree: to keep the Vehicle in good condition and repair; not to remove it from the address at which it is presently kept without your prior written consent; not to sell or transfer it or use it as Collateral in another transaction; not to use the Vehicle nor permit its use in any illegal manner; not to allow someone else to seize the Vehicle or create a lien (claim) on it; to give you immediate written notice of loss or damage to the Vehicle.

Trade-In and Downpayment: I guarantee that I own the Vehicle traded in, if any, and that it is free from any lien or security interest not shown in the "Trade-In" section. I also represent that I have made the downpayment and have not borrowed it.

Title and Security Interest: If the Vehicle is already titled or is to be titled, I guarantee that I am or will be the registered owner and your security interest shall appear as the only security on any certificate of title now or hereafter issued. I agree that you can apply for title certificates to show your security interest and I agree to assist you in doing so. I also give you permission to file a financing statement (notice of your security interest filed for public record) covering your security interest without my signature on it.

Waivers and Releases: You can waive or delay enforcing any of your rights without losing them. You can waive or delay enforcing a right as to one of us without waiving it as to the other. You need not give anyone notice of the waiver, delay or release. Your failure to file a security interest, failure to keep the Vehicle insured, release of a security interest or granting extensions of times of payment shall not affect my obligation under this Contract.

Applicable Law: This Contract shall be governed by New York Law. If any provision is found to be ineffective under any law or regulation, the remainder will still be binding and effective.

(The following notice shall not apply to any sale for other than personal, family, or household use.)

NOTICE: ANY HOLDER OF THIS CONSUMER CREDIT CONTRACT IS SUBJECT TO ALL CLAIMS AND DEFENSES WHICH THE DEBTOR COULD ASSERT AGAINST THE SELLER OF GOODS OR SERVICES OBTAINED PURSUANT HERETO OR WITH THE PROCEEDS HEREOF. RECOVERY HEREUNDER BY THE DEBTOR SHALL NOT EXCEED AMOUNTS PAID BY THE DEBTOR HEREUNDER.

WARRANTIES: If this Contract involves the sale of a new Vehicle, the Seller makes no warranty, either express or implied, including any implied warranty of merchantability or fitness for a particular purpose, except for any warranty set forth in the Buyer's Guide for used cars.

IF THIS CONTRACT INVOLVES THE SALE OF A USED VEHICLE, AS DEFINED UNDER 16 CFR PART 455, THE INFORMATION I SEE ON THE WINDOW FORM FOR THIS VEHICLE IS PART OF THIS CONTRACT. INFORMATION ON THE WINDOW FORM OVERRIDES ANY CONTRARY PROVISIONS IN THE CONTRACT OF SALE.

Third Party Guarantee: In consideration of your entering into this Contract with Buyer, I guarantee to you prompt payment of all sums due under this Contract if Buyer fails to pay them promptly. I understand that you can extend the terms of payment without notice to me, release any security which you may have, fail to keep the Vehicle insured, or fail to have your security interest recorded, and that this will not affect my duty to make the payments under this Contract if the Buyer defaults.

Witness _____   Guarantor _____

Address _____   Guarantor _____

ASSIGNMENT

For value received, the Seller hereby sells, transfers and assigns to Assignee named on the face hereof, its successors and assigns, all right, title and interest in this Contract and to the Vehicle described in this Contract and to all moneys due and to become due under this Contract and any guaranty made in connection with this Contract. Seller warrants that this Contract is genuine, unamended and enforceable without defense or counterclaim, that all parties to the Contract are over eighteen years of age and have legal capacity to execute the Contract, that the Buyer (or Co-Buyer) has accepted delivery of the Vehicle and it is registered and titled to the Buyer, that the Cash Downpayment has been paid to Seller and has not been borrowed to Seller's knowledge, that the Assignee is acquiring a purchase money security interest in the Vehicle free and clear of any lien, claim and encumbrance, and that if Assignee requests Seller to do so and pays Seller the appropriate fee, the Seller will immediately cause Assignee's name to appear on the Certificate of Title as the first and only lienholder. If Buyer has indicated he wishes any group credit insurance, Seller warrants that such coverage has been obtained and paid for and agrees to hold Assignee harmless from any claims with respect to such insurance, and promptly to make the appropriate refunds if such insurance is canceled and/or the Contract is prepaid. Upon a breach of any of the provisions in this assignment or if the Buyer, Co-Buyer or Guarantor notify (orally or in writing) Assignee that they have any claim or defense arising out of this Contract or under Sections 198-a or 198-b of the New York General Business Law — whether or not there is a default in payment — Seller agrees, on demand, immediately to repurchase this Contract for the unpaid balance including earned Finance Charges as of the date of repurchase. Seller agrees to hold harmless and indemnify Assignee for any loss sustained as a result of any claim or defense Buyer, Co-Buyer or Guarantor may have against Seller, whether or not this loss is sustained as a result of a judicial determination. Seller hereby consents to any extensions of time for payment; modification of terms; release or substitution of parties or Vehicle; and agrees that the Assignee's failure to perfect its lien on the Vehicle will not affect this assignment.

FULL RECOURSE ASSIGNMENT

Seller agrees, in addition to the warranties above, that in the event of default by Buyer in the full payment on the due date thereof of any instalment payable under the Contract or in the prompt performance of any other obligation to be performed under the Contract by Buyer, Seller will, upon demand by Assignee forthwith repurchase the Contract from Assignee for a repurchase price in cash equal to the full unpaid balance of the Contract as of the date of such repurchase, including any earned Finance Charge.

Auto Sales, Inc.
_____
Seller

Luida Stantru, President   September 1, 1988
Title   Date

OTHER ASSIGNMENT

Seller agrees, in addition to the warranties stated in the first Assignment section set forth above, that if the Buyer defaults in any manner under this Contract the following additional covenants shall apply, such covenants being more specifically defined in an agreement between Seller and Assignee.

_____   _____
Type of Assignment   Seller

_____   _____
Date   Title   (E2238)

BANCONSUMER FORM NY 220 SLC (Rev 6/86)   NOTICE: SEE OTHER SIDE FOR IMPORTANT INFORMATION.

189

SELECTED FORMS

<table>
<tr><td colspan="2">Type of Prop <u>RESIDENTIAL</u> Total Rooms <u>7</u></td></tr>
<tr><td>Lock Box No</td><td>No Bedrooms <u>3</u></td></tr>
<tr><td>Comm Split <u>50/50</u></td><td>No Baths <u>1/2</u></td></tr>
</table>

EXCLUSIVE RIGHT TO SELL AGREEMENT
Distributed by
STAMFORD MULTIPLE LISTING SERVICE, INC.
16 Third Street Stamford Conn 06905
TEL 327-3411

LISTING OFFICE USE

No. xxxxx

LOCATION OF LISTED PROPERTY <u>175 PARKWAY DRIVE</u> AREA # <u>9</u> LISTED PRICE <u>299 000.</u>
OWNER'S NAME <u>JOHN AND MARY DOE</u> EXPIRATION DATE <u>XXXXX</u>
OWNER'S ADDRESS <u>SAME AS ABOVE</u> TEL NO <u>XXXXXXX</u> BUS <u>XXXXXXX</u>
FURNISHED RENTAL _____ UNFURNISHED _____ TERM _____

THE OWNER(S) WHO SIGNED THIS AGREEMENT, REQUEST AND EMPLOY THE AGENT SHOWN BELOW TO SELL (OR LEASE) THE ABOVE MENTIONED PROPERTY AT THE PRICE SHOWN ABOVE, AND TO CIRCULATE THE LISTING THROUGH THE **STAMFORD MULTIPLE LISTING SERVICE, INC.**

THE AGENT AGREES TO PUT FORTH EFFORTS TO SELL THIS PROPERTY THROUGH THEIR OFFICE. THE LISTING IS TO BE RECEIVED WITHIN 24 HOURS AT THE **STAMFORD MULTIPLE LISTING SERVICE, INC.** TO BE CIRCULATED TO THE MEMBER OFFICES OF THE **STAMFORD MULTIPLE LISTING SERVICE, INC.**

THE OWNER(S) AGREE TO GIVE THE AGENT THE SOLE AND EXCLUSIVE RIGHT, SUBJECT TO THE CONDITIONS SET FORTH ON THIS FORM, TO SELL (OR LEASE) THE PROPERTY. IT IS CLEARLY UNDERSTOOD THAT IF THE OWNER(S) SELLS OR RENTS THE PROPERTY HIMSELF. HE MUST STILL PAY THE FULL SERVICE FEE TO THE LISTING AGENT

THE OWNER(S) AGREE TO REFER TO THE AGENT ALL INQUIRIES FROM BUYERS OR BROKERS

"NOTICE: THE AMOUNT OR RATE OF REAL ESTATE COMMISSIONS IS NOT FIXED BY LAW. THEY ARE SET BY EACH BROKER INDIVIDUALLY AND MAY BE NEGOTIABLE BETWEEN THE SELLER AND BROKER" (PUBLIC ACT 80-99)

THE OWNER(S) AGREE TO PAY THE AGENT A FEE OF <u>6</u> % OF THE AGREED SALES PRICE, OR IF LEASED <u>10</u> % OF THE FIRST YEAR'S GROSS RENTAL AND <u>5</u> % THEREAFTER, FOR FULL PERIOD OF OCCUPANCY PAYABLE UPON SIGNING OF LEASE VACANT LAND ONLY _____ % SHOULD THE TENANT PURCHASE THE RENTED PROPERTY. THE SELLING FEE SHALL BE DUE AND PAYABLE TO THE RENTING AGENT FROM THE OWNER(S)

THIS AGREEMENT WILL BE IN EFFECT STARTING <u>XXXXX</u> AND WILL END <u>XXXXX</u> IF DURING THE TERM OF THIS AGREEMENT A BROKER HAS INTRODUCED A BUYER TO THE PROPERTY, INTERESTED HIM IN THE PURCHASE THE BROKER'S RIGHT TO THE SERVICE FEE WITH RESPECT TO THE SALE MADE TO THIS BUYER SHALL NOT BE TERMINATED IF THE SALE IS CONSUMMATED WITHIN <u>3</u> MONTHS AFTER THIS AGREEMENT EXPIRES, AND NO NEW MULTIPLE LISTING AGREEMENT BECOMES EFFECTIVE DURING THAT SAME PERIOD

THE PURPOSE OF THIS AGREEMENT IS TO LIST THE ABOVE PROPERTY FOR SALE (OR LEASE) AND THE AGENT IS NOT RESPONSIBLE FOR MAINTENANCE OR UPKEEP OF THE PROPERTY OR FOR ANY PHYSICAL DAMAGE DONE TO THE PROPERTY WHILE THIS LISTING IS IN EFFECT. THE AGENT IS NOT RESPONSIBLE FOR THE ACCURACY OF THE INFORMATION SUPPLIED BY THE OWNER(S). TO THE AGENT

AGENT IS AUTHORIZED TO POST A SIGN YES ☐ NO ☐ INSTALL A LOCK BOX YES ☒ NO ☐ INITIALED <u>JD</u>

THIS AGREEMENT IS SUBJECT TO SECTION 46a-64 OF THE GENERAL STATUTES AS AMENDED (PUBLIC ACCOMMODATIONS ACT)

THE OWNER(S) AGREE TO PAY AGENT'S REASONABLE LEGAL FEES AND COSTS OF COLLECTION OF ANY COMMISSIONS THAT ARE DUE UNDER THIS AGREEMENT

Architecture <u>COLONIAL</u> Material <u>SHINGLE</u> Rms <u>7</u> Age <u>13 YRS</u>
Date of Occupancy <u>IMMEDIATE</u> Lot <u>80' X 300' (24,000 SF), LOCK BOX — VACANT</u>
1st Fl Foyer <u>X</u> Porch <u>DECK</u> LR <u>X</u> FP _____ DR <u>X</u> Kitchen <u>EAT-IN</u>
Den _____ FP _____ Bedroom _____ Bath <u>1/2</u> Playroom <u>X</u> W/FP Other _____
2nd Fl Bedroom <u>3</u> Baths <u>1</u> Other _____
3rd Fl _____ Attic <u>X</u>
Lower Level _____
Garage <u>1 CAR/EE</u> Cellar <u>FULL</u> Screens <u>X</u> Storms <u>X</u> Thermo _____ Heat <u>ELEC. HP</u> Cost <u>1700</u>
Septic <u>X</u> Sewer _____ Sewer Asst _____ Water <u>CITY</u> Taxes <u>2300./YR APPROX</u>
Tax Assessment Land <u>28,350</u> Dwelling <u>55,120</u> Other _____ Total <u>83,470</u>
New Homes Only INSULATION Type _____ Thickness _____ R-Value _____
Stove <u>ELEC.</u> Refrig <u>X</u> Dishwasher <u>X</u> Washer <u>X</u> Dryer <u>X</u>
SCHOOLS Elementary <u>NCR</u> Middle <u>TLR</u> High <u>SHS</u>
RENTED EQUIPMENT <u>HOT WATER HEATER - 8.00/MO</u> Zone District <u>C/S</u>
REMARKS: <u>BRICKED WALL IN SPACIOUS FAMILY ROOM. BUILT-INS ON A CUL-DE-SAC. CONVENIENT LOCATION. IMMACULATE CONDITION. CLOSE TO TRANSPORTATION</u>

THE UNDERSIGNED OWNER(S) HEREBY VERIFY THAT THEY HAVE LEGAL TITLE TO THIS PROPERTY AND HAVE THE RIGHT TO SELL OR LEASE THE ABOVE DESCRIBED PROPERTY

Accepted for <u>MAYBERRY REALTY</u> Signed this <u>X</u> day of <u>XXX</u> 19 <u>XX</u>
By <u>FRANK SMITH</u> <u>John Doe</u>
Firm Address <u>50 MAIN STREET</u> <u>MARY DOE</u>
City <u>STAMFORD</u> State <u>CT</u> Zip <u>06901</u> <u>SAME AS ABOVE</u>
Telephone No <u>XXX-XXXX</u>

NOTE: THE INFORMATION SHOWN ABOVE IS AS GIVEN BY THE SELLER AND INTENDED TO BE ACCURATE BUT NOT GUARANTEED BY THE AGENT. THIS IS A LEGALLY BINDING CONTRACT. IF NOT UNDERSTOOD, SEEK LEGAL ADVICE

LISTING FIRM'S COPY

REAL ESTATE BROKER'S AGREEMENT

STANDARD CONSTRUCTION AGREEMENT

The following form, supplied by the American Institute of Architects, appears also in the "AIA Handbook," or Architect's Handbook of Professional Practice. The forms appearing there have been revised periodically, and the Institute cautions that "when using AIA forms, the user should ascertain the latest edition." The one presented here is AIA Document A107—1987.

Beginning with Article 7 of the form, the material consists largely of text, considerably abbreviated and rearranged, from the "General Conditions of the Contract for Construction" (AIA Document A201). The AIA Handbook traces the history of this document to its origin in a Uniform Contract of 1888. It is said to be "a recognized standard of the American construction industry." In its 1987 edition, it represents a consensus of leaders in the industry, resulting from a century of testing in practice and in the courts.

The Conditions of the Contract (General, Supplementary and other) are said to form three of the six parts of any construction contract, the others being the Drawings, the Specifications, and the Owner–Contractor Agreement. "The General Conditions of the Contract are standardized contractual provisions describing the rights, responsibilities and relations of parties to the Construction Contract, as well as the related duties and responsibilities of the Architect, and are generally exclusive of procedural provisions. . . . For the most part, the General Conditions are suitable for both private or public work. . . . The Supplementary Conditions, drafted in collaboration with the Owner and the Owner's legal counsel for each project, modify or extend the General Conditions as the special details of each project may require. . . . 'Other' Conditions refers to situations where a standard set of Supplementary Conditions must be further complemented." Handbook, Chapter 13.

The Institute discourages any use of the General Conditions except in full, and in the printed form supplied by it. "The value of AIA Document A201 lies partly in the fact that its frequent users—architects, contractors, subcontractors and owners—become thoroughly familiar with its provisions, have confidence in their fairness, and recognize its format at a glance. . . . [I]ndividual practitioners are ill-advised to substitute their own provisions without expert advice since they may thereby unknowingly weaken the relationships among the document's provisions or between AIA Document A201 and the Agreements and other coordinated documents mentioned earlier." Ibid.

The text of the General Conditions extends to some 15 pages.

T H E   A M E R I C A N   I N S T I T U T E   O F   A R C H I T E C T S

AIA Document A107

Abbreviated Form of Agreement Between Owner and Contractor

For CONSTRUCTION PROJECTS OF LIMITED SCOPE where the Basis of Payment is a STIPULATED SUM

1987 EDITION

THIS DOCUMENT HAS IMPORTANT LEGAL CONSEQUENCES; CONSULTATION WITH AN ATTORNEY IS ENCOURAGED WITH RESPECT TO ITS COMPLETION OR MODIFICATION.

This document includes abbreviated General Conditions and should not be used with other general conditions. It has been approved and endorsed by The Associated General Contractors of America.

AGREEMENT

made as of the   day of   in the year of
Nineteen Hundred and

BETWEEN the Owner:
(Name and address)

and the Contractor:
(Name and address)

The Project is:
(Name and location)

The Architect is:
(Name and address)

The Owner and Contractor agree as set forth below.

AIA DOCUMENT A107 • ABBREVIATED OWNER-CONTRACTOR AGREEMENT • NINTH EDITION • AIA® • © 1987
THE AMERICAN INSTITUTE OF ARCHITECTS, 1735 NEW YORK AVENUE, N.W., WASHINGTON, D.C. 20006

A107-1987   **1**
[E2239]

SELECTED FORMS

ARTICLE 1
THE WORK OF THIS CONTRACT

1.1 The Contractor shall execute the entire Work described in the Contract Documents, except to the extent specifically indicated in the Contract Documents to be the responsibility of others, or as follows:

ARTICLE 2
DATE OF COMMENCEMENT AND SUBSTANTIAL COMPLETION

2.1 The date of commencement is the date from which the Contract Time of Paragraph 2.2 is measured, and shall be the date of this Agreement, as first written above, unless a different date is stated below or provision is made for the date to be fixed in a notice to proceed issued by the Owner.
(Insert the date of commencement, if it differs from the date of this Agreement or, if applicable, state that the date will be fixed in a notice to proceed.)

2.2 The Contractor shall achieve Substantial Completion of the entire Work not later than
(Insert the calendar date or number of calendar days after the date of commencement. Also insert any requirements for earlier Substantial Completion of certain portions of the Work, if not stated elsewhere in the Contract Documents.)

, subject to adjustments of this Contract Time as provided in the Contract Documents.
(Insert provisions, if any, for liquidated damages relating to failure to complete on time.)

ARTICLE 3
CONTRACT SUM

3.1 The Owner shall pay the Contractor in current funds for the Contractor's performance of the Contract the Contract Sum of
Dollars
($), subject to additions and deductions as provided in the Contract
Documents.

AIA DOCUMENT A107 • ABBREVIATED OWNER-CONTRACTOR AGREEMENT • NINTH EDITION • AIA® • © 1987
THE AMERICAN INSTITUTE OF ARCHITECTS, 1735 NEW YORK AVENUE, N.W., WASHINGTON, D.C. 20006

A107-1987 2
[E2240]

SELECTED FORMS

3.2 The Contract Sum is based upon the following alternates, if any, which are described in the Contract Documents and are hereby accepted by the Owner:

(State the numbers or other identification of accepted alternates. If decisions on other alternates are to be made by the Owner subsequent to the execution of this Agreement, attach a schedule of such other alternates showing the amount for each and the date until which that amount is valid.)

3.3 Unit prices, if any, are as follows:

ARTICLE 4
PROGRESS PAYMENTS

4.1 Based upon Applications for Payment submitted to the Architect by the Contractor and Certificates for Payment issued by the Architect, the Owner shall make progress payments on account of the Contract Sum to the Contractor as provided below and elsewhere in the Contract Documents. The period covered by each Application for Payment shall be one calendar month ending on the last day of the month, or as follows:

4.2 Payments due and unpaid under the Contract shall bear interest from the date payment is due at the rate stated below, or in the absence thereof, at the legal rate prevailing from time to time at the place where the Project is located.

(Insert rate of interest agreed upon, if any.)

(Usury laws and requirements under the Federal Truth in Lending Act, similar state and local consumer credit laws and other regulations at the Owner's and Contractor's principal places of business, the location of the Project and elsewhere may affect the validity of this provision. Legal advice should be obtained with respect to deletions or modifications, and also regarding requirements such as written disclosures or waivers.)

SELECTED FORMS

ARTICLE 5
FINAL PAYMENT

5.1 Final payment, constituting the entire unpaid balance of the Contract Sum, shall be made by the Owner to the Contractor when the Work has been completed, the Contract fully performed, and a final Certificate for Payment has been issued by the Architect.

ARTICLE 6
ENUMERATION OF CONTRACT DOCUMENTS

6.1 The Contract Documents are listed in Article 7 and, except for Modifications issued after execution of this Agreement, are enumerated as follows:

6.1.1 The Agreement is this executed Abbreviated Form of Agreement Between Owner and Contractor, AIA Document A107, 1987 Edition.

6.1.2 The Supplementary and other Conditions of the Contract are those contained in the Project Manual dated
, and are as follows:

Document	Title	Pages

6.1.3. The Specifications are those contained in the Project Manual dated as in Subparagraph 6.1.2, and are as follows:
(Either list the Specifications here or refer to an exhibit attached to this Agreement.)

Section	Title	Pages

AIA DOCUMENT A107 • ABBREVIATED OWNER-CONTRACTOR AGREEMENT • NINTH EDITION • AIA® • 1987
THE AMERICAN INSTITUTE OF ARCHITECTS, 1735 NEW YORK AVENUE, N.W., WASHINGTON, D.C. 20006

A107-1987   4
[E2242]

195

6.1.4 The Drawings are as follows, and are dated   unless a different date is shown below:
(Either list the Drawings here or refer to an exhibit attached to this Agreement.)

Number   **Title**   **Date**

6.1.5 The Addenda, if any, are as follows:

Number   **Date**   **Pages**

Portions of Addenda relating to bidding requirements are not part of the Contract Documents unless the bidding requirements are also enumerated in this Article 6.

6.1.6 Other documents, if any, forming part of the Contract Documents are as follows:
(List any additional documents which are intended to form part of the Contract Documents.)

AIA DOCUMENT A107 • ABBREVIATED OWNER-CONTRACTOR AGREEMENT • NINTH EDITION • AIA® • © 1987
THE AMERICAN INSTITUTE OF ARCHITECTS, 1735 NEW YORK AVENUE, N.W., WASHINGTON, D.C. 20006   **A107-1987** **5**
[E2243]

SELECTED FORMS

GENERAL CONDITIONS

ARTICLE 7
CONTRACT DOCUMENTS

7.1 The Contract Documents consist of this Agreement with Conditions of the Contract (General, Supplementary and other Conditions), Drawings, Specifications, addenda issued prior to the execution of this Agreement, other documents listed in this Agreement and Modifications issued after execution of this Agreement. The intent of the Contract Documents is to include all items necessary for the proper execution and completion of the Work by the Contractor. The Contract Documents are complementary, and what is required by one shall be as binding as if required by all; performance by the Contractor shall be required only to the extent consistent with the Contract Documents and reasonably inferable from them as being necessary to produce the intended results.

7.2 The Contract Documents shall not be construed to create a contractual relationship of any kind (1) between the Architect and Contractor, (2) between the Owner and a Subcontractor or Sub-subcontractor or (3) between any persons or entities other than the Owner and Contractor.

7.3 Execution of the Contract by the Contractor is a representation that the Contractor has visited the site and become familiar with the local conditions under which the Work is to be performed.

7.4 The term "Work" means the construction and services required by the Contract Documents, whether completed or partially completed, and includes all other labor, materials, equipment and services provided or to be provided by the Contractor to fulfill the Contractor's obligations. The Work may constitute the whole or a part of the Project.

ARTICLE 8
OWNER

8.1 The Owner shall furnish surveys and a legal description of the site.

8.2 Except for permits and fees which are the responsibility of the Contractor under the Contract Documents, the Owner shall secure and pay for necessary approvals, easements, assessments and charges required for the construction, use or occupancy of permanent structures or permanent changes in existing facilities.

8.3 If the Contractor fails to correct Work which is not in accordance with the requirements of the Contract Documents or persistently fails to carry out the Work in accordance with the Contract Documents, the Owner, by a written order, may order the Contractor to stop the Work, or any portion thereof, until the cause for such order has been eliminated; however, the right of the Owner to stop the Work shall not give rise to a duty on the part of the Owner to exercise this right for the benefit of the Contractor or any other person or entity.

ARTICLE 9
CONTRACTOR

9.1 The Contractor shall supervise and direct the Work, using the Contractor's best skill and attention. The Contractor shall be solely responsible for and have control over construction means, methods, techniques, sequences and procedures and for coordinating all portions of the Work under the Contract, unless Contract Documents give other specific instructions concerning these matters.

9.2 Unless otherwise provided in the Contract Documents, the Contractor shall provide and pay for labor, materials, equipment, tools, construction equipment and machinery, water, heat, utilities, transportation, and other facilities and services necessary for the proper execution and completion of the Work, whether temporary or permanent and whether or not incorporated or to be incorporated in the Work.

9.3 The Contractor shall enforce strict discipline and good order among the Contractor's employees and other persons carrying out the Contract. The Contractor shall not permit employment of unfit persons or persons not skilled in tasks assigned to them.

9.4 The Contractor warrants to the Owner and Architect that materials and equipment furnished under the Contract will be of good quality and new unless otherwise required or permitted by the Contract Documents, and that the Work will be free from defects not inherent in the quality required or permitted, and that the Work will conform with the requirements of the Contract Documents. Work not conforming to these requirements, including substitutions not properly approved and authorized, may be considered defective. The Contractor's warranty excludes remedy for damage or defect caused by abuse, modifications not executed by the Contractor, improper or insufficient maintenance, improper operation, or normal wear and tear under normal usage. If required by the Architect, the Contractor shall furnish satisfactory evidence as to the kind and quality of materials and equipment.

9.5 Unless otherwise provided in the Contract Documents, the Contractor shall pay sales, consumer, use, and other similar taxes which are legally enacted when bids are received or negotiations concluded, whether or not yet effective or merely scheduled to go into effect, and shall secure and pay for the building permit and other permits and governmental fees, licenses and inspections necessary for proper execution and completion of the Work.

9.6 The Contractor shall comply with and give notices required by laws, ordinances, rules, regulations, and lawful orders of public authorities bearing on performance of the Work. The Contractor shall promptly notify the Architect and Owner if the Drawings and Specifications are observed by the Contractor to be at variance therewith.

9.7 The Contractor shall be responsible to the Owner for the acts and omissions of the Contractor's employees, Subcontractors and their agents and employees, and other persons performing portions of the Work under a contract with the Contractor.

9.8 The Contractor shall review, approve and submit to the Architect Shop Drawings, Product Data, Samples and similar submittals required by the Contract Documents with reasonable promptness. The Work shall be in accordance with approved submittals. When professional certification of performance criteria of materials, systems or equipment is required by the Contract Documents, the Architect shall be entitled to rely upon the accuracy and completeness of such certifications.

9.9 The Contractor shall keep the premises and surrounding area free from accumulation of waste materials or rubbish caused by operations under the Contract. At completion of the Work the Contractor shall remove from and about the Project waste materials, rubbish, the Contractor's tools, construction equipment, machinery and surplus materials.

9.10 The Contractor shall provide the Owner and Architect access to the Work in preparation and progress wherever located.

9.11 The Contractor shall pay all royalties and license fees; shall defend suits or claims for infringement of patent rights and shall hold the Owner harmless from loss on account thereof, but shall not be responsible for such defense or loss when a particular design, process or product of a particular manufacturer or manufacturers is required by the Contract Documents unless the Contractor has reason to believe that there is an infringement of patent.

9.12 To the fullest extent permitted by law, the Contractor shall indemnify and hold harmless the Owner, Architect, Architect's consultants, and agents and employees of any of them from and against claims, damages, losses and expenses, including but not limited to attorneys' fees, arising out of or resulting from performance of the Work, provided that such claim, damage, loss or expense is attributable to bodily injury, sickness, disease or death, or to injury to or destruction of tangible property (other than the Work itself) including loss of use resulting therefrom, but only to the extent caused in whole or in part by negligent acts or omissions of the Contractor, a Subcontractor, anyone directly or indirectly employed by them or anyone for whose acts they may be liable, regardless of whether or not such claim, damage, loss or expense is caused in part by a party indemnified hereunder. Such obligation shall not be construed to negate, abridge, or reduce other rights or obligations of indemnity which would otherwise exist as to a party or person described in this Paragraph 9.12.

9.12.1 In claims against any person or entity indemnified under this Paragraph 9.12 by an employee of the Contractor, a Subcontractor, anyone directly or indirectly employed by them or anyone for whose acts they may be liable, the indemnification obligation under this Paragraph 9.12 shall not be limited by a limitation on amount or type of damages, compensation or benefits payable by or for the Contractor or a Subcontractor under workers' or workmen's compensation acts, disability benefit acts or other employee benefit acts.

9.12.2 The obligations of the Contractor under this Paragraph 9.12 shall not extend to the liability of the Architect, the Architect's consultants, and agents and employees of any of them arising out of (1) the preparation or approval of maps, drawings, opinions, reports, surveys, Change Orders, Construction Change Directives, designs or specifications, or (2) the giving of or the failure to give directions or instructions by the Architect, the Architect's consultants, and agents and employees of any of them provided such giving or failure to give is the primary cause of the injury or damage.

ARTICLE 10
ADMINISTRATION OF THE CONTRACT

10.1 The Architect will provide administration of the Contract and will be the Owner's representative (1) during construction, (2) until final payment is due and (3) with the Owner's concurrence, from time to time during the correction period described in Paragraph 18.1

10.2 The Architect will visit the site at intervals appropriate to the stage of construction to become generally familiar with the progress and quality of the completed Work and to determine in general if the Work is being performed in a manner indicating that the Work, when completed, will be in accordance with the Contract Documents. However, the Architect will not be required to make exhaustive or continuous on-site inspections to check quality or quantity of the Work. On the basis of on-site observations as an architect, the Architect will keep the Owner informed of progress of the Work and will endeavor to guard the Owner against defects and deficiencies in the Work.

10.3 The Architect will not have control over or charge of and will not be responsible for construction means, methods, techniques, sequences or procedures, or for safety precautions and programs in connection with the Work, since these are solely the Contractor's responsibility as provided in Paragraphs 9.1 and 16.1. The Architect will not be responsible for the Contractor's failure to carry out the Work in accordance with the Contract Documents.

10.4 Based on the Architect's observations and evaluations of the Contractor's Applications for Payment, the Architect will review and certify the amounts due the Contractor and will issue Certificates for Payment in such amounts.

10.5 The Architect will interpret and decide matters concerning performance under and requirements of the Contract Documents on written request of either the Owner or Contractor. The Architect will make initial decisions on all claims, disputes or other matters in question between the Owner and Contractor, but will not be liable for results of any interpretations or decisions rendered in good faith. The Architect's decisions in matters relating to aesthetic effect will be final if consistent with the intent expressed in the Contract Documents. All other decisions of the Architect, except those which have been waived by making or acceptance of final payment, shall be subject to arbitration upon the written demand of either party.

10.6 The Architect will have authority to reject Work which does not conform to the Contract Documents.

10.7 The Architect will review and approve or take other appropriate action upon the Contractor's submittals such as Shop Drawings, Product Data and Samples, but only for the limited purpose of checking for conformance with information given and the design concept expressed in the Contract Documents.

10.8 All claims or disputes between the Contractor and the Owner arising out or relating to the Contract, or the breach thereof, shall be decided by arbitration in accordance with the Construction Industry Arbitration Rules of the American Arbitration Association currently in effect unless the parties mutually agree otherwise and subject to an initial presentation of the claim or dispute to the Architect as required under Paragraph 10.5. Notice of the demand for arbitration shall be filed in writing with the other party to this Agreement and with the American Arbitration Association and shall be made within a reasonable time after the dispute has arisen. The award rendered by

7 A107-1987
AIA DOCUMENT A107 • ABBREVIATED OWNER-CONTRACTOR AGREEMENT • NINTH EDITION • AIA® • 1987
THE AMERICAN INSTITUTE OF ARCHITECTS, 1735 NEW YORK AVENUE, N.W., WASHINGTON, D.C. 20006
[E2245]

198

SELECTED FORMS

the arbitrator or arbitrators shall be final, and judgment may be entered upon it in accordance with applicable law in any court having jurisdiction thereof. Except by written consent of the person or entity sought to be joined, no arbitration arising out of or relating to the Contract Documents shall include, by consolidation, joinder or in any other manner, any person or entity not a party to the Agreement under which such arbitration arises, unless it is shown at the time the demand for arbitration is filed that (1) such person or entity is substantially involved in a common question of fact or law, (2) the presence of such person or entity is required if complete relief is to be accorded in the arbitration, (3) the interest or responsibility of such person or entity in the matter is not insubstantial, and (4) such person or entity is not the Architect or any of the Architect's employees or consultants. The agreement herein among the parties to the Agreement and any other written agreement to arbitrate referred to herein shall be specifically enforceable under applicable law in any court having jurisdiction thereof.

ARTICLE 11
SUBCONTRACTS

11.1 A Subcontractor is a person or entity who has a direct contract with the Contractor to perform a portion of the Work at the site.

11.2 Unless otherwise stated in the Contract Documents or the bidding requirements, the Contractor, as soon as practicable after award of the Contract, shall furnish in writing to the Owner through the Architect the names of the Subcontractors for each of the principal portions of the Work. The Contractor shall not contract with any Subcontractor to whom the Owner or Architect has made reasonable and timely objection. The Contractor shall not be required to contract with anyone to whom the Contractor has made reasonable objection. Contracts between the Contractor and Subcontractors shall (1) require each Subcontractor, to the extent of the Work to be performed by the Subcontractor to be bound to the Contractor by the terms of the Contract Documents, and to assume toward the Contractor all the obligations and responsibilities which the Contractor, by the Contract Documents, assumes toward the Owner and Architect, and (2) allow to the Subcontractor the benefit of all rights, remedies and redress afforded to the Contractor by these Contract Documents.

ARTICLE 12
CONSTRUCTION BY OWNER OR BY SEPARATE CONTRACTORS

12.1 The Owner reserves the right to perform construction or operations related to the Project with the Owner's own forces, and to award separate contracts in connection with other portions of the Project or other construction or operations on the site under conditions of the contract identical or substantially similar to these, including those portions related to insurance and waiver of subrogation. If the Contractor claims that delay or additional cost is involved because of such action by the Owner, the Contractor shall make such claim as provided elsewhere in the Contract Documents.

12.2 The Contractor shall afford the Owner and separate contractors reasonable opportunity for the introduction and storage of their materials and equipment and performance of their activities, and shall connect and coordinate the Contractor's construction and operations with theirs as required by the Contract Documents.

12.3 Costs caused by delays, improperly timed activities or defective construction shall be borne by the party responsible therefor.

ARTICLE 13
CHANGES IN THE WORK

13.1 The Owner, without invalidating the Contract, may order changes in the Work consisting of additions, deletions or modifications, the Contract Sum and Contract Time being adjusted accordingly. Such changes in the Work shall be authorized by written Change Order signed by the Owner, Contractor and Architect, or by written Construction Change Directive signed by the Owner and Architect.

13.2 The Contract Sum and Contract Time shall be changed only by Change Order.

13.3 The cost or credit to the Owner from a change in the Work shall be determined by mutual agreement.

ARTICLE 14
TIME

14.1 Time limits stated in the Contract Documents are of the essence of the Contract. By executing the Agreement the Contractor confirms that the Contract Time is a reasonable period for performing the Work.

14.2 The date of Substantial Completion is the date certified by the Architect in accordance with Paragraph 15.3.

14.3 If the Contractor is delayed at any time in progress of the Work by changes ordered in the Work, by labor disputes, fire, unusual delay in deliveries, abnormal adverse weather conditions not reasonably anticipatable, unavoidable casualties or any causes beyond the Contractor's control, or by other causes which the Architect determines may justify delay, then the Contract Time shall be extended by Change Order for such reasonable time as the Architect may determine.

ARTICLE 15
PAYMENTS AND COMPLETION

15.1 Payments shall be made as provided in Articles 4 and 5 of this Agreement.

15.2 Payments may be withheld on account of (1) defective Work not remedied, (2) claims filed by third parties, (3) failure of the Contractor to make payments properly to Subcontractors or for labor, materials or equipment, (4) reasonable evidence that the Work cannot be completed for the unpaid balance of the Contract Sum, (5) damage to the Owner or another contractor, (6) reasonable evidence that the Work will not be completed within the Contract Time and that the unpaid balance would not be adequate to cover actual or liquidated damages for the anticipated delay, or (7) persistent failure to carry out the Work in accordance with the Contract Documents.

15.3 When the Architect agrees that the Work is substantially complete, the Architect will issue a Certificate of Substantial Completion.

15.4 Final payment shall not become due until the Contractor has delivered to the Owner a complete release of all liens arising out of this Contract or receipts in full covering all labor, materials and equipment for which a lien could be filed, or a bond satisfactory to the Owner to indemnify the Owner against such lien. If such lien remains unsatisfied after payments are made, the Contractor shall refund to the Owner all money that the Owner may be compelled to pay in discharging such lien, including all costs and reasonable attorneys' fees.

15.5 The making of final payment shall constitute a waiver of claims by the Owner except those arising from:

.1 liens, claims, security interests or encumbrances arising out of the Contract and unsettled;

.2 failure of the Work to comply with the requirements of the Contract Documents; or

.3 terms of special warranties required by the Contract Documents.

Acceptance of final payment by the Contractor, a Subcontractor or material supplier shall constitute a waiver of claims by that payee except those previously made in writing and identified by that payee as unsettled at the time of final Application for Payment.

ARTICLE 16
PROTECTION OF PERSONS AND PROPERTY

16.1 The Contractor shall be responsible for initiating, maintaining, and supervising all safety precautions and programs in connection with the performance of the Contract. The Contractor shall take reasonable precautions for safety of, and shall provide reasonable protection to prevent damage, injury or loss to:

.1 employees on the Work and other persons who may be affected thereby;

.2 the Work and materials and equipment to be incorporated therein; and

.3 other property at the site or adjacent thereto.

The Contractor shall give notices and comply with applicable laws, ordinances, rules, regulations and lawful orders of public authorities bearing on safety of persons and property and their protection from damage, injury or loss. The Contractor shall promptly remedy damage and loss to property at the site caused in whole or in part by the Contractor, a Subcontractor, a Sub-subcontractor, or anyone directly or indirectly employed by any of them, or by anyone for whose acts they may be liable and for which the Contractor is responsible under Subparagraphs 16.1.2 and 16.1.3, except for damage or loss attributable to acts or omissions of the Owner or Architect or by anyone for whose acts either of them may be liable, and not attributable to the fault or negligence of the Contractor. The foregoing obligations of the Contractor are in addition to the Contractor's obligations under Paragraph 9.12.

16.2 The Contractor shall not be required to perform without consent any Work relating to asbestos or polychlorinated biphenyl (PCB).

ARTICLE 17
INSURANCE

17.1 The Contractor shall purchase from and maintain in a company or companies lawfully authorized to do business in the jurisdiction in which the Project is located insurance for protection from claims under workers' or workmen's compensation acts and other employee benefit acts which are applicable, claims for damages because of bodily injury, including death, and from claims for damages, other than to the Work

itself, to property which may arise out of or result from the Contractor's operations under the Contract, whether such operations be by the Contractor or by a Subcontractor or anyone directly or indirectly employed by any of them. This insurance shall be written for not less than limits of liability specified in the Contract Documents or required by law, whichever coverage is greater, and shall include contractual liability insurance applicable to the Contractor's obligations under Paragraph 9.12. Certificates of such insurance shall be filed with the Owner prior to the commencement of the Work.

17.2 The Owner shall be responsible for purchasing and maintaining the Owner's usual liability insurance. Optionally, the Owner may purchase and maintain other insurance for self-protection against claims which may arise from operations under the Contract. The Contractor shall not be responsible for purchasing and maintaining this optional Owner's liability insurance unless specifically required by the Contract Documents.

17.3 Unless otherwise provided, the Owner shall purchase and maintain, in a company or companies lawfully authorized to do business in the jurisdiction in which the Project is located, property insurance upon the entire Work at the site to the full insurable value thereof. This insurance shall be on an all-risk policy form and shall include interests of the Owner, the Contractor, Subcontractors and Sub-subcontractors in the Work and shall insure against the perils of fire and extended coverage and physical loss or damage including, without duplication of coverage, theft, vandalism and malicious mischief.

17.4 A loss insured under Owner's property insurance shall be adjusted with the Owner and made payable to the Owner as fiduciary for the insureds, as their interests may appear, subject to the requirements of any applicable mortgagee clause.

17.5 The Owner shall file a copy of each policy with the Contractor before an exposure to loss may occur. Each policy shall contain a provision that the policy will not be cancelled or allowed to expire until at least 30 days' prior written notice has been given to the Contractor.

17.6 The Owner and Contractor waive all rights against each other and the Architect, Architect's consultants, separate contractors described in Article 12, if any, and any of their subcontractors, sub-subcontractors, agents and employees, for damages caused by fire or other perils to the extent covered by property insurance obtained pursuant to this Article 17 or any other property insurance applicable to the Work, except such rights as they may have to the proceeds of such insurance held by the Owner as fiduciary. The Contractor shall require similar waivers in favor of the Owner and the Contractor by Subcontractors and Sub-subcontractors. The Owner shall require similar waivers in favor of the Owner and Contractor by the Architect, Architect's consultants, separate contractors described in Article 12, if any, and the subcontractors, sub-subcontractors, agents and employees of any of them.

ARTICLE 18
CORRECTION OF WORK

18.1 The Contractor shall promptly correct Work rejected by the Architect or failing to conform to the requirements of the Contract Documents, whether observed before or after Substantial Completion and whether or not fabricated, installed or completed, and shall correct any Work found to be not in accordance with the requirements of the Contract Documents within a period of one year from the date of Substantial Com-

AIA DOCUMENT A107 • ABBREVIATED OWNER CONTRACTOR AGREEMENT • NINTH EDITION • AIA® • © 1987
THE AMERICAN INSTITUTE OF ARCHITECTS, 1735 NEW YORK AVENUE, N.W., WASHINGTON, D.C. 20006
[E2247]

pletion of the Contract or by terms of an applicable special warranty required by the Contract Documents. The provisions of this Article 18 apply to Work done by Subcontractors as well as to Work done by direct employees of the Contractor.

18.2 Nothing contained in this Article 18 shall be construed to establish a period of limitation with respect to other obligations which the Contractor might have under the Contract Documents. Establishment of the time period of one year as described in Paragraph 18.1 relates only to the specific obligation of the Contractor to correct the Work, and has no relationship to the time within which the obligation to comply with the Contract Documents may be sought to be enforced, nor to the time within which proceedings may be commenced to establish the Contractor's liability with respect to the Contractor's obligations other than specifically to correct the Work.

ARTICLE 19
MISCELLANEOUS PROVISIONS

19.1 The Contract shall be governed by the law of the place where the Project is located.

19.2 As between the Owner and the Contractor, any applicable statute of limitations shall commence to run and any alleged cause of action shall be deemed to have accrued:

  .1 not later than the date of Substantial Completion for acts or failures to act occurring prior to the relevant date of Substantial Completion;

  .2 not later than the date of issuance of the final Certificate for Payment for acts or failures to act occurring subsequent to the relevant date of Substantial Completion and prior to issuance of the final Certificate for Payment; and

  .3 not later than the date of the relevant act or failure to act by the Contractor for acts or failures to act occurring after the date of the final Certificate for Payment.

ARTICLE 20
TERMINATION OF THE CONTRACT

20.1 If the Architect fails to recommend payment for a period of 30 days through no fault of the Contractor, or if the Owner fails to make payment thereon for a period of 30 days, the Contractor may, upon seven additional days' written notice to the Owner and the Architect, terminate the Contract and recover from the Owner payment for all Work executed and for proven loss with respect to materials, equipment, tools, and construction equipment and machinery, including reasonable overhead, profit and damages applicable to the Project.

20.2 If the Contractor defaults or persistently fails or neglects to carry out the Work in accordance with the Contract Documents or fails to perform a provision of the Contract, the Owner, after seven days' written notice to the Contractor and without prejudice to any other remedy the Owner may have, may make good such deficiencies and may deduct the cost thereof, including compensation for the Architect's services and expenses made necessary thereby, from the payment then or thereafter due the Contractor. Alternatively, at the Owner's option, and upon certification by the Architect that sufficient cause exists to justify such action, the Owner may terminate the Contract and take possession of the site and of all materials, equipment, tools, and construction equipment and machinery thereon owned by the Contractor and may finish the Work by whatever method the Owner may deem expedient. If the unpaid balance of the Contract Sum exceeds costs of finishing the Work, including compensation for the Architect's services and expenses made necessary thereby, such excess shall be paid to the Contractor, but if such costs exceed such unpaid balance, the Contractor shall pay the difference to the Owner.

SELECTED FORMS

ARTICLE 21
OTHER CONDITIONS OR PROVISIONS

SAMPLE

This Agreement entered into as of the day and year first written above.

OWNER   CONTRACTOR

_____   _____
(Signature)   *(Signature)*

_____   _____
(Printed name and title)   *(Printed name and title)*

11 A107-1987   **AIA DOCUMENT A107** • ABBREVIATED OWNER-CONTRACTOR AGREEMENT • NINTH EDITION • AIA® • © 1987
THE AMERICAN INSTITUTE OF ARCHITECTS, 1735 NEW YORK AVENUE, N.W., WASHINGTON, D.C. 20006
[E2249]

3/87

†